SECURING LAND RIGHTS
COMMUNAL LAND REFORM IN NAMIBIA

Romie Vonkie Nghitevelekwa

UNAM PRESS
UNIVERSITY OF NAMIBIA

University of Namibia Press
www.unam.edu.na/unam-press
unampress@unam.na
Private Bag 13301
Windhoek
Namibia

First published:	2020
Cover Art:	Harvesting time by Elia Shiwoohamba
Cover design:	Jigsaw Graphic Design and Layout
Copy-editing:	Hettie Human
Design and layout:	Jigsaw Graphic Design and Layout

ISBN 978-99916-42-62-8

With financial support by the German Research Foundation (DFG) through the collaborative research center 'Future Rural Africa', funding code TRR 228/1

Future Rural Africa

Funded by
DFG Deutsche
Forschungsgemeinschaft
German Research Foundation

Distribution
In Namibia by Namibia Book Market: www.namibiabooks.com
Internationally by the African Books Collective: www.africanbookscollective.com

SECURING LAND RIGHTS
COMMUNAL LAND REFORM IN NAMIBIA

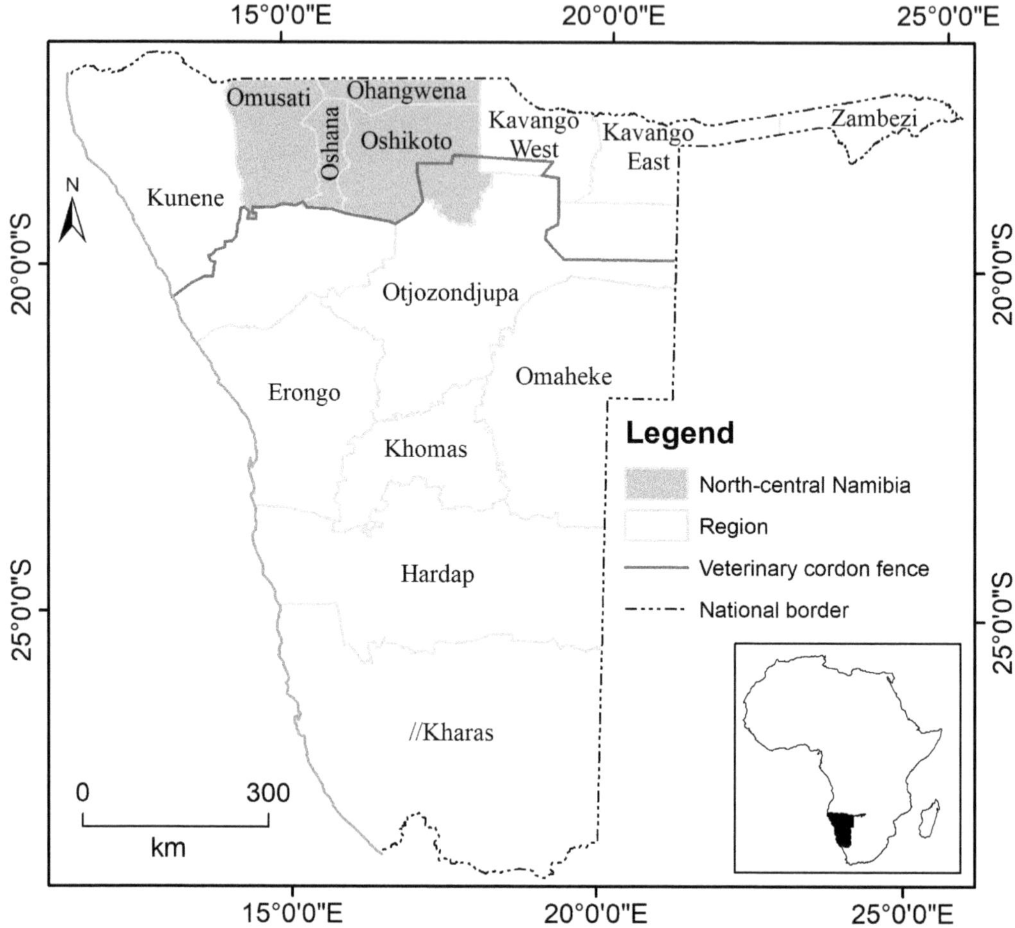

Namibia's administrative and political regions showing the north-central regions (grey shading), the ethnographic setting for this research, and the veterinary cordon fence also known as the Red Line.

Contents

List of Figures vii

List of Tables viii

List of Colour Photographs ix

Abbreviations x

Foreword xi

Preface xiii

1 Setting the Scene **1**

Trajectory of land tenure reform in Africa 3

Genesis of a land reform agenda for Namibia 16

New standpoints on a land reform model for Namibia 18

Independence and development of the land reform programme in Namibia 19

Enactment of a law for communal land in Namibia 24

2 North-Central Namibia's Ethnographic Setting **29**

Demographical and physical setting 29

Political setting 32

Socio-economic setting 36

Territorial restructuring 39

Economic restructuring 47

3 Customary Land Tenure System in Practice **55**

Settling in the area 56

Allocating, sharing, and distributing the land 60

Relating to the land, transferring land, and inheriting land 68

Dividing landholdings, multiple landholdings, banking the land 74

Working the land 75

Farming in *ofuka* areas 83

When not tilling the land 85

4 Emerging Land Markets **89**
Nature, extent, and hotspots of land markets in communal areas 90
Urban and rural land questions: two sides of one coin 94
The disguised nature of land markets in communal areas 96
Polarised views on land markets in communal areas 96

5 Institutions and Processes in Tenure Reform **99**
Communal land boards 100
Traditional authorities 103
Land rights application 104
Land rights ratification 106
Status of land rights registration 110
Dealing with land disputes and conflicts 111

6 Registration of Customary Land Rights **115**
Issuing customary land rights certificates 115
Surety for life and lifetime security 121
Gender equity 121
Land rights registration amidst diverse mechanisms of access to land 126
Excluding other customary uses of land 129

7 Registration of Rights of Leasehold **131**
Rights of leasehold for general business enterprises 131
Rights of leasehold for agricultural purposes 132

Conclusion 143

References 147

Glossary 156

Index 158

List of Figures

Frontispiece:	Namibia's administrative and political regions	iv
Figure 1.1:	Homelands proposed by the Odendaal Commission showing Mangetti Block farming units in Ovamboland	6
Figure 2.1:	Percentage of households indicating subsistence farming as main sources of livelihoods	50
Figure 2.2:	Regional disaggregation of households indicating subsistence farming as main source of livelihood	51
Figure 2.3:	Percentage of households with off-farm and subsistence farming as main sources of livelihoods	52
Figure 3.1:	Ondobe and Okongo areas	55
Figure 3.2:	The tree from which Ondobe derived its name	57
Figure 3.3:	Eudaneko district meeting	60
Figure 3.4:	Pearl millet in a field in Ondobe area	78
Figure 3.5:	A pond in Ondobe area	78
Figure 3.6:	Women squeezing juice from a pile of marula in Omunyekadi Village	81
Figure 3.7:	Pension distribution in Ondobe	82
Figure 6.1:	A village meeting session	116
Figure 6.2:	Members of the village celebrating *Oshipe*	116
Figure 7.1:	Areas gazetted for small-scale commercial farming units in 2007	134

List of Tables

Table 2.1: Communal Conservancies in North-Central Namibia 45

Table 2.2: Community Forests in North-Central Namibia 45

Table 2.3: Fees Levied for Different Land Uses by Uukwaluudhi Traditional Authority 49

List of Colour Photographs

1. Traditional and modern fences
2. The author enthusiastically explaining her project to a farmer in Ondobe area
3. Centenary commemoration of King Mandume's death
4. Information banners about land rights registration
5. Cattle in *ofuka* area
6. A tractor threshing *omahangu* in *ofuka* area
7. A pond of water fenced within a customary landholding in Ondobe area
8. A homestead in Ondobe area
9. A granary locally called *eshisha*
10. A fence cordoning off a customary landholding on communal land
11. A *Berchemia discolor (Omuve)* tree creating shade for the midday hours in Ondobe area
12. Typical narrow corridor allowing movement of people and cattle from one area to another

13 a & b. Individualised and fenced off landholdings with better rangeland conditions

14. An older woman working in her field
15. An aerial view of a village adjacent to Ondangwa Town

Abbreviations

CBNRM	Community-based natural resource management
GIZ	Deutsche Gesellschaft für Internationale Zusammenarbeit
KfW	Kreditanstalt für Wiederaufbau
NGO	Non-governmental organisation
PCLD	Programme for Communal Land Development
SWAPO	South West Africa People's Organisation
UN	United Nations
UNIN	United Nations Institute for Namibia

Foreword

For the last 30 years, Namibia has been implementing a land reform programme. In the freehold sector, it seeks to address historical injustices by improving access to agricultural land for "previously disadvantaged" Namibians. In the non-freehold or communal areas, land reform aims to remove uncertainties about legitimate access and rights to land by introducing the registration of customary land rights in regional land registers. Despite about 50 per cent of Namibia's population still regarding access to communal land as being important, not enough research has been carried out in the various regions of Namibia to understand how local customary tenure systems for land and natural resources operate. Romie Nghitevelekwa's book is a welcome contribution to our understanding of customary tenure to individualised and communal rights. Based on extensive field research, the book introduces the reader to the complex nature of accessing land held under customary tenure and the nature of such rights. The discussion of various aspects of customary tenure takes place against the background of Namibia's land reform programme and, in particular, how the policy and legal framework impact social equity and tenure security.

Informing her approach is the conviction that customary tenure does not represent a second-class tenure, as is often averred. Instead of recommending that customary tenure is abolished in favour of formal and freehold land title, she argues that its recognition in law is fundamental to promoting equity. In this context, she also dismisses popular claims that customary tenure is not secure enough to encourage investment.

The book presents a much more nuanced discussion of how people obtain access to land than is normally assumed, by differentiating between landholders whose rights are registered and land users who derive secondary tenure rights from landholders, often through kinship networks. This underlines the point that in customary tenure systems, different people have different rights over the same land parcel. Such secondary tenure rights are not protected by current legislation – a situation that has the potential to increase the vulnerability of those who depend on them, particularly women. The individualisation of customary land rights, through a process of registration, is likely to impact negatively on a system that, through its flexibility, facilitates the sharing of benefits arising from accessing land more widely.

Importantly, the book also shows that customary tenure systems are constantly adapting to new socio-economic realities. One such transformation involves the individualisation of communal pastures, and represents a response by the state to the demand by an elite group who wish to possess their own farms. To facilitate this desire, the Communal Land Reform Act (2002) introduced a new form of tenure, namely, long-term leasehold. The other, less well-known change that the author discusses is the gradual commoditisation of customary land rights. Although it operates illegally, an emerging land market in non-freehold areas opens new ways of accessing land through money transfers. This practice is currently happening, particularly in villages adjacent to local authority areas with a high demand for residential land, and raises the important policy question: how should the state deal with this illegal trading of customary land rights?

This book is indispensable reading for scholars and land activists alike, in particular at this specific juncture, where the country is reforming its land policy and legal framework. It draws attention to important questions relating to land governance in non-freehold areas that need further discussion and consideration in a new land policy and law.

Wolfgang Werner, Windhoek
Retired Associate Professor, Department of Land and Property Sciences,
Namibia University of Science and Technology (NUST)

Preface

This book is a result of doctoral research conducted between 2013 and 2017, and deals with communal land and tenure reform in north-central Namibia's communal areas. Tenure reform is part of communal land reform, a process that aims to secure land rights on communal land. I analyse the implications of tenure reform for people's lived realities and social equity in terms of access to land and rights over land under the customary tenure system. My aim was to explore and examine people's lived experiences of communal land reform, and the changes resulting from the different restructuring processes that are underway. The book enters Namibia's scholarly landscape at a time when land reform is a strategic topic. Communal land and its reform need critical reflection, since the majority of Namibia's population depends on communal land in one way or another, and the demand for communal land for different purposes continues to increase.

Field research presented in this book was undertaken between 2013 and 2017. The key research participants were land users, landholders, traditional authorities, members of the Communal Land Boards, officials of the then Ministry of Land Reform[1] at central and regional levels, and experts in the land sector. Data were collected through various avenues, including village meetings and events, district meetings, Communal Land Board meetings, through informant interviews, informal discussions, semi-structured interviews, questionnaire-based surveys, observation, and participant observation. To understand the status of customary tenure systems, land use, security of tenure and the implications of communal land reform, documentary analysis was also imperative to examine historical settings and circumstances that inform contemporary practices.

In his book, titled *Decolonising the Mind: The Politics of Language in Literature*, Ngũgĩ wa Thiong'o states that

> Work, any work, even literary creative work, is not the result of an individual genius but the result of a collective effort. There are so many inputs in the actual formation of an image, an idea, a line of argument and even sometimes the formal arrangements. The very words we use are a product of a collective history. So, too, is the present work (1986, pp. x–xi).

1 In March 2020, the Ministry of Land Reform as a stand-alone ministry ceased to exist. Land reform has been incorporated into the ministry now called Ministry of Agriculture, Water and Land Reform.

The extract from wa Thiong'o speaks directly to this book. First and foremost, this book would not have been possible without the contributions of the landholders, land users, village headmen, district senior headmen and all those that participated in my research. Thank you all for opening your homes and sharing your experiences with me. My doctoral research was supported by the German Research Foundation (DFG) and the Swiss National Science Foundation (SNSF), through a collaborative and multidisciplinary project titled *Communal Land Reform in Namibia – Implications of Individualisation of Land Tenure.* This collaborative project was undertaken through the University of Freiburg in Germany, and the universities of Basel and Fribourg in Switzerland. This book is a result of the study component undertaken through the University of Freiburg under the supervision and guidance of Prof. Gregor Dobler, whose critical eye, direction, and continuous encouragement allowed me to perfect my arguments. Other senior academics in the project were Prof. Olivier Graefe, Prof. Klaus Kuhn and Dr Lena Bloemertz, whose direction and support brought multidisciplinarity to the project. My co-researchers, Dr Laura Weidman and Brice Prudat, offered great companionship throughout the process. My work has benefited immensely from colleagues at the Institut für Ethnologie in Freiburg, namely, Dr Mirjam Lücking, Ms Olivia Klimm, Dr Martin Büdel, Mr Yannick van den Berg and Dr Margarete Brüll and, at the University of Basel and the Basler Afrika Bibliographien (BAB), Dr Vladimir Wingate, Dr Luregn Lenggenhager, Dr Dag Henrichsen and Mr Reto Ulrich. On a more personal level, Gregor and Rita, Lena and Christophe, Laura and Sammy all hosted me while I was in Europe. The Furuholm family in Sweden was instrumental in the last stage of the write-up.

Here at home, immense support came from Dr Jeremy Sylvester, Dr Volker Winterfeldt, Ms Barbara Winterfeldt, Dr Martha Akawa, Prof. Jairos Kangira, the University of Namibia in general, and, in particular, my colleagues in the Department of Sociology, namely, Ms Ndeshi Namupala, Dr Ellison Tjirera, Ms Maria Kaundjua, Dr Artwell Nhemachena, Prof. Lucy Edwards-Jauch, Ms Lydia Kauari and Dr Kola Omomowo. Encouragement by Prof. Heike Becker of the University of the Western Cape meant a lot to me. I owe appreciation to the University of Namibia Press and, in particular, Dr Jill Kinahan and Ms Naitsikile Iizyenda for their support during the publication process and to an anonymous reviewer for constructive review comments. I am thankful to Mr Fillemon Shatipamba and Prof. Martin Hipondoka for their assistance with the maps in the book. I am also grateful to Hettie Human, the copyeditor of this book.

I acknowledge and thank my seniors in the land sector, especially Prof. Wolfgang Werner, for review comments and for the foreword to this book; Dr John Mendelsohn and Mr Willem Odendaal, and officials of the then Ministry of Land Reform and the Programme for Communal Land Development (PCLD). Former officials of

PCLD, in particular *Tate* Mulofwa, Mr Marcel Meijs, Dr Claus-Peter Hager and Dr Elke Matthaei of Deutsche Gesellschaft für Internationale Zusammenarbeit (GIZ), all contributed to the discussions that benefited this book.

In addition to being the result of extensive field research for my doctoral studies and several commissioned studies, the book represents the associated local experiences of being what is called a citizen social anthropologist. Being a citizen social anthropologist did not only benefit me methodologically; the implications of being a citizen anthropologist underscore my direct participation in the very activities I was researching. The studies commissioned and from which I derived empirical data for this book include studies of the then Ministry of Land Reform through the Programme for Communal Land Development (PCLD) and the Konrad-Adenauer-Stiftung. In March 2015, I was appointed as a member of the Ohangwena Communal Land Board. Being a member of this Land Board provided opportunities for close-up participant observation during the process of land rights registration. The commissioned projects, especially those of the Konrad-Adenauer-Stiftung, employed the quantitative research design we used to undertake a survey that involved a sample of 400 women in the four regions of north-central Namibia. This project involved generating data on women's access to land and rights over land. Similarly, the project commissioned under the PCLD led to the generation of data on emerging land markets in communal areas. Experiences and results from these commissioned projects are all integrated in the book.

The research process and this book would not have been possible without my family and friends. My friends, Nangula, Nakuti, Nelago, Katuli, Mekondjo, Linea, Magano, Tala, Josephine, Beata, Eufemia, Selma, and Gloria, you are all my pillars. My girls, who kept my home together, Ndahambelela, Nangombe, Beata, Takatsu, Iyaloo and mee Maita, I owe all to you. My siblings, Manickie, Angula, Kayoso, Maria and Ilifa, this is dedicated to you. My mother, *Meme* Hilma Iimene, and father, *Tate* Lucas Nghuulikwa, my aunts, *Meme* Kandali and especially *Meme* Ruusa Shigwedha Negonga, thank you for the foundation you built for me. To the late *Tate* Festus Negonga, what can I say, except thank you very much to you and *Meme* Negonga – you opened this world for me. *Tate* Festus, may your soul continue to rest in peace. *Kuku* Gwamungolo, *Tate* Fillemon Negonga and your family, you are indeed family. My cousins, Taatsu, Ndatega, Nailoke, Shilongo, Kettu, and Mbushandje (Romie Uahengo), Veiko, Max, Mbushandje (Romie Negonga), Isia, Selma, Fenny, Hileni and Cele, and Mkwaanime also deserve heartfelt thanks. My mother in-law, *Meme* Rebecca Shetu, and my in-laws, your support means the world to me.

I saved the best for last, my family: my husband, Kondjeni, and my children, Meitavelo, Tuwilika and Tunehafo. Kondjeni, thank you for keeping our home together in my absence. I appreciate your continuous encouragement. Meitavelo, you were part of the process from the beginning. Tuwilika, you were part of the writing process, and Tunehafo, you were part of the book completion process. You were and continue to be my pillars. You are the reason I strive further. I dedicate this piece of work to you. To you all I say, *tangi unene*!

"I will praise thee, O Lord, with my whole heart, I will shew forth all thy marvellous works." Psalm 9:1

1
Setting the Scene

Land tenure reform is part of the communal land reform programme, itself a component of the broader land reform programme in Namibia that includes both communal land reform and freehold (agricultural) commercial land reform. Communal land reform started in 2002/2003, after the enactment and gazetting of the Communal Land Reform Act, 2002[2] which states that communal land is vested in the state for the socio-economic benefit of the people residing in communal areas (Republic of Namibia, 2002). This legal vesting principle is intended to provide a safety net for the people residing in communal areas, especially the "landless and those with insufficient access to land who are not in formal employment or engaged in non-agriculture [sic] business" (Republic of Namibia, 2002, p. 11). Before the Act came into force, communal land in Namibia was administered solely under customary tenure systems of the different traditional authorities. Customary tenure systems dominate in most rural African settings, where it is used "to express and order ownership, possession, and access, and to regulate use and transfer" of land (Wily, 2011, p. 1). It is within the context of customary systems that land tenure reform is introduced to change "the legal and administrative manner in which land rights are recognised and regulated" (Wily, 2000, p. 1).

Social equity is central for tenure reform in Namibia. Hence, I examine the implications of land tenure reform for people's lived realities and social equity. Upon studying the trajectory of tenure reform in Africa at large, it became evident that the rationale of tenure reform has been to abolish customary and communal tenure systems in favour of individualised titled tenure. As I show, however, tenure reform, as steered through communal land reform in Namibia, does not seek to abolish customary tenure systems. Tenure reform through communal land reform recognises rights granted through customary systems for what they are, and not in relation to individualised titled tenure.

I use north-central Namibia as an ethnographic setting for my analysis. North-central Namibia is a setting in transition, one undergoing several restructuring processes, both territorial and socio-economic. Demographically, 38% of the Namibian population lives in the four north-central regions of the country (Namibia Statistics Agency, 2017). These transitions and restructuring processes have direct

2 No. 5 of 2002.

bearing on customary land tenure, including access to land, security of tenure and land use. To assist comprehension of these changes, I analyse customary land tenure at a micro level by studying villages in a geographical area I term Ondobe area, and in former frontier areas, or areas that were once described as *ofuka* (wilderness areas). My analysis of customary land tenure at a micro level focuses on the processes of accessing land (through allocations, sharing and distribution), dividing the land, banking the land, working the land and other dynamics concerning land relations.

What is apparent from my analysis is that land is not only important for meeting material needs, but also for maintaining social relations. Equally, social relations and, in particular, the economy of sharing through land, is key to the livelihoods of many people, especially the landless and, more particularly, women. I underscore this strength of the customary tenure system. In a setting in transition, however, new processes of accessing land and relating to land beyond customary tenure have emerged. One example of these new processes is the emergence of market-based transactions (land markets) that aid access to land – a practice that the Communal Land Reform Act, 2002 prohibits, but which continues unchecked. The transitions and changes observed on communal land in north-central Namibia have not only increased demand for land, but have also diversified land use from being largely oriented to meeting subsistence needs, to a combination of this with commercially-oriented land uses, such that commodification of land and land use is apparent. These dynamics beg for equitable security of tenure. Therefore, I trace the process of land rights registration, which is a key process of communal land and tenure reform that aims to bring about security of tenure on communal land. The process of land rights registration entails changes in the institutional landscape of communal land administration, recognition, and ratification of land rights. Changes also include new processes of dealing with and adjudicating land-related disputes and conflicts. I analyse the provision of security of tenure through statutory processes and embed this process and its outcomes in the diverse mechanisms of access to land and complex land relations inherent in customary tenure systems. While individualised titled tenure (or freehold tenure) is not the intention of tenure reform in communal areas, general individualisation of tenure is taking place. This is evident in the increasing individualisation of land, and fencing of large tracts of communal pastures in the frontier zones of north-central Namibia. Individualisation of communal pastures has taken place at the agency of land users, and the state has come into play through the registration of rights of leasehold for agricultural purposes, thereby providing statutory security of tenure. Granting rights of leasehold for agricultural purposes introduces another type of tenure in communal areas, though one that is oriented to commercialisation. I therefore follow the process of land rights registration on communal land and investigate the implications of different land rights that have been formalised on communal land in people's lived realities and social equity.

Trajectory of land tenure reform in Africa

Evolutionary approaches to land tenure reform

Land tenure reform has been on the agenda of development in sub-Saharan Africa for many decades. The turn of the 20th century was marked by African populations being dispossessed of land, strict boundaries being introduced, and dual land tenure systems being created. In Namibia, for example, land dispossession commenced in 1883, when Adolf Lüderitz, a German trader, acquired land in southern Namibia from the Nama chief, Joseph Fredericks. Subsequent dispossession of land followed throughout the time of German and South African colonial administrations, and resulted in unequal distribution and ownership of land. At the end of colonialism and apartheid in 1990, more than 36.2 million hectares of land was occupied by some 6,292 farming households, which supported an estimated 2% of the population, while 33.5 million hectares of land was occupied by 150,000 families, and supported more than 70% of the total population (Republic of Namibia, 1991a). Land dispossession resulted in injustices in the form of what Fraser (1996) calls *mal*distribution of land. *Mal*distribution of land, or the blatantly unequal distribution of resources in Namibia, is a direct result of a socially constructed and unjust political economy. Dual land tenure systems were created by the introduction of a new land tenure system of individualised private ownership, or freehold land tenure. This new system existed parallel to the customary land tenure systems. White settlers owned land privately, with full title deeds to land, while African people held only rights of occupation and use (Amoo, 2014). Thus, land tenure systems came to be characterised by the indigenous people-settler dichotomy. Under customary tenure systems, landholdings were not deemed to be property, and indigenous Africans were therefore denied property in land (Peters, 2013a). According to Chanok (1991), by "deeming African landholding *not* property, the colonial regimes sought to prevent legal challenge to its claims on 'conquered' territory" (cited by Peters, 2013a, p. 539).

The attitudes of colonial agents to indigenous land tenure systems involved value judgement; they placed indigenous (customary) tenure on a value hierarchy and measured it against the individualised private ownership or freehold tenure system. Customary land tenure systems were perceived as static, rigid, insular, inflexible, incompatible, and insecure, because of the "absence of clearly defined and enforceable property rights" (Deininger & Feder, 2014, p. 8; Peters, 2009, p. 1318). These systems were, furthermore, perceived to present a constraint on agricultural productivity, to inhibit individual investment in land, credit markets, using land as security and/or collateral for small farmers and, broadly, inhibitory to economic growth and general social progress (Bassett, 1993; Peters, 2009).

The individual within the communal tenure system was interpreted to have no security of tenure, and security of tenure was regarded as an incentive for investment, and necessary for efficiency and productivity (Peters, 2009). Additionally, customary land tenure systems were associated with too many people having claim to and interest in the same parcel of land, which was regarded as discouraging to land improvements (Bassett, 1993). Insecurity of tenure has been, furthermore, associated with "unsustainable use and degradation of natural resources" (Deininger & Binswanger, 1999, p. 250). This inference aligns with the economic theory called the tragedy of the commons. According to Garrett Hardin, who coined the term,

> The inherent logic of the commons remorselessly generates tragedy... Ruin is the destination toward which all men rush, each pursuing his own interest in a society that believes in the freedom of the commons. Freedom in a commons brings ruin to all (1968, p. 1244).

The idea of the inferiority of customary land tenure systems to individualised and private forms of tenure was influenced by notions of proprietary ownership, which resulted from enclosure events that swept across Western Europe in the 19th century (Bassett, 1993, p. 6). During that time, enclosures were viewed as an inevitable response to the need for greater efficiency in agricultural production (Peters, 2009). These attitudes reflect and mark the advent of an individualised and private land ownership tenure system as the dominant culture, which worked against the communal and customary form of land tenure system, which was considered inferior. Using Fraser's conception of social justice, which I equate to social equity, treating communal and customary land tenure systems as inferior to the individualised and private land ownership tenure system represents symbolic injustices "created through a discursive framework of binary oppositions" (Fraser, 1996, p. 9). Colonial agents in Africa linked land tenure systems to agricultural productivity and overall social progress and used this linkage as justification for land tenure reform. By viewing customary land tenure as inhibitory to agricultural productivity and general social progress, the proposed tenure reform, therefore, sought to abolish and/or convert the customary land tenure systems in Africa to individualised and private land ownership (Bassett, 1993). This process represents the evolutionary model of tenure change, where converting to individualised and private property was deemed "the necessary next stage of the civilising process" (Peters, 2013a, p. 539). The logic was to "replace customary systems with titling and private property rights, which were posited as necessary preconditions for modernization and development" (Peters, 2009, p. 1318). In this frame of conviction, colonial officials were convinced that individual freehold title was the way to wrest African farming and, more generally, the African way of life, out of its "backward" state (Peters, 2013a, p. 540). The reformists, therefore, adopted a common model of agrarian change that involved titling of land rights, and ignored and, ultimately, undermined the distinctive differences between and within African settings (Bassett, 1993).

This evolutionary model of change in tenure was effected through law reform and tenure reform programmes in dozens of independent African countries during the 1960s, and continued into the 1970s, so vigorously that these years are regarded as the "land reform decades" (Bassett, 1993, p. 11), during which land policy reforms proliferated. African countries that had just gained their independence included Kenya, Tanzania, Burkina Faso, Malawi, and Mozambique, all of which embraced land tenure reform. Land tenure reform agendas were spearheaded by Kenya, with its Swynnerton Plan, which launched "privatization at scale through systematic individualization, titling, and registration" (Wily, 2011, p. 2). Reforms in Tanzania took a different route, and involved nationalising expatriates' estates, abolishing freehold tenure, outlawing land sales, and implementing the Ujamaa and other villagisation programmes, which involved aggregating village hamlets to facilitate the provision of services to the peasantry (Wily, 2011, p. 2). Similarly, in Senegal, land reform "redefined the country's land tenure systems in the interests of nationalized African communalism" (Wily, 2011, p. 2). The land reform decades also saw international donors and development agencies and, in particular, the World Bank, adopting land policies. Early in the 1950s, the United Nations (UN) General Assembly had already adopted a resolution on land reform: Resolution 401 (V)[3] (Ochieng, 2020). Through Resolution 401 (V), the General Assembly held the view that "agrarian conditions which persisted in many underdeveloped countries constituted a barrier for their economic development" (United Nations, 1951, p. 27). To address this barrier, the General Assembly recommended

> analysis of the degree to which unsatisfactory forms of agrarian structure and, in particular, systems of land tenure, in the underdeveloped countries and territories impede economic development and thus depress the standard of living especially of agricultural workers and tenants and of small and medium-sized farmers.

The General Assembly, therefore, called for the institution of several measures to address these barriers, one of them being land reform. The resolutions and resulting policies adopted by international organisations all followed the trend of modernising land tenure in underdeveloped countries, including those in Africa. The World Bank, for example, adopted a policy document, titled *Land Reform: Sector Policy Paper*, which was published in 1975. This document became influential for land policy in Africa, and also formed part of the World Bank's agenda for structural adjustment (Manji, 2006).

While modernisation of land tenure was widespread in Africa, especially in newly independent countries, other countries, for example, Namibia and South

3 UN General Assembly Resolution 401 (V): Land reform (adopted 20 November 1950).

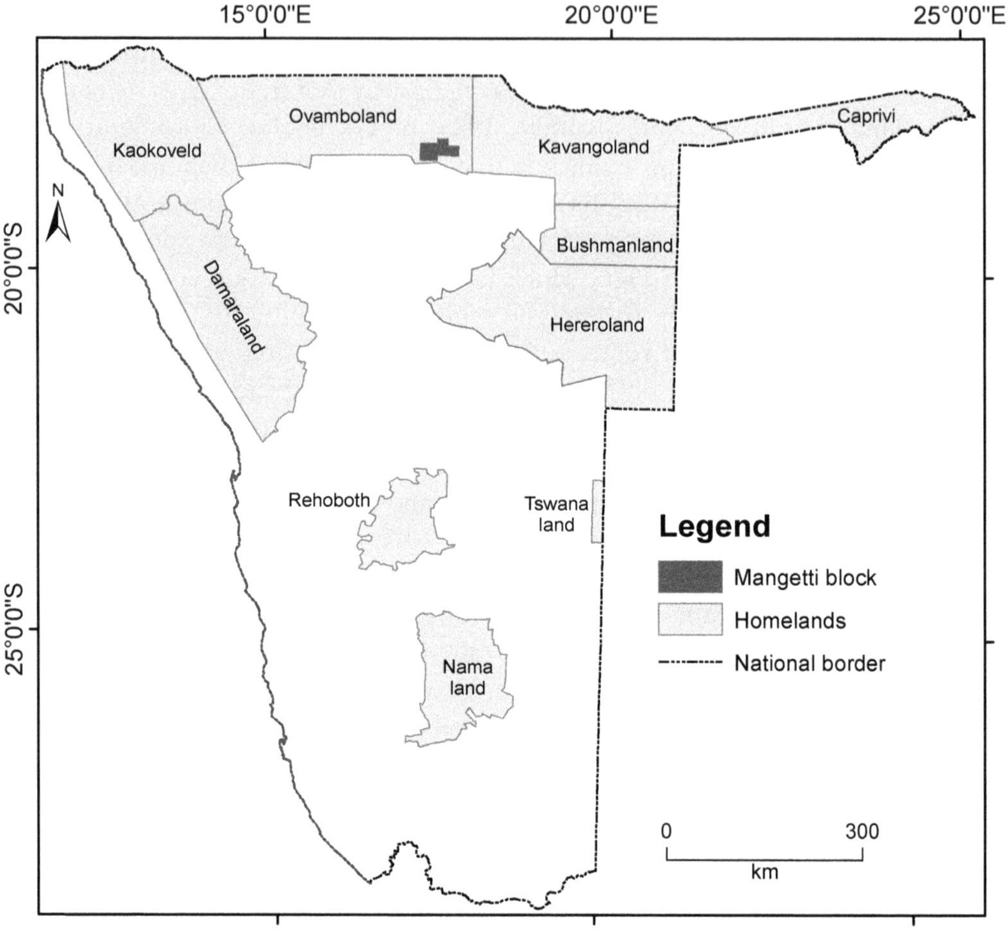

Fig 1.1: Homelands proposed by the Odendaal Commission (1964) showing Mangetti Block farming units in Ovamboland.

Africa, which were still under apartheid at the time, maintained the dual systems of freehold and communal land tenure (under customary tenure). Nevertheless, the modernisation approach and paradigm also reached Namibia, although it took a different route. This process is particular to the recommendations of the Odendaal Commission. In 1962, the South African apartheid regime commissioned an inquiry, titled *Commission of Enquiry into South West Africa Affairs*, under Franz Hendrik Odendaal. The Commission recommended economic development programmes with two aims: one, to strengthen the modern economy in the areas occupied by the White population; and two, to bring about selective transformations in the areas occupied by the indigenous population (Odendaal, 1964). For the indigenous communities, the Commission made recommendations for accelerated development, which would transform their traditional socio-cultural backgrounds (Odendaal, 1964). Transformation of traditional socio-cultural backgrounds was intended to give the non-White population groups "the opportunity, necessary assistance and encouragement to find an outlet for their new experience and capabilities" (Odendaal, 1964, p. 429). This process was viewed as the transition from a subsistence economy, or a system of self-support and an economy of supplying their own needs to a money economy peculiar to the system of the Whites (Odendaal, 1964, p. 425). This process was to be applied in respect of agriculture, whereby a policy was to be adopted to guide indigenous communities towards greater agricultural productivity through "gradual adaptation of their traditional and economic institutions" (Odendaal, 1964, p. 80).

The economic development programmes that were subsequently introduced as a result of the Odendaal Commission were published in the document titled *South West Africa: A Five-Year Plan for the Development of the Native Areas*, in 1965. The implications of the transformation recommended by the Odendaal Commission and the five-year plan have been extensively analysed, particularly by Wolfgang Werner. The economic development programmes that were introduced as a result of the Commission's recommendations brought about far-reaching transformation, including tenure reformation in terms of access to land whereby individualisation of large tracts of communal land was introduced to encourage the development of small-scale commercial farming units. Individualisation of communal land first started in Hereroland and was later replicated in other communal areas (Werner, 2015, p. 73). In north-central Namibia, 96 farming units (known as *Owambo Mangetti* or Mangetti Block) were surveyed and allocated to individuals on the initiative of state agents (Werner, 2015) (see Map 1.1).

Individualisation of communal land in the 1960s set a precedent for communal land enclosures, which continue to haunt communal areas today. Following the modernisation narrative of the time, individualisation was seen as necessary to improve animal husbandry (Werner, 2015, p. 73). Tapscott and Hangula argue that this process marked the beginning of the colonial state's efforts to create a class of owners of large areas of land in communal areas (1994, p. 6). The process of communal land individualisation essentially involved alienation of land, which meant a loss of land used as buffer zones, especially during times of drought. The precedent set for the enclosure of communal land is evident in the Ondonga Traditional Authority. In the 1970s, the Ondonga "tribal authority", as it was called then, started authorising the fencing of communal land under its jurisdiction (Werner, 2015). These authorisations set patterns for livestock owners to fence communal land in the name of improving livestock husbandry and promoting commercialisation (Tapscott & Hangula, 1994; Werner, 2015). While agricultural development and progress in other parts of Africa were linked to the transformation of communal and customary land tenure systems, in Namibia, transformations were oriented to establishing individual tenure through long-term leasehold, without necessarily converting to freehold. In this way, Namibia's reform differed from reform observed in other African countries.

In Namibia, the Odendaal Commission recommended the transformation of communal to individual tenure, and not necessarily customary into freehold. Additionally, these were selective transformations applied to selected areas of communal land. Land use in large parts of communal areas remained oriented to subsistence. The imperatives of colonial control in Namibia were in the form of so-called indirect rule through chiefs, a process that was politically expedient (Peters, 2013a). Granting freehold status to African landholders would "mean the loss of the right to expropriate lands and the ability to regulate agricultural practices on the reserves" (Bassett, 1993, p. 9). Thus, landholders remained tenants of the state, and held land under customary tenure systems; they were denied property in land, and lived in parallel with White settlers, who held land under freehold tenure, which was the dominant and superior form of tenure. According to Basset (1993), this dual system was implemented for political reasons for African landholders and for economic reasons for the White settlers. Thus, while the Odendaal Commission's recommendations might seem to embody the elements of a modernisation approach to land tenure reform, it drew its impetus from the separatist policies of the South African apartheid government, rather than from the "trickle down" theory favoured by the World Bank and other donors. For Namibia, granting freehold status to the many landholders living in the communal areas would have hindered the very purpose that communal areas served for the colonial economy, that of acting as labour reservoirs.

Criticism of evolutionary approaches to land tenure reform

During the 1970s, conventional development thinking on land tenure systems faced criticism. The criticism related primarily to the basis of the premises and outcomes of the land policies and programmes that had been introduced (Peters, 2013a). At the centre of the criticism was that the land reform programmes that had been introduced failed to achieve the promised results of agricultural investment and, therefore, increased productivity. The problems of tenure that were considered to have a bearing "on agricultural productivity mainly because they influence on-farm investment decisions and determined efficiency of resource use", could not be proven (World Bank, 1975, p. 38). In fact, it was argued that agricultural production stagnated during the land reform decades (Bassett, 1993). The land policies "did not facilitate the use of land for collateral for small farmers" (Peters, 2013a, p. 541). Similarly, the premise that customary tenure was inhibitory to investment was rejected. Empirical findings reported that "cash cropping by small farmers, such as cocoa production on customary land in West Africa", were clear cases of small farmers investing in their land, even in the absence of individualised titled property (Peters, 2013a, p. 541). This critical research literature indicated that "agricultural intensification and commercial production were not inhibited by customary landholding as much as by broader social and political-economic conditions at local, regional and international levels" (Peters, 2013a, p. 541). Migot-Adholla, Hazell, Blarel, and Place (1991) tested the relationship between indigenous tenure arrangements and agricultural productivity in Kenya, Ghana, and Rwanda. One of their findings was that there was "a weak relationship between individualisation of land rights and land yields" (Migot-Adholla et al., 1991, p. 156).

Second, the premise that communal land tenure systems exclude individual rights was proven false. A third critique was that conventional tenure reform programmes that were implemented were linked to social inequities. These reforms "encouraged speculation in land by outsiders, thus displacing the very people – the local users of the land who were supposed to acquire increased security through titling" (Peters, 2013a, p. 541). These reforms ignored overlapping and multiple land uses that exist within customary tenure systems and, therefore, exacerbated land-related conflicts, and reinforced patterns of unequal access to land based on gender, age, ethnicity, and other social differences (Peters, 2013b, p. 547).

Critics, furthermore, claimed that under customary tenure systems, households could acquire rights of exclusion and transfer as population pressure and/or levels of commercialization increased (Bruce & Migot-Adholla, 1994, p. 4). This claim was true in the past, and it is true today; thus, conceptions of communal land continue to belie the actual nature of tenure systems in rural Africa. Land called communal land is increasingly dwindling, giving way to individualised holding of land, under which landholders claim clearly defined rights, in particular, rights of exclusion.

Critical questions have been posed about the assumed rigidity, insularity, inflexibility, incompatibility and insecurity of communal and/or customary land tenure systems by authors such as Cohen (1980), Boserup (1981), Noronha (1985), Feder and Norohna (1987) and Bruce (1988) as summarised and cited in Bruce and Migot-Adholla, (1994); also see Mafeje, (1976). All these authors emphasise the dynamisms of the customary tenure arrangements, and show how these arrangements have, historically, adapted to economic and technological change (Bruce & Migot-Adholla, 1994). Researchers report cases, especially in West Africa, of cash cropping and price responsiveness, in particular regarding cocoa production by farmers on customary land, which "reject premises that customary tenure inhibited investment in agricultural production and agricultural commercialisation" (Peters, 2004, p. 274). Place and Hazell, in a study in Ghana, Kenya and Rwanda, conclude that, "with a few exceptions, land rights were not found to be a significant factor in determining whether or not farmers made land-improving investments or used yield-enhancing inputs" (1993, pp. 18, 19). Critics have shown that "the relationship between security and productivity is complicated by social and political processes that appear to have a greater impact on investments than formal tenure considerations" (Bassett, 1993, p. 2). Therefore, "the notion that tenure reform is the panacea to Africa's agrarian ills is an old idea that ignores critical social dynamics that strongly influence how productive resources are acquired, utilized, contested, and mobilized" (Bassett, 1993, p. 2). Even researchers at the World Bank, such as Deininger and Binswanger, agree that "efficiencies losses associated with communal tenure systems may be more modest than generally assumed" (Deininger & Binswanger, 1999, p. 258). Additionally, although communal land tenure may not be tradable, "rentals – and often sales – within the community (and possibly beyond) are normally allowed, providing scope for efficiency-enhancing transfers" (Deininger & Binswanger, 1999, p. 258).

A fitting conclusion from the considerable amount of literature critiquing abolitionist approaches to African land tenure systems is captured by Migot-Adholla et al., namely, that the differences between African land tenure systems, dubbed traditional, and Western land tenure systems, dubbed modern, should not be perceived in terms of opposite extremes, but as points along a continuum between communal rights systems and privatised rights systems (Migot-Adholla et al., 1991, p. 171). The conventional view of the relationship between land tenure systems and agricultural change has been proven to be a fallacy, and not fitting for African contexts. The call is, therefore, to follow less Eurocentric models and approaches to tenure reform. The core argument emanating from the arguments above highlights the social nature of land access and control, which calls for land tenure to be understood in terms of relations between people.

Neo-evolutionary approaches to land tenure reform

The criticism discussed above led to a shift in the hegemonic view of communal and/or customary land tenure. For example, Deininger and Binswanger acknowledge that, as a result of "more intensive study of communal tenure systems in a broader framework and the recognition that these systems perform multiple functions" (1999, p. 258), there has been a reassessment of previous positions, which has led to a shift, especially by development agencies' official positions on customary landholding (Peters, 2004, p. 270). This shift meant the way forward is that

> instead of reinforcing an often artificial binary between private and communal rights or between the traditional and modern or trying to privatize land rights to 'modernize' land tenure in an environment where few of the conditions for such modernization are present, policy makers should focus on ways

> to increase secure property rights within given constraints (Deininger & Binswanger, 1999, p. 259).

This approach is argued to "allow a more flexible evolution of the structure of property rights while at the same time restoring some of the traditional social functions of land through secondary common property uses" (Deininger & Binswanger, 1999, p. 269). This shift is evident in the World Bank's policies, especially those of the late 1980s, though even 1975 policies hint at this shift. The 1975 policy, for example, acknowledges that

> The position of the World Bank in regard to land reform has changed over the past decade, reflecting a reconsideration of the objectives of development and the most appropriate strategies for attaining those objectives. The objectives are now generally accepted to be increased productivity and employment, and social justice. Land reform can be consistent with these objectives and, in some situations, may well be a necessary condition for their realization (World Bank, 1975, p. 38).

The reconsideration referred to in the extract above reflects the inclusion of social equity/justice, which has been largely absent from the classical land reform agenda. In 1989, the World Bank released a policy document, titled *Sub-Saharan Africa: From Crisis to Sustainable Growth*, which, in the section on redefining land rights, acknowledges that "the rights of African farmers over land vary between the extremes of communal and individual ownership" (World Bank, 1989, p. 104). With this statement, the World Bank acknowledges that individual rights are not absent from what is dubbed communal tenure systems. The new view recognises the "adaptive and flexible character of [communal tenure] that, over time, allows for 'evolution' towards more efficient forms of landholding" (Peters, 2004, p. 270).

Notwithstanding these reconsiderations, land reform proponents, including the World Bank, maintain a position claiming a causal relationship between tenure security and agricultural productivity. In the 1989 report, for example, the World Bank states that "farmers must be given incentives to change their ways. One most important incentive is the right to permanently cultivate land and bequeath or sell it. Secure land rights also help rural credit markets to develop, because land is good collateral" (World Bank, 1989, p. 104). The report maintains, furthermore, that for agricultural modernisation to succeed, freehold titling and codification of traditional tenure systems are necessary. The key agenda remains the "promotion of privatized and individualized property rights" (Borras, 2006, p. 110).

The proponents of land reform defend classical land reform approaches, and claim that undesirable outcomes "were more caused by policy distortions and imperfections in other markets than by the operation of land markets per se" (Deininger & Binswanger, 1999, p. 269). The prohibition of land market interventions, for example, "has greatly reduced opportunities for the poor to rent land" (Deininger & Binswanger, 1999, p. 269). Thus, the proponents still "posit 'a framework of secure, transparent and enforceable property rights as the critical precondition for investment and economic growth'" (Peters, 2004, p. 276). Peters (2009, p. 1319) concludes, rightly, that this is just an "old idea clad in new language". She asserts, furthermore, that this "should not be interpreted as merely empty verbiage but as part of what has been dubbed 'post-modern liberalism', a curious 'potpourri' of pro-poor, pro-participatory approaches combined with promotion of global free trade" (Peters, 2004, p. 270). Pro-poor, participatory approaches, therefore, have been promoted as the "solution to persistent landlessness and poverty in the countryside of most developing countries" (Borras, 2006, p. 99).

These ideas were given elevated prominence by the internationally acclaimed economist, Hernando de Soto (2000). De Soto's central view is that non-Western countries are poor because the majority of their assets and/or property rights are not formalised. People in these countries have assets, they have entrepreneurial ingenuity, but their assets lack representational value. According to De Soto, people in the so-called Third World are helplessly trapped in obsolete ways, which prevent capitalism from delivering to them the same wealth it has delivered to the West (De Soto, 2000, p. 5); they are not able to benefit from capitalism because of their inability to generate capital (De Soto, 2000, p. 5). De Soto posits, furthermore, that most people from the so-called Third World already have or "possess the assets they need to make a success of capitalism" (De Soto, 2000, p. 6); the problem is that they hold these assets in defective forms: houses built on land the ownership rights of which are not adequately recorded, and

> because the rights to these possessions are not adequately documented, assets cannot readily be turned into capital, cannot be traded outside the narrow local circles where people know and trust each other, cannot be used as collateral for a loan and cannot be used as a share against an investment (De Soto, 2000, p. 6).

In contrast, De Soto claims, countries in the West are advanced in their economies because "every parcel of land, every piece of equipment or store of inventories is represented in a property document that is a visible sign of a vast hidden process that connects all these assets to the rest of the economy" (De Soto, 2000, p. 6).

Through this "representational process, assets can lead an invisible parallel life alongside their material existence" (De Soto, 2000, p. 6), including being used as collateral for credit. By this process, the West injects life into assets and makes them generate capital. The so-called Third World lacks this representational process. People in the so-called Third World have assets but lack the process to represent their property and create capital. Without representation, their assets are dead capital. According to De Soto, this is the "mystery of capital". The logical solution is, therefore, to bring the assets into a formal property system by recording them and "embodying them in a title" (De Soto, 2000, p. 45). De Soto asserts that without formal property from which economic potential can be extracted, the assets of developing and former communist countries are like water in a lake high in the Andes: an untapped stock of potential energy (De Soto, 2000, p. 46). Capital is born by representing in writing, in a title, a security, a contract and other records, the most economically and socially useful qualities *about* the asset, as opposed to the more striking visual aspects of the asset (De Soto, 2000, p. 48). Through doing this, we step out of "the material world into the conceptual universe where capital lives" (De Soto, 2000, p. 48).

In Namibia, views similar to those of De Soto have found prominence in land reform discourse. Political figures have incorporated De Soto's view in their speeches. In 1996, during the Consultative Conference on Communal Land Administration, in her welcoming address, the former minister of the then Ministry of Lands, Resettlement and Rehabilitation at the time underscored challenges facing communal areas. In her words, "under the current arrangements, communal land farmers cannot use the land they occupy as collateral for borrowing money for development from commercial institutions" (Iivula-Ithana, 1997, p. 12). She added that "a way must be found to bring communal land in the mainstream of national development efforts" (Iivula-Ithana, 1997, p. 12). Similarly, in his opening address, the then president of Namibia, Dr Sam Nujoma, at the same conference explained that

> investors can only have confidence in investing in communal areas if we have a rural land administration system that provides people with rights to land tenure. We know that currently most farmers cannot raise loans because they cannot use their land as collateral (Nujoma, 1997, p. 15).

Nujoma emphasised that, "for significant economic development to take place in communal lands, farmers should be able to raise loans in order to improve present production levels" (1997, p. 13). These sentiments were expressed again at a Cabinet retreat, which was held in Swakopmund in 2005. The following points are two of the recommendations that emerged from the retreat:

1. In view of uncertainty about land ownership, which makes investment difficult and discourages innovation and risk-taking, the issue of long-term tenure for both communal and commercial farmland should be clarified;
2. Housing and home ownership in rural areas, as well as tradable land rights in communal areas, should be promoted in order to encourage ownership of land

> and enable civil servants, such as teachers and police and military personnel, to own land and use housing finance schemes to acquire homes in rural areas (Republic of Namibia, 2005a, pp. 20, 21, 32).

The Cabinet retreat, furthermore, expressed the view that, although reform through the Communal Land Reform Act, 2000 addresses communal land administration and land rights insecurity, the establishment of communal land boards does not mean rural people would be able to use land as collateral to acquire financing. This is because the customary tenure system does not provide for such transactions (Republic of Namibia, 2005a, pp. 20, 21, 32).

Beyond political and policymaking circles, similar views of the limitations of customary tenure have come under the umbrella theme of unlocking the economic potential of communal land. In 2012, the Bank of Namibia hosted an annual symposium with the theme, *Unlocking the Economic Potential of Communal Land*. This theme was chosen "because of the need for policy discourse and actions on how to make the communal land economically viable" (Research Department of the Bank of Namibia, 2012, p. 5). Some of the questions that the symposium aimed to answer included, firstly, "could providing tradable property use or ownership rights, similar to those of commercial land... increase the economic potential of communal land?", and secondly, "what have been the experiences of other developing economies in converting from customary land system into tradable land rights?" (Research Department of the Bank of Namibia, 2012, p. 5).

De Soto's view perpetuates symbolic injustices against customary tenure systems. The view is still underpinned by value hierarchy and cultural domination in favour of individualised, private land tenure, in contrast to customary land tenure systems. The view is based on a "status order of society and culturally defined hierarchies of status", and regards customary land tenure as inferior and private ownership as superior (Fraser, 1996, p. 32). Thus, De Soto's view, like evolutionary and/or neo-evolutionary views, still conforms to the desire to convert customary tenure systems into individual, private ownership of land. Clearly, customary land tenure systems are still interpreted as inhibitory to investment in the land and to general social progress. Customary land tenure systems are not understood or interpreted in their own right.

Opposition to the neo-evolutionary approaches of land tenure reform

Just like the evolutionary approaches to land tenure reform, the neo-evolutionary model of tenure change, or post-modern liberal idea of tenure change and De Soto's views, in particular, have attracted strong criticism. To present these criticisms, I draw on the pertinent work of Ben Cousins and colleagues (2005). The authors of this work argue that De Soto's policy prescriptions are "highly misleading" and "may be inappropriate for the poorest and most vulnerable in... society, and have negative rather than positive impacts on their security and well-being" (Cousins et al. 2005, pp. 1, 14). Furthermore, De Soto's views do not "adequately acknowledge that titling programmes have been tried (at huge costs) all over the developing world and failed to produce the results he predicts; in fact, many titling schemes have been shown to *disadvantage* the poor" (Cousins et al., 2005, p. 2). De Soto and the entire neo-evolutionary model of tenure change fail to "accommodate other property systems, and the unsettling implications for mainstream property systems are skirted, not confronted" (Cousins et al., 2005, p. 2). It also fails to recognise differentiation among populations: "the poor and the 'extra-legal' sector are portrayed as homogenous, where in reality they are highly differentiated – some of the poor are entrepreneurs, but others are landless rural workers who own virtually no assets at all" (Cousins et al., 2005, p. 2). This criticism reflects what Fraser (1996) calls the recognition of difference, as opposed to universalist recognition. The recognition of difference is a pragmatic approach to addressing *mis*recognition. A pragmatic approach focuses on "what sorts of recognition is [sic] needed to overcome specific, existing obstacles to participatory parity" (Fraser, 1996, p. 33). In Namibia, this participatory parity is inhibited by several factors. In other words, viability of communal land cannot be solved by reforming tenure alone. Several structural inequalities have to be addressed, particularly factors relating to access to markets, road, and water infrastructural development.

Just as the evolutionary models of tenure change overemphasised efficiency, productivity and agricultural development, De Soto, under the umbrella of the neo-evolutionary tenure change, is criticised for solely acknowledging the capital formation function of property, and undermining and ignoring the other functions, such as securing livelihoods and social identity (Cousins et al., 2005, p. 2).

Cousins and colleagues, therefore, issue a call to "policy makers ...[to] resist the temptation to seek simplistic solutions to poverty of the kind offered by de Soto" (2005, p. 5). Tenure reform remains necessary, but it is a difficult task and, alone, it cannot reduce poverty and bring about prosperity. Instead, the advice is to build a

> better understanding of the complexity of multiple, informal tenures within the 'extra-legal' sector, in all their diversity, and acknowledge at the outset that they are fundamentally different to the individualised, exclusive, private property systems of Western capitalism (Cousins et al., 2005, p. 6).

Critics acknowledge that the lack of legal recognition of property rights can result in insecurity of tenure and, therefore, laws and policies promoting tenure security are required (Cousins et al., 2005, p. 5). Security of tenure is not to be realised by integrating existing systems into the property mainstream, but through "supporting social practices that have widespread legitimacy" (Cousins et al., 2005, p. 5). Prevailing social practices are underpinned by features that should be recognised, supported, and strengthened. The social embeddedness of tenure helps to secure livelihoods and define identity (Cousins et al., 2005, p. 5). Critics, however, take on one positive suggestion from De Soto's view that what is needed is adjustment of the dominant framework, to accommodate extra-legal property, in order to build a bridge between the legal and the extra-legal (Cousins et al., 2005, p. 5). I argue, too, that what is required is to create a level playing field between private tenure and customary land tenure systems, that allows parity of participation, without reducing or integrating one into the other; Fraser refers to a field of "multiple, debinarized, fluid, ever-shifting differences" (1995, p. 82). This "debinarized" field represents a radical move to "combat the denial of 'property' to the many forms of customary tenure under which millions of resource users in Africa hold land" (Peters, 2013a, p. 557). It provides the "basis for preventing further misappropriation by more powerful agents, domestic and foreign" (Peters, 2013a, p. 557).

Genesis of a land reform agenda for Namibia

The land question formed the basis of Namibia's liberation struggle against its occupation by apartheid South Africa (Republic of Namibia, 1991a; Werner, 2001), and deliberations on the desired independent, centralised land reform, as a vehicle for transformation in Namibia. The centrality of land reform is evident in several studies undertaken and reports published in the 1970s and 1980s, particularly by the United Nations Institute for Namibia (UNIN), an educational institution set up by the United Nations for Namibia, in Lusaka, Zambia. Two of the studies and subsequent reports by UNIN are key. In 1979, UNIN published a detailed report, titled *Toward Agrarian Reform: Policy Options for Namibia.* The report provides policy options for agrarian reform for an independent Namibia, and, in particular, identified land reform as the "precondition for change in the productive structure and in the standard of living of the rural masses" (United Nations Institute for Namibia, 1979, p. v). Subsequently, in 1986, UNIN published a second comprehensive report, titled *Namibia: Perspectives for National Reconstruction and Development.* The 1986 report also identified land reform as the "means to achieve thorough-going socio-economic transformation through elimination of exploitative relations, both traditional and capitalistic" (United Nations Institute for Namibia, 1986, pp. 133–134). The centrality of land reform was also evident in the strategic documents of the South West People's Organisation (SWAPO). The strategic forecast and framework for an independent Namibia for SWAPO integrally concerned justice in land relations (United Nations Institute for Namibia, 1986; Werner, 2001). As a vehicle for transformation, land reform was to bring about a just society and a just Namibia, through land distribution and ownership, dual land tenure systems and differentiated economic orientations.

In terms of the dual land tenure system, the 1979 UNIN report, in particular, discouraged communal land and customary tenure systems, and a freehold land tenure system for an independent Namibia. The report states specifically that "the customary communal land tenure as presently practised in the homelands would... be unsatisfactory for an independent Namibia" (United Nations Institute for Namibia, 1979, p. 41). The report also states that freehold land tenure system should be discouraged, as it "creates socially unacceptable structures" (United Nations Institute for Namibia, 1979, p. 41). Clearly, the objectives and forecast for an independent Namibia disregarded the dual land tenure system. The desired options were those that leaned towards public ownership of land through nationalisation of land – a more socialist-oriented option. With this option, the vision was that the state would own the land and grant different kinds of rights for different uses, including that of agricultural production. This restructuring pattern surrounded the strategic goal and framework of equity/justice. The envisaged restructuring pattern, furthermore, represented a long-term vision of which the aim was not radical change, but gradual implementation, in order to avoid conflict with production, that is, agricultural production. The long-term view of policy concerning agrarian transformation in an independent Namibia emphasises the need for a mix of policies that maintains the agricultural production base and, at the same time, dismantles unjust land relation structures.

Liberation movements that advocated for land reform commensurate with the tenets of socialism drew their inspiration from the events of the time, and, especially, changes in other southern African countries. Inspiration came from the newly independent nations of Mozambique and Angola which attained their independence in 1975. Furthermore, the preference for a socialist-oriented land-reform option was influenced by SWAPO's alignment to the Soviet Union, which had supported SWAPO to achieve its liberation agenda (Jauch & Tjirera, 2017). However, hopes for socialist-oriented land reform, as exemplified by Mozambique and Angola, were to be dashed by the counter-revolutionary wars in those countries, by the fall of communism and, more specifically, by the weakening of Soviet power in the early 1980s. The weakening of the Soviet bloc and the events leading up to the fall of the Berlin Wall led to major changes for nationalist movements like SWAPO, freeing them from a socialist-oriented ideology to pursue a path more suited to their nationalist agenda. It can therefore be argued that, though the land policies pursued by SWAPO in the 1960s and 1970s were socialist in nature, SWAPO itself was, first and foremost, a nationalist movement and secondarily, a socialist one.

New standpoints on a land reform model for Namibia

From the 1980s, the discourse on a model for land reform changed. Discourse on land reform takes place within the context of prevailing political and economic ideological contexts. In the 1980s, the land reform discourse changed from a socialist-oriented agenda, to become aligned with a neoliberal agenda. There was a gradual shift from a discourse advocating land reform aligned with the tenets of socialism, to one influenced by neoliberal standpoints. The shift related, in particular, to the redistributive tenets of land reform, and to alignment with a capitalist economic and neoliberal theoretical stance to property, that is, in respect of private property. Evidence of this change is found in SWAPO's *Economic Policy Position Document,* which was released in 1988, and in the election manifesto of 1989 (Jauch & Tjirera, 2017, p. 145). According to *The Namibian,* this SWAPO policy document

> no longer called for nationalization of key industries but instead promised fair and just compensation in those instances where state acquisition of assets from private hands is considered necessary for the rebuilding and restructuring of Namibia's national economy (27 January 1989, cited by Jauch & Tjirera, 2017, p. 145).

The standpoint that nationalisation would not be pursued became clearer in 1989, after it was recommended and accepted that the Constituent Assembly would adopt the 1982 Constitutional Principles as the guiding framework for drafting the Namibian Constitution (Zongwe, 2019, p. 71). These Constitutional Principles were proposed by the Western Contact Group (comprising Canada, France, United Kingdom, United States, and West Germany). Of particular importance to the 1982 Constitutional Principles was the Bill of Rights, which included rights to property or the protection of property rights, more particularly, private property held under freehold title. The Bill of Rights reads, "there will be a declaration of fundamental human rights, which will include the rights... to protection from arbitrary deprivation of private property or deprivation of private property without just compensation" (United Nations Security Council, 1982). According to Kaapama (2007), the 1982 Constitutional Principles precluded SWAPO from pursuing radical socioeconomic transformation and bringing about redistributive justice. The Constitutional Principles became the foundation on which Article 16 of the Namibian Constitution, on the protection of property rights, is based. These principles form the legal foundation for the adoption of market-related economic policies, the so-called mixed economy, and neoliberal-oriented land reform. All in all,

> The international community's imposition of the 1982 constitutional principles is seen as an *alibi* to safeguard vested socioeconomic interests

> that were established through colonial theft and plunder and as providing an inappropriate basis for pursuing meaningful national reconciliation based on the principles of restorative justice and for promoting equitable and sustainable national development processes (Kaapama, 2007, p. 34).

According to Okoth-Ogendo (2000, cited by Kaapama, 2007, p. 35), adopting a neoliberal model was not only peculiar to Namibia; its adoption was generally a "prerequisite for the accommodation of emerging and/or reformed states within the context of the international politics of development aid, aid that was instantaneously needed to kick-start their reconstruction processes". Note that the 1982 Constitutional Principles and, today, the Namibian Constitution, are silent on the protection and securing of customary land rights; instead, the focus is on private property held under freehold title.

Independence and development of the land reform programme in Namibia

At independence in 1990, Namibia inherited socio-economic inequalities that manifested in skewed land distribution and ownership, dual systems of land tenure, and economic orientations to land use. These inequalities in relation to land were characterised by the minority of the population owning the majority of the land, while the majority of the population lived on a minority of the land. The duality of the land tenure system comprised, first, the freehold tenure system under which land is privately owned and protected, meaning that landholders have individual titles to land, and that land rights are bankable; and, second, communal land, under which there are no freehold titles – instead, use rights are allocated to individuals and household units by traditional authorities under customary tenure systems without any statutory protection. The two land tenure systems are associated with the third manifestation of injustice in land relations, that is, a differentiated economic orientation of land use. A freehold land tenure system is oriented to commercial purposes, while a communal tenure system is oriented to subsistence. Both the dual nature of tenure systems and the differentiated economic orientations to land use represent "first and second class systems" (Hamutenya, 1997, p. 32). I do not regard the customary tenure system or communal land as inferior to private ownership, nor do I promote what happened in other African countries, namely, calls for its abolition. There is irrefutable evidence from across the continent that people are not primarily poor because of customary tenure, but because of a lack of support services. What is problematic is attitudes towards customary tenure, as explained above, and the lack of statutory security of tenure under the customary system that is exacerbated, especially in the context of numerous restructuring processes. In a socio-economic survey undertaken in preparation for the 1991 land conference, Namibian people from different communal areas were asked about their perceptions of security of tenure. One of the questions in the survey was: "Can anyone take your land away from you?" (The Namibian Economic Policy Research Unit, 1991). A quarter of the respondents from north-central Namibia (Owambo) who participated in the survey indicated that they could lose their land. The respondents specified that the traditional authorities in Owambo "effectively control the land… and after the death of the head of household, they do take land away from the household unless the wife and children can again find the payment for the right to use it" (The Namibian Economic Policy Research Unit, 1991, p. 182). A related question was: "Under what circumstances could someone take your land away?" (The Namibian Economic Policy Research Unit, 1991, p. 183). In response to this question, most respondents indicated that they believed they could lose their land, and about a quarter of the respondents from north-central Namibia believed that they could lose their land "when government takes it for redistribution" (The Namibian Economic Policy Research Unit, 1991, p. 183); women believed that the death of their male affine (either husband or father) would result in their losing their land. These responses reveal just some of the insecurities that have long characterised customary tenure systems.

To address injustices in land relations, the government of independent Namibia embarked on a programme of land reform. As discussed in the preceding section, various options for land reform had already been deliberated before independence, starting with the option to nationalise, and moving to a neoliberal approach. In his presentation during the 1996 Consultative Conference on Communal Land Administration, the late Hidipo Hamutenya explained three options at hand. These were, one, nationalisation of land, two, a complete process of land alienation and privatisation of all communal land, and three, continuing the *status quo* of the dual land tenure system (Hamutenya, 1997). These options all had far-reaching implications, and none of them were seen to offer a comfortable policy choice for Namibia (Hamutenya, 1997, p. 32). For example, nationalisation was viewed to carry the risk of instigating panic and destabilising the commercial subsector, of which commercial agriculture formed the basis and was an important source of the country's revenue. At independence, for instance, nationally, agriculture contributed about 8.5% to the gross national product, and 24% of the national workforce was employed in that sector (Sherbourne, 2014). If the commercial sector were to be destabilised, large-scale retrenchments would result. Alienation and privatisation of communal land was not perceived to be a good option either, as it would result in large-scale dispossession of land and destitution of the majority of the population, while a few of the elite would retain benefits. About 120,000 rural households depended on communal land for their sustenance; these people eked out a living from the land. It was feared that privatisation would create widespread socio-economic insecurity and, therefore, political instability (Hamutenya, 1997). In spite of its shortcomings, the communal land tenure system was recognised as a system which provided a safety net for many people.

Because of the shortcomings inherent in the first two options (nationalisation of all land and privatisation of communal land), the government of an independent Namibia therefore opted to maintain the status quo of a dual land tenure system (Hamutenya, 1997). Hamutenya (1997) failed to include in his justification for maintaining the status quo the events of the 1980s that had led Namibia to choose a so-called mixed economy, as enshrined in the Constitution and, more importantly, the choice of a neoliberal approach to property rights. Thus, the three options were not choices at independence: the status quo had already been accepted before then and had its provenance in 1980s politics, and geopolitics at a global level.

Hamutenya (1997) indicated that the status quo would be maintained temporarily, but would be reformed gradually. Only when the Namibian economy had been sufficiently diversified and expanded and could offer the majority of the population alternative employment in sectors other than subsistence agriculture, would changes in this sector be viable. His long-term vision was certainly that of a "unitary land system that will provide a full range of tenure arrangement systems which would have equal status and validity before the law as the freehold system" (Hamutenya, 1997, p. 32). Retaining communal land in an independent Namibia was premised on the tenets of equity, which had long dominated the strategic frame of land reform in Namibia. Land reform in Namibia, thus, comprises distinct arms: one that is located within the neoliberal agenda of promoting and protecting private property, and another that is located within the social equity agenda, and which targets communal land.

Precursors of the land reform programme were national consultations on the land question, which had been initiated in 1990, and which culminated in the National Conference on Land Reform and the Land Question in 1991. The objective of the conference was to achieve consensus on the land question, which would provide a solid foundation for the formulation of a policy and programme of action on land reform (Republic of Namibia, 1991). The conference produced consensus resolutions for land reform that addressed both freehold and communal land. These were non-legally binding consensus resolutions. The conference "tried to find a balance between concerns for addressing colonial dispossession, equity and efficiency" (Cousins & Scoones, 2010). Efficiency concerns centred on approaches to a land redistribution model that were expected to address past injustices of land dispossession that had resulted in the skewed distribution of land, while not disturbing the commercial agricultural sector, for fear of destabilisation. The idea was to maintain efficiency in the functioning of the commercial agricultural sector. Equity was central, and the goals were to redistribute land to previously disadvantaged people and, ultimately, address the racially weighted land distribution; and to secure land tenure and rights to resources for households and individuals holding land under customary land tenure systems. While the aim in the freehold areas was to redistribute land, the aim in the communal areas was to recognise customary tenure regimes as legal in their own right and equivalent in the eyes of national law to the freehold/leasehold culture (Werner, 2015; Wily, 2000, p. 2). These aims, I argue, underscore claims for redistribution and claims for recognition – the "co-fundamental and mutually irreducible dimensions of justices [and/or of social equity]" (Fraser & Honneth, 2003, p. 3).

The immediate focus of the programme of land reform was on the freehold areas, in other words, on the claims for redistribution. This focus was justified because this was where inequality was most blatantly visible (Graefe et al., 2012). At the 1991 land conference, the future of Namibia's communal areas and land was on the agenda. During the conference, the then prime minister, Hon. Hage Geingob, reiterated that the conference needed to give serious attention to land policy and administration in the communal areas and, particularly, to the protection of communal rights to land of poorer members of society. At the conference, 13 of the 24 consensus resolutions pertained to communal land. Consensus pertaining to communal land concerns the following thematic issues:

1. The future role of communal areas
2. Access to communal land
3. Access to land for disadvantaged communities
4. Rights of women in regard to access to land and land rights
5. Governance institutions for land allocation and administration
6. Security of tenure
7. Illegal fencing
8. Dual grazing
9. Payment for access to land
10. Game conservation and farmers' rights
11. Transfer of large communal farmers to commercial land
12. The stock control barrier (Red Line)
13. The role of NGOs and cooperatives

While reforms on freehold land had commenced right after independence, reforms on communal land remained in discussion rooms for the first 12 years of independence. Werner fittingly states that, during the first 12 years of independence, "a veritable legal vacuum existed with respect to the administration of communal land" (2011, p. 39). This means that, until 2002, when the Communal Land Reform Act was passed, and March 2003, when it was put in force, there was no statutory legal framework to guide land administration in communal areas. Traditional authorities continued to allocate land according to their respective customary laws. The administration of communal land remained outside the realm of statutory law. This legal vacuum has had serious implications for access to land and land relations in general. Odendaal (2011, p. 12) observes that "powerful interest groups often used this policy and administrative vacuum to their advantage and ignored customary land tenure rights to fence off large tracts of communal land".

All along, two types of tenure system and land use could be observed in communal areas: On the one hand, individual rights to land are allocated to households for residence and cropping; and on the other hand, commonages are used for grazing. Individualised landholdings, for which landholders had rights that were legitimated by traditional authorities, are relatively secure, until a change in life circumstances occurs, as referred to by the respondents in the survey discussed above; women, in particular, faced insecurity of tenure when their spouses died. Additionally, as a result of the legal vacuum, commonage suffered the consequences of land individualisation, in particular, land in uninhabited areas which was seasonally used for grazing. Odendaal (2011, p. 11) argues that "in the absence of statutory legal law on communal land, poor communal livestock farmers and traditional authorities had no statutory law remedy to defend their rights". This argument applies to poor communal livestock farmers, however, traditional authorities have had a direct role in the process of land individualisation, as they allocate land. Their participating roles were exposed after the legal framework for communal land, which prohibits fencing off large tracts of communal land, was passed. Landholders who had fenced off large tracts of land claimed that their land was the result of legitimate claims, as they had been allocated these lands by traditional authorities.

Overall, the main conclusion that can be drawn from the legal vacuum on communal land for the first 12 years of independence is that powerful interest groups accumulated land at the expense of the poor. Fencing off large tracts of land has direct implications for the livelihoods of subsistence farmers. These implications can be witnessed today, as poor farmers are forced to graze their livestock in the corridors between fences of large individualised tracts of land, which become degraded and are ever shrinking. Appropriation of large tracts of land in communal areas affects many land users, some of whom state that "everywhere you go it is just fences after fences", "we are left to graze our livestock in the corridors between fences", "village headmen have been allocating large landholdings, even when they know our commonages are shrinking" (interview with landholder, OM65_2015)[4].

4 Codes denote the first letters of the village name and the year of interview.

The counterargument offered by landholders who have fenced large tracts of land is that they lack options, because land reform in the freehold land areas has been too slow and has not delivered on the promise to integrate large communal farmers, as had been agreed at the 1991 land conference. Large communal farmers are defined as farmers who have accumulated a large number of livestock. The Affirmative Action Loan Scheme, one of the redistribution mechanisms for freehold land, uses ownership of 150 large stock units (livestock) as a proxy for large farmers. Large communal farmers with 150 or more large stock units, therefore, put a great deal of grazing pressure on communal land. Communal land carries too much livestock for it to be environmentally sustainable. Therefore, the problem of large-scale individualisation of land in communal areas is exacerbated by a lack of access to land in freehold commercial agricultural areas.

Enactment of a law for communal land in Namibia

The process of bringing communal land administration within the realm of statutory law has been characterised by conflicting opinions. These conflicting opinions go hand in hand with the argument that communal land reform is perhaps a far bigger challenge than land reform in commercial areas (Graefe et al., 2012). When reconstructing the events leading up to the enactment of the communal land law, the contestation and criticism reported in the media can be categorised as criticism of a lack of transparency and the bureaucratisation of the process; the communal land bill failing to address sufficiently the issue of social equity, but favouring elites; and the communal land bill favouring the organs of the modern state and disadvantaging traditional authorities.

After the 1991 land conference, discussions over communal land were next subjected to collective discussion in 1994, when the People's Land Conference was organised under the auspices of non-governmental organisations (NGOs). This conference yielded results in the form of many resolutions, but carried no political weight and accordingly, the resolutions did not translate into policymaking. The 1996 Consultative Conference on Communal Land Administration, jointly organised by the government and the University of Namibia, focused on communal land matters in particular. In her opening remarks, the then minister of Lands, Resettlement and Rehabilitation, Hon. Pendukeni Iivula-Ithana, stated that the conference was the "first of its kind in Namibia where various stakeholders in communal matters have come together to discuss issues pertaining to communal land" (Iivula-Ithana, 1997, p. 11). According to the minister, the conference was held "to find a common ground on how to proceed further in bringing communal land in the mainstream of the national development agenda" (Iivula-Ithana, 1997, p. 11). Central to the agenda of the conference was the discussion of the Communal Land

Bill. Deliberations on the Bill were marked by dissent, several proposals, rejections of certain provisions, and proposals for new amendments. Dissenting voices came particularly from traditional authorities concerning the creation of the regional land boards and the roles of traditional leaders in communal land administration. During the deliberations, all the traditional authorities were given the opportunity to give their statements, especially on the Communal Land Bill on the table. In a collective statement by the traditional authorities of north-central Namibia, the late *omukwaniilwa,* Immanuel Eliphas Kauluma, made it clear that "[traditional authorities] cannot be made to be back-yard boys of what should be technical and advisory bodies, namely, the Regional Land Boards" (Traditional Authorities from Owambo, 1997, p. 69). *Omukwaniilwa* continued that traditional authorities have "a long standing responsibility and are, therefore, more authoritative than appointed land professionals technicians [sic]" (Traditional Authorities from Owambo, 1997, p. 69). Through this statement, the traditional authorities of north-central Namibia therefore demanded that the government inform them directly whether they were needed (Traditional Authorities from Owambo, 1997). In relation to the creation of the regional land boards, the Bill provided that these bodies would be responsible for regulating and exercising control over the occupation and use of communal land. Hence, the traditional authorities saw this provision as removing their functions and entrusting these functions to organs of the modern state. Because of these dissenting voices, the government reviewed the provisions to legally centralise the roles of traditional authorities in land allocation and communal land administration in general.

After the 1996 conference, the Bill spent the following six years between the drafters, public hearings, and the two chambers of Parliament, the National Assembly, and the National Council. There were still contestations in the public sphere, which were aired in the media. The contentions and rejections, back-and-forth proposals and amendments of the Bill included allegations of a lack of consultation at the regional level, comparing the process to the colonial Land Act (*The Namibian,* 1999), claims that the Bill failed to address the issue of fencing of communal land by government officials and wealthy members of society *(The Namibian,* 2001), and, in particular, accusations that the "Bill did not adequately deal with illegal fencing carried out prior to its enactment and it lacks explicitness on the fencing issue" (Maletsky, 2000a). Large areas of communal land continued to be fenced off, leaving little space for poverty-stricken communal farmers to graze their livestock (*The Namibian*, 2001). Those who rejected the Bill argued that it "would deprive more indigenous people of the right to land ownership" (*The Namibian,* 1999). These criticisms refer to claims that the Bill favoured the interests of elites, and disadvantaged the rural poor and, therefore, lacked social equity. According to Werner (2011), the debates between the proponents and opponents on the fencing of communal land were conflated into rights and equity issues, which compromised the usefulness of these debates.

Others argued that the Bill "failed to address the imbalances of the colonial Land Act, which previously discriminated against indigenous people" (*The Namibian*, 1999). Still others supported the legal provision of placing the responsibility for land administration in the hands of the "land boards only, and it must be taken away from the traditional leaders who exploited their communities by embracing colonial laws" (*The Namibian*, 1999). Critics raised further concerns over the lack of transparency of the process. When the Bill was tabled in Parliament in 2000 and passed on to the National Council, people were still arguing that the Bill had failed to consider a wide range of inputs. It was reported, for example, that the Bill was passed after ignoring inputs of "2 055 individuals and organisations consulted on the Bill" (Maletsky, 2000a). Additionally, the Bill did not address the "concerns raised by some 800 communal farmers who marched on Parliament" (Maletsky, 2000a); it was passed after "ignoring the views of previously marginalised communal farmers" (Maletsky, 2000b). Critics also argued that "the Bill will adversely affect the future administration and management of communal land in the country" (Maletsky, 2000b). Some critics confirmed that law on communal land was long overdue and the proposed legislation would impact the lives of rural communities throughout the country; however, the fact that the Bill did not address certain concerns "could undermine its aims" (Maletsky, 2000b).

The critics called on the National Council, in which they placed their hopes, to consider their proposals. In May 2000, the National Council rejected the Bill, based on fundamental defects, and argued that it would make the poor even poorer. During the sitting when the Bill was discussed, the National Council rejected the Bill on the basis that sections could have adverse and far-reaching impacts, in particular, the section that provides for the granting of rights of leasehold (Shigwedha, 2000a). The argument was that granting rights of leasehold on communal land is a potentially dangerous step, as it may lead to substantial areas of communal land being claimed by a few financially strong persons or institutions (Shigwedha, 2000b), leaving poor people with only a few or no common grazing areas (Shigwedha, 2000a). The National Council, furthermore, raised the issue of people who were fencing communal land, illegally and unfairly, and stated that the Bill did not address this matter authoritatively. The National Council proposed that the Bill include provisions of

> setting out the maximum size of 10 hectares as the largest piece of land that may be granted in respect of communal land, other than communal land where exclusive agricultural activities are undertaken – which contributes greatly to the country's economy (Shigwedha, 2000b).

What is clear from the dissenting voices and criticism of the Communal Land Bill is that the issue of social equity was considered to be central. The majority of Namibian people saw communal land as a safety net for the poor. The criticisms were ultimately about the struggles and politics of recognition. People demanded recognition of the role of communal land in rural people's lives, and were therefore calling for strong protection of land rights in communal areas. In the year 2002, the Communal Land Reform Act, No 5 of 2002 was finally passed and gazetted on 1 March 2003. This marked the beginning of the implementation of communal land reform in Namibia, which comprises two arms: securing tenure, and integrating communal farmers into the commercial agricultural economy. This book traces this process, criss-crossing north-central Namibia, to understand people's lived realities and experiences, locating communal land reform within the broader tenure reform that has swept across Africa.

2

North-Central Namibia's Ethnographic Setting

North-central Namibia presents an ideal case for examining the changing nature of the customary tenure system and communal land reform, and for exploring the increasing competition for land, as well as the increasing diversity of land uses. Thirty-eight percent of the Namibian population reside there, and compared to other regions, it is the geographical area with the greatest number of land rights registered through communal land reform.

Demographical and physical setting

The region called north-central Namibia is commonly referred to as *Owambo,* and it is predominantly inhabited by the Aawambo people. In spite of the changes that have occurred through migration from and to other parts of Namibia, and deliberate changes by the independent government of Namibia to reorganise society beyond an ethnic orientation, Owambo is a physical, geographical and socio-cultural reference area. The two dominating physical features of north-central Namibia are the Cuvelai Delta and Etosha Pan, hence, it is alternatively referred to as the Cuvelai-Etosha Basin. The Cuvelai is a network of drainage channels that spreads out across southern Angola and, after crossing the Namibian border, converging through hundreds of what are locally called *iishana* (singular *oshana)* which flow into the Etosha Pan (Mendelsohn et al., 2000, p. 1). *Iishana* are shallow pans that are filled with water during the rainy season, but which are dry the rest of the year (Mendelsohn et al., 2013). Etosha Pan, in turn, is a huge salt pan that seldom holds water; it is a product of wind erosion and salt deposition over millions of years (Mendelsohn et al., 2000).

North-central Namibia has shallow groundwater and relatively fertile soils. Its climate is semi-tropical, and annual rainfall varies between about 650 mm in the far east to about 300 mm in the far west (Mendelsohn, 2006). These conditions made it possible for the Aawambo to settle in the area; over hundreds of years they have been able to cultivate crops, farm with livestock and access fresh water (Mendelsohn et al., 2013). People in north-central Namibia confirm this claim by asserting that people settled where there was a water source: *omeya oo haa shili ovanhu* (water encourages people to settle); Siiskonen (1990, p. 43) confirms that "water conditions... clearly determined the location of settlements in the Etosha Pan flood plain".

North-central Namibia covers about 84,450 square kilometres or 8.4 million hectares, which is roughly 10% of Namibia's total surface area (Angombe et al., 2016). Mendelsohn et al. (2013) describe it as covering 97,620 square kilometres, or about 9.7 million hectares, which is roughly 12% of Namibia's surface area. Explorers and missionaries who arrived in the area in the mid-19th century observed and estimated that the population numbered about 50,000 people (Siiskonen, 1990). In the latter half of the 19th century, and at about the turn of the 20th century, the population was estimated to have grown to about 100,000 people (Siiskonen, 1990). The population continued to grow throughout the 20th century. The inter-censal demographic survey report published in 2016 estimated that north-central Namibia was home to over 850,000 inhabitants, which is about 38% of the country's total population (Namibia Statistics Agency, 2017a).

With a population of over 850,000 people, north-central Namibia is the most populous and densely populated area in Namibia, with an average density of 14.3 persons per square kilometre, which is above the national population density average, which is estimated at 2.6 persons per square kilometre. North-central Namibia's population density is considered to be "greater than in any other rural areas in south-western Africa" (Mendelsohn et al., 2013, p. 19). There are variations in population density between the four regions in north-central Namibia: Ohangwena with 23.9 persons per square kilometre, Oshana with 21.9 persons per square kilometre, Omusati with 9.4 persons per square kilometre and Oshikoto with 5.0 persons per square kilometre (Namibia Statistics Agency, 2017a). The majority of the population in north-central Namibia (80%) resides in rural areas, though there are regional variations: In Ohangwena, 94% of the population resides in rural areas, in Oshikoto, 84%, in Oshana, 54%, and in Omusati, 95% (Namibia Statistics Agency, 2017a).

Emmanuel Kreike (2004) divides the area conceptually using the local terms of *ofuka/okuti* and *oshilongo. Ofuka/okuti* refers to wilderness areas, while *oshilongo* refers to human-created environments. These terms refer to the variable distribution of the population in the area, in that *ofuka/okuti* areas are characterised by low population densities, and *oshilongo* areas by high population densities. The terms also differentiate between land use, in that *ofuka/okuti* areas were predominantly used for livestock farming with *eehambo* (cattle posts), while *oshilongo* areas were for homesteads and crop production. *Ofuka/okuti* areas constituted frontiers at the periphery. As agro-pastoralists, the Aawambo have long practised seasonal migration, which involved men moving cattle from *oshilongo* to *ofuka/okuti* in search of better grazing grounds, as is common practice for agro-pastoralists who live in dry lands in Africa. This practice is explained by Yuichiro Fujioka, who states that agro-pastoralists of Africa "tend to have highly mobile lifestyles and use natural resources widely and sparsely" (2010, p. 129). While the binary of *ofuka/okuti* and *oshilongo* existed, and is still used in everyday language today, many socio-economic and environmental changes have taken place. These changes render the distinctions between *ofuka/okuti* and *oshilongo* less valid. Areas that used to be described as *ofuka/okuti* have been transformed into *oshilongo,* or now largely exhibit *oshilongo* characteristics. People have established permanent villages with infrastructure, population size and density have increased, and urban localities locally referred to as *eedolopa* are even being proclaimed (by means of local authority areas) in geographical areas once regarded as *ofuka/okuti.* Two examples of the latter transformations are Okongo village in eastern Ohangwena Region, which is now a village council and on its way to becoming a town, and Omuthiya village in Oshikoto Region, which is now a fully-fledged town and the regional capital.

Population growth in north-central Namibia has stimulated demand for land and, in particular, individualised landholdings. Village headmen who are responsible for allocating land complain that there is no more land to allocate to new applicants. Landholders, in turn, complain that land is in short supply, and often subdivide their landholdings to provide land for their adult children, at least for residential purposes. For purposes of cultivation, landholders commonly assert that "they (young adults) can go and find land in *ofuka.*" However, even this instruction is being challenged, as available land in the so-called *ofuka* areas is dwindling too. What we are witnessing in north-central Namibia, therefore, and especially in the densely populated areas, is land being fragmented into smaller holdings that are now increasingly being used for residential purposes, thereby reducing the land available for crop production purposes. This process of land fragmentation is not confined to north-central Namibia, but is evident across Africa, as observed by Peters who argues that, "in the more densely populated regions in countries in eastern and southern Africa, the average size of landholdings on customary land has drastically dropped, with consequent increase in landless and squatter groups" (2013b, p. 548).

The instruction by parents that young adults should go to *ofuka* to get land for cultivation has been put into practical action. Hence, areas once regarded as *ofuka* have subsequently become fully-fledged permanent villages with individualised landholdings and large individualised farms, representing a move away from the open commonages that previously were used for seasonal grazing. Cox, Kerven, Werner and Behnke report on this change by explaining that "driven by population pressure, people have been migrating out of the *oshanas,* first grazing their animals (and coming to know the area), then settling, and finally forming officially recognised villages" (1998, p. 179). Verlinden and Kruger argue that "population increase in settled areas starts migration to more fertile land units in previous prime grazing areas causing a conflict between grazing and cropping" (2007, p. 179).

Political setting

Before the advent of colonialism, north-central Namibia comprised eight polities that made up independent kingdoms ruled by *aakwaniilwa/eehamba* (kings), who were assisted by *omalenga* (headmen). These polities were Oukwanyama, Ondonga, Uukwambi, Ongandjera, Ombalantu, Uukwaluudhi, Uukolonkadhi and Eunda. They were separated by large stretches of wilderness or woodland zones, which varied in breadth (Dobler, 2014, p. xxi; Siiskonen, 1990, p. 41). These woodland zones decreased in size as the population, and demand for crop fields or individualised landholdings, increased. The kingship and Aawambo society at large were and are still organised and structured according to kinship, along matrilineal lines and clans (Williams, 1994). Under colonialism, the Aawambo, especially the Ovakwanyama, were separated by the border line dividing Angola, then a Portuguese colony, from what is today called Namibia, initially a German colony, and later a British mandate under the administration of South Africa. The establishment of the border line resulted in some Ovakwanyama living on the Angolan side, and others within what is now Namibia. During German colonial rule, encounters with Europeans in the area were confined to meetings with explorers and missionaries, visits to mission stations and missionary work; and as a result of early labour migration to farms, towns and mines in central Namibia. In 1906, the area was declared a native reserve. Administratively, the area remained beyond the German colonial government's control until the outbreak of World War I (Dobler, 2014) when, in 1915, South African troops invaded German South West Africa, and the region came under South African control. Between 1915 and 1932, South Africa established an administrative presence in the area, subjugated the kingdoms, and integrated the kings and headmen into a system of indirect rule (Dobler, 2014, p. xxii). Officially, the area was governed by a White native commissioner who, under the system of indirect rule, governed through the kings and headmen. The kings and headmen were backed by the colonial power if they kept to its rules, and were displaced if they did not (Dobler, 2014, p. xxii). During South Africa's administration and, in particular, since 1968, the area was transformed from a native reserve into a self-governing homeland called Ovamboland, thereby joining other homelands that were created as a result of the Odendaal Commission's recommendations (Odendaal, 1964). Under the self-governing system, the kings and chiefs became the ministers of the homeland government (Dobler, 2014; Shiweda, 2011). By adhering to the colonial power's rules, the kings and headmen maintained control over the people and land. The kings and headmen maintained their power to control access to and allocate land in their respective jurisdictions.

After Namibia became independent in 1990, the colonial dispensation's system of organising and administratively defining Namibia on ethnic grounds was revoked. Soon after independence, the independent government instituted the Delimitation Commission to delineate the country into regional and local political units, the boundaries of which were to be "geographical only, without reference to the race, colour or ethnic origins of the inhabitants" (Republic of Namibia, 1990, p. 60). This was a concerted move away from the homeland policy of the apartheid regime, which had divided Namibia according to ethnic/tribal and racial lines, and based "political order [and belonging] on institutionalised ethnicity" (Dobler, 2014, p. 17). The Delimitation Commission divided Namibia into 13 regions, later 14, when Kavango Region was divided into Kavango East and Kavango West. Namibia comprises a two-tier modern governance system made up of central and decentralised governance. Decentralised governance is made up of the 14 political and administrative regions, four of which are found in north-central Namibia: Ohangwena, Omusati, Oshana and Oshikoto.

These political and administrative regions of Namibia were established in accordance with Articles 102 and 103 of the Constitution for the purpose of regional and local government (Republic of Namibia, 1990). Each region is headed by a regional governor, who is appointed by the president to represent the president in the region. Furthermore, each region is divided into constituencies for electoral, decentralised governance and development purposes. Constituencies were also delineated by the Delimitation Commission and in accordance with Article 106 of the Constitution. Individual constituencies are headed by councillors who are elected by the people within the respective boundaries of constituencies.

In addition to the modern, decentralised state governance system, the Namibian Constitution provides for the establishment of a council of traditional leaders to advise the president, particularly on matters relating to the control and utilisation of communal land (Republic of Namibia, 1990). This constitutional provision made possible the statutory institutionalisation of traditional authorities in the country. Traditional authorities in Namibia function under the Traditional Authorities Act, 2000.[5] North-central Namibia comprises eight traditional authorities, namely, Ombalantu, Ombadja, Ondonga, Ongandjera, Oukwanyama, Uukolonkadhi, Uukwaluudhi and Uukwambi. The people under these traditional authorities share many "socio-economic, cultural and political traits" (Dobler, 2014, p. xix). The boundaries of traditional authorities overlap the four political and administrative regions. Parts of Ohangwena Region fall under Oukwanyama and Ombadja, and others under the Ondonga traditional authorities; Oshikoto Region has some areas falling under the Oukwanyama and others under the Ondonga traditional authorities. Some areas of Oshana Region fall under the Uukwambi, Ondonga and

5 No. 25 of 2000.

Oukwanyama traditional authorities. Omusati Region has areas falling under the Ombalantu, Ongandjera, Uukwaluudhi and Uukolonkadhi traditional authorities.

Traditional authorities are hierarchical, socio-political institutions that comprise layered levels of authority: The supreme leader is locally called *ohamba/ omukwaniilwa*; senior traditional councillors are sometimes referred to as senior headmen, locally called *omalenga* (pl.) *elenga* (sing.); and traditional councillors, who are sometimes referred to as village headmen and locally called *oovene vomikunda* (pl.) *mwene womukunda* (sing.); and *ookapatashu* (representatives of village headmen in the different parts of villages). *Ookapatashu* are not provided for in the Traditional Authorities Act, but by the customary leadership system. The hierarchical structure of the Oukwanyama Traditional Authority, for example, consists of the supreme leader, the *ohamba,* who appoints *omalenga,* who preside over districts locally referred to as *oikandjo* or *oilongo.* Between 2013 and 2017, at the time of my fieldwork, there were 11 *oikandjo* in Oukwanyama Traditional Authority. One of the *oikandjo* or districts where I worked is Eudaneko, which comprised 39 villages. The *omalenga* appoint village headmen (*oovene vomikunda),* who preside over villages (*omikunda*). In this case, appointing merely entails inauguration, formalising and/or legitimising village headmen, while the actual appointing of village headmen traditionally takes place in the matrilineal family social space. Positions of village headmen are inherited along consanguinity lines. Consanguinity is a kinship term that refers to relations through common bloodlines. Consanguinity is juxtaposed to affinal, which refers to relations through marriage. In all the villages I worked, the village headmen at the time were related, by common bloodlines, to the founders of their respective villages. The village headmen I interviewed asserted that "this village was founded by my great grandfather grandfather/father". They would often assert in the local language that *ondi li moipundi ya tate/ya tatekulu,* roughly translated as "I am on my father's/ grandfather's throne". It is important to note that today this practice is slowly being challenged, as village members are starting to demand democratic process in the appointment of village headmen, in other words, that the headmen be elected.

In order to be legitimated by the senior headman, the village headman pays what is locally referred to as *ombadu yekaya* (*omakaya* refers to tobacco) to the senior headman. In return, village headmen receive *ombadu yekaya* for allocating land in their respective villages. Using tobacco as means of payment or for services rendered in north-central Namibia is an old practice that was introduced by the missionaries (Peltola, 2002), and which was gradually adopted as payment for access to land. As monetary exchange was introduced and intensified under the contract labour system, access to land was also monetised, but the practice was still referred to as *ombadu yekaya.* During this time, contract workers returned from their contracts with tobacco as gifts for their traditional leaders, and would present village headmen with tobacco when they were allocated land. A village headman in one of the villages I worked narrated the history of giving *ombadu yekaya*:

> Villages were expensive, and not all clans could afford them – *omikunda okwa li di na ondilo, ka kwali ha di dulika komapata keshe.* In the old tradition, people used to pay 12 cattle, artefacts of *Ovawambo,* the artefacts that have been bequeathed to us, the clans' artefacts that are so rare and priceless. I have no knowledge of where they came from. These included ivory amulets, those which are not adorned by poor man. One would even ask you to present a horse, knowing that you do not have it at all. That was how expensive villages were. With education and the establishment of the modern state, things have changed. Headmen are no longer asked a lot. Now they look at the size of the village and the bigger the village the more the number of cattle one has to pay. Like this village, there are almost 200 *omaumbo* [households], but the neighbouring villages only have about 70 *omaumbo.* The highest payment that one can make is eight cattle, that is for biggest villages now.

Giving *ombadu yekaya* bestows a sense of owning the village. Headmen of some of the villages where I worked often referred to *omukunda wange* (my village). In Chapter 6, which deals with the land registration process, I explain that when village headmen give consent for land rights registration, they write *onde mu pa epitikilo a kale momukunda wange* (I have given him/her permission to be in my village), or *onde mu pa edu momukunda wange* (I have given him/her land in my village). As shown in Chapter 3, village headmen giving *ombadu yekaya* to a senior headman has direct implications for access to land. In all the villages, village headmen appoint *ookapatashu,* who are their representatives in different sections of villages, and they form what is called the village leadership, or locally *elelo lomukunda.* One of the village headmen explained the hierarchy of the traditional authority (particularly Oukwanyama Traditional Authority) as follows:

> The kingdom *(ouhamba)* is big; therefore, the *ohamba* cannot lead alone. The hierarchy follows that the *ohamba* delegates senior councillors, senior councillors delegate village headmen and village headmen delegate *ookapatashu.* The *ookapatashu* represent the village headmen in the different sections of villages and they report to the village headmen. The village headmen represent the *ohamba* at the village level and they report to the senior councillors. The senior councillors represent the *ohamba* at the district level. The senior councillors form the cabinet of the traditional authority. They report to the *ohamba* as in the ministers reporting to the president of a country.

Traditional authorities, as institutions, are mandated to administer land, allocate and cancel land rights, solve local disputes, and maintain customary laws in their respective areas of jurisdiction (Mendelsohn et al., 2013, p. 137). The functions of land administration in particular, land rights allocation and cancellation of land rights vests in the traditional authorities as legally mandated by the Communal Land Reform Act, 2002 (Republic of Namibia, 2002). All actors in the traditional authorities' hierarchical structure have specific powers and functions – which I call layered authority – which they exercise at their respective levels in relation to land administration and land-related dispute resolution. In the context of the customary system, and within this hierarchical structure, it is the village headmen and *ookapatashu* who are directly involved in land allocation, not *ohamba,* and not *omalenga.* Village headmen and *ookapatashu* regulate access to land and are responsible for legitimating land rights for land users in their respective villages. The mandates of *ohamba* and *omalenga* include all matters relating to the designation and re-designation of communal land for various purposes within their respective territorial units, as well as the function of maintaining a direct link between people on the ground, and the state (Nghitevelekwa, 2016). They are the links between outside actors (including the government) and their respective traditional communities. Contestations can arise between the different levels of the traditional authority, especially in cases of encroachment into the functions at different levels. For example, during my fieldwork, several village headmen under Oukwanyama Traditional Authority complained about senior headmen, *omalenga,* who were engaged in land allocation, a function that is not in their jurisdiction.

Socio-economic setting

North-central Namibia's life worlds include both rural and urban settings, however, rural settings dominate. Like many other rural African settings, the rural economy in north-central Namibia is agrarian-based. People's livelihoods are dependent on farming and, therefore, land has been "the most important form of property and productive resource" (Siiskonen, 2009, p. 5). All rural land is legally designated as communal land, administered through both customary and statutory laws and, therefore, by both the traditional authorities and state institutions. Although land is designated as communal, there are mixed tenure arrangements which range from individualised landholdings for residential and cropping purposes; the undivided but shrinking share of commonages for grazing; large individualised tracts of land, mostly for livestock farming; fenced-off land, mostly for livestock farming shared by more than one village; designated areas for community conservation, and small individualised holdings that are used for commercial and business enterprises. The sizes of the landholdings used for different purposes vary substantially. These may be less than a hectare to about 20 hectares of individualised landholding for residential and cropping; a few square metres to 10 hectares of individualised landholdings for commercial and business enterprises; 100 hectares to 4,000 hectares of individualised land used for livestock farming, and up to 11,000 hectares for group tenure. The large-scale individualised land used for livestock farming refers to the small-scale farms found in the far eastern Ohangwena and Oshikoto regions, and includes communal farmers who have accumulated a large number of stock and farm beyond subsistence, but also land used for commercial purposes related to farming.

In an agrarian setting, people in north-central Namibia produce a variety of crops on their lands. *Omahangu* (pearl millet) is the most important crop grown, and it serves as a staple. Other crops are sorghum, beans, pumpkins, watermelons, and groundnuts. People farm with cattle, goats, and donkeys, though cattle are the most significant. Crop production takes place on individualised landholdings, while livestock grazing has long taken place on open and undivided commonages in the villages/*oshilongo* areas and in *ofuka/okuti* areas. While the majority of the population till the land, livestock farming is characterised by great variation in terms of ownership (Mendelsohn, 2006). This means not all agricultural households own livestock. In 2006, in Ohangwena Region, for example, only 39% of agricultural households had more than 30 cattle, 34% of agricultural households had between one and 30 cattle, and 59% of agricultural households had no cattle at all (Mendelsohn, 2006). The 2011 Population and Housing Census Survey shows similar variations in Ohangwena Region: Only 44% of agricultural households were engaged in livestock farming, while 79% of agricultural households were engaged in crop production (Namibia Statistics Agency, 2011, p. 69). More recently, the Namibia Census of Agriculture 2013/14 Communal Sector Revised Report reveals that only 31.7%, 33.1%, 34.1% and 39.2% of agricultural households in the Ohangwena, Omusati, Oshana and Oshikoto respectively, reported owning livestock (Namibia Statistics Agency, 2019a).

Despite these variations, livestock farming and cattle, in particular, are important for the socio-economic livelihoods of the Aawambo. Cattle serve a variety of purposes and values, ranging from providing draught power and manure for fertilising crop fields; a source of milk and meat for consumption; means to pay *lobola* (bride price); means to pay *ombadu yekaya* for landholding and for the village; and means of exchange to acquire *omahangu* through barter, especially during low-yield years. Cattle are, furthermore, valued for the ceremonial economy, for example, to slaughter at ceremonial events such as weddings and funerals. They are used as means to confer status in society and could be an indicator of wealth. Livestock conveys authority in the homestead and within the community, for men in particular (Winterfeldt, 2013). Cattle are a source of cash when it is needed to meet specific cash-related needs. For example, some farmers sell cattle to pay the university expenses of their children who are studying at institutions of higher learning. In addition, one head of cattle is a "standard unit of charge for fines or compensation in respect of traditional laws and customs" (Hinz & Namwoonde, 2010, p. 189). Even if the person who is charged does not have cattle, the extended family, often the maternal family, takes up the responsibility to ensure that the fine is paid, either in the form of cattle or cash. While I was doing fieldwork in one of the villages, people were mobilising resources for renovating their local church. Several members of the church pledged heads of cattle as their contributions. In March 2013, I participated in the commemoration of Mandume Day, a day to celebrate the late King Mandume ya Ndemufayo of the Ovakwanyama people. Many people from different parts of Oukwanyama contributed cattle for the event. This diversity of uses for cattle confirms the assertion that "livestock is very important agronomically, economically, [socially] and culturally to rural producers" (Verlinden & Kruger, 2007, p. 179). Cattle are valued for production purposes, consumption purposes, as units of payment and commercial exchange, and for the ceremonial economy, which is, ultimately, about reproducing and maintaining social relations. Farmers often emphasised that, *Just like you have your money in the bank or your insurance with insurance companies, for us, our insurance is our cattle or cattle are our bank, when different needs arise, we turn to our cattle.* In Pierre Bourdieu's terms, the value of cattle in north-central Namibia transcends economic, social, and cultural values, and therefore has symbolic value (Bourdieu, 1986).

While cropping is done on landholdings that have been allocated to households on the basis of individualised land rights, livestock farming has long operated on commonage on the basis of group rights. Different types of commonages are identified in north-central Namibia: commonages in the *iishana* of the Cuvelai drainage system; the open saline grasslands locally known as *ombuga* to the south of the Cuvelai drainage system, and the woodlands that surround villages in eastern Ohangwena and northern Oshikoto regions. For commonages in the Cuvelai drainage landscape, access is determined by membership of a particular village – people who are from a specific village can graze their livestock in the commonage of that particular village. There are clear boundaries between villages, demarcated by specific landmarks known to all village members. In some cases, conflicts over boundaries between villages and even traditional authorities occur, in which cases there are overlapping claims to commonage rights. Commonage rights in *ombuga* and woodland areas used to be open to all farmers. For example, the woodlands that fall under the jurisdiction of the Oukwanyama Traditional Authority do not only accommodate livestock farmers from Oukwanyama, although, in practice, contestations exist about the access of others and often lead to disputes. The commonages in both the Cuvelai landscape and the woodland areas have been affected and transformed as a result of population growth, growing settlements, individualisation of landholdings for cropping and homesteads, and individualisation of land for grazing purposes. This trend presents an uncertain future for the livestock economy, which depends on open commonage.

Territorial restructuring

Since independence, "various forms of state power and governmental legislations have formally exposed the territory of Namibia to many processes of spatial restructuring and development" (Becker, 2006, p. 26). Communal areas, in particular, manifest this territorial or spatial restructuring, evidenced by different processes and outcomes that produce kaleidoscopic complexities and various uses of land. Becker (2006) regards these processes and outcomes as part of production of space and territoriality. North-central Namibia, as the most populous geographical area of Namibia, is a hotspot for these different uses of land.

Mushrooming of local authority areas

One of these uses of land is illustrated by the introduction of local authority areas/urban areas in areas that were once largely rural. In 1992, the government of the newly independent Namibia passed the Local Authorities Act, 1992.[6] The Act works to turn rural spaces into urban spaces. The Act defines urban spaces as all the areas that have been proclaimed as settlements, village councils, town councils and municipalities by the Ministry of Rural and Urban Development. The pioneer urban localities in north-central Namibia, Ondangwa and Oshakati, were established in the 1960s. Since the country became independent, however, north-central Namibia has seen a rapid increase in the number of urban localities, now exceeding 20. These urban localities consist of one municipality, Tsumeb, in Oshikoto Region, and 11 towns: Omuthiya and Oniipa in Oshikoto; Eenhana, Helao Nafidi (including Engela, Omafo, Ohangwena and Onhuno) in Ohangwena Region; Ondangwa, Ongwediva and Oshakati in Oshana; and Okahao, Oshikuku, Outapi and Ruacana in Omusati Region, and the following settlement areas and village councils: Onayena, Onethindi, Onyuulaye, Oshigambo, Oshivelo in Oshikoto; Omungwelume, Ongenga, Ongha in Ohangwena; Eheke and Uukwangula in Oshana; and Ogongo, Okalongo, Onesi and Tsandi in Omusati. New urban centres continue to emerge, for example, Okongo in the eastern part of Ohangwena Region was proclaimed in 2015, and Ongha, in the western part, is in the process of being proclaimed. Year in, year out, existing urban localities expand in space, and the government gazettes extension areas to existing urban localities. The current figures for areas proclaimed as local authority areas

6 No. 23 of 1992.

represent about 69,000 hectares, which is about 2% of north-central Namibia. The area of land now falling under local authority areas seems insignificant. However, seen in combination with other processes that involve alienation of communal land, resulting implications for customary land rights are significant. Once an area has been proclaimed as a local authority area, it ceases to be part of communal land; this exclusion is provided for by the Communal Land Reform Act, 2002, which states that

> Where a local authority area is situated or established within the boundaries of any communal land area the land comprising such local authority area shall not form part of that communal land area and shall not be communal land (Republic of Namibia, 2002, p. 9).

Establishing new local authority areas and expanding boundaries of existing local authority areas result in the alienation of communal land. Proclamation of land as local authority area also has alienation effects in terms of governance, in that this function moves from one institution to another. Traditional authorities lose their jurisdiction and power over the land, while local authorities gain control and power over those lands. Proclamation of land as local authority area has direct impacts on the landholders in terms of their customary land rights and land as a physical asset, including land-based resources, such as fruit trees. These impacts are partly minimised through compensation, as per the Compensation Policy Guidelines for Communal Land adopted in 2009. The policy guidelines give different options of compensation, among which is ownership of residential erven (plots) in the proclaimed area, or receiving alternative land of similar extent elsewhere, to continue with farming activities (Republic of Namibia, 2009, p. 4). In 2020, landholders were compensated at N$ 5,000 per hectare for cultivated land and N$ 2,500 per hectare for uncultivated land. In addition, landholders are compensated on the investment they have made on the land. Detailed compensation structures for different investments on the land are set out in the Compensation Policy Guidelines for Communal Land (see Republic of Namibia, 2009, p. 9). There is also compensation for land-based resources, such as fruit trees landowners have planted on the land. The trees with highest compensation are indigenous or naturally growing trees on landholdings, such as *omwoongo* (*sclerocarya birrea*), *omwandi* (*diospyros mespiliformis*), *omulunga* (*hyphaene petersiana*) and *omuve* (*berchemia discolor*), for which compensation is in excess of N$ 10,000 for each tree. The only exception in terms of indigenous trees or naturally growing trees is the *omukwiyu (ficus sycomorus),* for which the compensation value is N$ 2,500, probably because these trees are less common and, hence, the fruits are not commonly utilised and the total income per season is lower than that for other indigenous trees. Indigenous trees are differentiated from exotic and planted trees, such as mango, lemon, orange, and guava, for which compensation values are less than N$ 10,000 each. Then, there is what is called the disturbance allowance, which is 15% of the total value of compensation, and which should not exceed N$ 15,000. There is no compensation for grazing land that is shared by communal farmers.

Proclamations of local authority areas have resulted in numerous land-related disputes, which take the forms of jurisdictional disputes, territorial disputes involving traditional authorities, and compensation grievances involving landholders. Many landholders complain about receiving unfair compensation for giving up their landholdings to local authorities. Research reported in the *Status of National Legal Frameworks for Valuing Compensation for Expropriated Land: An Analysis of Whether National Laws in 50 Countries/Regions Across Asia, Africa, and Latin America Comply with International Standards on Compensation Valuation* (Tagliarino, 2017) concludes that Namibia, together with Angola, Liberia and Nicaragua, is lagging behind in terms of compensation valuation indicators, because their "national laws mostly fail to adopt international standards on the valuation of fair compensation" (p. 19). International standards on the valuation of compensation centralise the principles of fairness and justice. This provides that "a person should not be forcibly removed from his or her land for a public purpose without payment of compensation that is commensurate of his or her losses" (Tagliarino, 2017, p. 3). The international standards are intended to "protect affected landholders from impoverishment and other risks, including landlessness, joblessness, food insecurity, increased morbidity, and marginalisation" (Tagliarino, 2017, p. 3). Unfair compensation is a result of communal land being rendered as what Cousins (1999) refers to as invisible capital. He argues that the true social, economic, and ecological value of natural resources on communal land is often underestimated. Furthermore, valuation for compensation does not consider the multiple uses of land in communal areas, beyond the material. Among the uses of land that are not considered in compensation are those that are social, for example, identity and belonging, and the length of time that a landholder has lived on the land. Few of these uses are monetised (Cousins, 1999).

Proclamation of local authority areas is often done in the name of bringing about development. In this case, the state uses what is called *eminent domain*, that is, using its juridical power to change from one land type and land use to another – changing from communal land to townland, and/or for public development purposes. The current logic of proclamations is that local authority areas are conceived of as spaces for development and transformation; these are areas that offer "services, goods, labour, ideas, identities, communication and decentralised governance" (Becker, 2006, p. 24). According to the current logic of development planning used for proclaiming local authority areas, economic intent is its preoccupation. This logic regards "towns and cities as the engines of economic growth" (Hesselberg, 2005,

p. 493). According to Becker, "the economic intent of such planning turns (semi-) arid landscapes into commercial commodities and transforms the social practice, ultimately, even the socio-cultural identity of all people involved; subsequently, constructing new spatialities" (2006, p. 23). Areas that have been proclaimed are integrated or become commodified spatialities or commodified territories. The very logic of what a town is, and what kinds of activities in terms of land uses should be practised within town boundaries, relates to commodification. As Becker (2006) explains, processes of transformation, in the form of local authority proclamations, are accompanied by rural polarisation of winners and losers. The losers are the land users and landholders whose landholdings and customary land rights are appropriated, and people who will not be able to function and subsist in a commodified space. Living in townlands requires someone to have access to monetary income, not only to pay for municipal services, but for basic livelihood – in other words, to survive in a commodified space. This idea is conceptualised within what we call primitive accumulation, where "a more publicly owned [resource] is enclosed into private ownership, and existing claimants are expelled (or have rights attenuated) to become a proletariat separated from land and nature, releasing resources for private capital" (Fairhead et al., 2012, p. 238).

Local authority areas and/or urban settings offer too few employment opportunities for incoming populations, who live there as a result of migration or integration. These areas are becoming spaces in which unemployment and poverty are reproduced. The general trend, as captured by the labour force survey, is an increase in unemployment rates in urban areas throughout the country. In 2014, unemployment in urban areas was estimated at 25.9%, and it increased to 30.3% in 2016 (Namibia Statistics Agency, 2017b). The continuing trend of increasing high rates of unemployment in urban areas is revealed further in the 2018 labour force survey report. The report estimated that unemployment rates in urban areas stood at 33.4% – an increase by 3.1% from 2016 (Namibia Statistics Agency, 2019b). A lack of employment opportunities and, therefore, the inability to survive in a commodified space, has produced what is seen in many urban settings: a sprawl of informal settlements and the urbanisation of poverty. Furthermore, what is also seen in local authority areas is that local councils accumulate debt, and need central government to bail them out, mostly because people do not have money to pay the councils for services rendered. Where communal land has been turned into the property of a local authority, land uses change to commercial and capital-oriented land uses. By-laws prohibit and criminalise certain land uses, for example, keeping poultry or livestock. The extent of land people have access to decreases, for example, from five hectares under communal land, to 300 or 400 square metres under the local authority. The cost of accessing land, and taxes on land, become unaffordable, especially for the urban poor, as these are based on the market price. For example, communal land can be accessed for a standard payment/ *ombadu yekaya* of N$ 600.00, and an annual payment of N$ 20.00 for land tax/ *iifendela yedu.* In contrast, the cost of accessing land, and the monthly rates and taxes within the local authority areas, is market-based. These changing dynamics represent threats to certain land uses that have long been the subsistence base of many people, and open avenues for inequalities in access to land, whereby only people with access to financial resources of a certain magnitude can afford land in local authority areas. Thus, the planning logics that are biased towards urbanity (urban life) and the resulting inability of most people to afford life in commodified spaces "exemplify human vulnerability experienced in light of change" (Becker, 2006, p. 24). What is certain, however, is that people do not remain idle victims of change, but are resilient. People adopt strategies that involve engaging in what has come to be known as the informal economy, and/or they become involved in illegal land markets. Engaging in illegal land markets is a strategy forged to reap benefits from communal land before it is appropriated into townlands (Mendelsohn & Nghitevelekwa, 2016).

I agree with Chigbu who argues that "rural development in sub-Saharan Africa is still based on modernisation approaches" (2013, p. 812). I interpret this to mean that the dominant approaches to change are urban-biased, seeking to transform or develop what is rural into what is urban. Together with other dynamics, these approaches contribute to an ongoing "future is urban" narrative. I agree, furthermore, with Chigbu's proposal to develop rural areas rurally, or for rural purposes. Improvements in rural conditions are an important element of development. However, these improvements "should aim to make rural lives and the environment sustainable, while preserving rural identities [in their different manifestations]" (Chigbu, 2013, p. 812). We can achieve this by adopting an approach called rurality as a choice, which, Chigbu argues, we can attain through "heritagisation of rural areas, introduction of rurality-based vision planning, and organisation of campaigns for the protection of rural heritages, among others" (Chigbu, 2013, p. 812).

Areas for community-based conservation

Communal areas or rural areas in north-central Namibia are now far from being areas of crop and livestock farming only. Like many other parts of Namibia, north-central Namibia's communal areas boast areas with diverse land uses, including community-based conservation. Community-based conservation areas have clear boundaries declared by law, either as communal conservancies or community forests. Community conservation areas are established under the flagship programme known as community-based natural resource management (CBNRM).

This programme is part of the agenda to decentralise decision-making to local levels, in this case, decision-making on environmental protection and conservation of natural resources. This is, ultimately, conceived to improve rural livelihoods. In the CBNRM programme, "community-based wildlife conservation has been promoted as a land-use that complements traditional subsistence agriculture" (Naidoo et al., 2016, p. 628), thus, it has both environmental and socio-economic goals. The CBNRM programme involves "devolving use and management rights over wildlife and other resources to local communities who are self-organised into communal conservancies" (Boudreaux, 2010, p. 1). Devolution of rights over natural resources is done through legal empowerment of people in rural areas by acts of parliament, for instance, the Nature Conservation Amendment Act, 2017 (Republic of Namibia, 2017),[7] and the Forest Amendment Act, 2005 (Republic of Namibia, 2005b).[8]

In 2020, north-central Namibia has six conservancies registered and gazetted through the Ministry of Environment, Forestry and Tourism. The first conservancy was registered in 2003, which was followed by others, registered in 2005 and 2009. In total, the six conservancies make up about 12,892 square kilometres (about 1,289,200 hectares), which is about 24% of north-central Namibia's communal land. These six are among the 86 registered communal conservancies in Namibia, which, collectively, cover 166,045 square kilometres (16,604,500 hectares or about 20.2% of Namibia's total surface area). It is estimated that communal conservancies in Namibia support a population of around 227,941 people, which is about 10% of the total population (statistics adapted from the Ministry of Environment, Forestry and Tourism & Namibia Association of CBNRM Support Organisation, 2019). Communal conservancies comprise multiple uses of land. For example, within the jurisdictional boundary of Okongo Communal Conservancy in Ohangwena Region, lie areas for individualised customary landholdings that are used for homesteads and cropping, two community forests and a core area for wildlife protection.

There are eight community forests in north-central Namibia, registered and gazetted through the then Ministry of Agriculture, Water and Forestry[9] between 2006 and 2013. These forests are part of the 42 registered community forests that cover around 9.6% of the total surface area of Namibia. In many cases, community forests overlap communal conservancies and, in fact, 95.5% of the forest area outside of conservancies covers only 0.4% of Namibia's total surface area (Ministry of Environment, Forestry and Tourism & Namibia Association of CBNRM Support Organisation, 2019). Tables 2.1 and 2.2 list these communal conservancies and

---

7 No. 3 of 2017.

8 No. 13 of 2005.

9 Since March 2020, Forestry has been moved to the ministry now called Ministry of Environment, Forestry and Tourism.

community forests in north-central Namibia, with their total areas, population and natural resources (data acquired from various sources, including unpublished project reports and http://www.nacso.org.na/conservancies).

Table 2.1: Communal conservancies in north-central Namibia

Communal Conservancies			
Name	**Size in hectares**	**Population**	**Natural resources**
Okongo Community Conservancy	134,000	2,676	Elephant, duiker, kudu, steenbok
King Nehale Conservancy	50,800	4,756	Blue wildebeest, gemsbok, giraffe, kudu, springbok
Iipumbu ya Tshilongo Conservancy	154,800	2,296	Common duiker, guineafowl, kudu, scrub hare, springbok
Sheya shUushona Conservancy	506,600	3,198	Elephant, duiker, hartebeest, hyena, kudu, lion, springbok, steenbok
Uukwaluudhi Conservancy	143,700	836	Black-faced impala, black rhino, duiker, eland, elephant, giraffe, hartebeest, kudu, plains zebra, springbok
Uukolonkadhi–Ruacana Conservancy	229,300	33,534	Black-faced impala, crocodile, elephant, hippo, mountain zebra, ostrich, springbok

Table 2.2: Community forests in north-central Namibia

Community Forests			
Name	**Status**	**Population**	**Size in hectares**
Okongo	Gazetted	1,250	75,000
Omufitu Wekuta	Gazetted	1,200	29,197
Ehangano	Emerging	450	13,600
Omundaungilo	Emerging	1,100	23,210
Oshikushithilonde	Emerging	1,300	87,836
Ongandjera	Emerging	35,354	128,200
Uukolonkadhi	Gazetted	12,000	111,700
Uukwaluudhi	Emerging	25,000	174,800
Oshaampula	Gazetted	1,136	807
Ohepi	Gazetted	1,680	2,495
Onkumbula	Emerging	400	56,456

Debates around community-based conservation are polarised into studies that are critical of nature conservation, agrarian activities, and socio-economic activities. In a study covering 77 communal conservancies in Namibia, Naidoo et al. (2016) provide a quantitative analysis of the trade-offs of and synergies that result from tourism and hunting as a core activity of communal conservancies (in terms of benefits from conservation). This study reveals that benefits from conservation for local communities take various pathways. For example, conservation generates benefits at different times of a conservancy's life span, and benefits flow to different beneficiaries, ranging from community management committees and the community at large, to individual employees. These benefits come in different forms (income from conservancy management, food in the form of meat for community members, and salaried jobs at lodges) (Naidoo et al., 2016, p. 634). In totality, these authors found that tourism and hunting make substantial and differentiated contributions to the economic welfare of rural residents in terms of employment creation and wages; residents also participate in the management of the natural resources (Naidoo et al., 2016). The agrarian critical studies, on the other hand, see community-based conservation as part of "green grabbing" (Fairhead et al., 2012), which, according to Fairhead et al., may take place in different ways: "wholesale alienation of land and in others the restructuring of rules and authority in the management of resources that may have profound alienating effects" (2012, p. 237). Namibia remains a role model for community conservation, because designating areas for environmental ends at community level does not result in alienation and appropriation of land from people. As indicated above, the model presents multi-layered and multiple-use landscapes. For example, in Omusati Region, the Uukolonkadhi Conservancy comprises many land uses: a wildlife core area, community forest, communal land for individualised landholdings for residence and cropping, tourism enterprises and others. The changes residents experience in relation to alienation effects involve the restructuring of rules for land use, for example, changes in rules of allocation, whereby no allocations can be done in the wildlife core areas or community forest core area, and rules relating to the harvesting of forest-based products. Many conservancies and community forests are characterised by constant clashes between agriculture (including livestock farming) and conservation goals and, therefore, contestations. However, from either side of the debate, what is sure at this point is that designation of conservation areas provides another dimension to the diversification of land use in many communal areas, including north-central Namibia.

Areas designated for agricultural purposes

As in other regions with communal areas in Namibia, agriculture (crop production and livestock farming) has been the mainstay of the rural economy in north-central

Namibia. As explained in the previous sections, the environmental landscape has been conceived to comprise of *oshilongo* and *ofuka* areas. The *ofuka* areas are confined to the livestock economy, first, as cattle posts, which have, over the years, been appropriated into individualised farms. While these transformations have been at the agency of large communal farmers, together with traditional authorities, the state has come to play a role in these dynamics by designating areas for agricultural purposes. This is also the case in north-central Namibia, where several areas have been designated for agricultural purposes. In Ohangwena, such an area lies on the far eastern side of the region. The designated area is collectively referred to as Ohangwena Small Scale Commercial Farms, and comprises Okongo East and Okongo West, together covering about 60,000 hectares. In Omusati, Ongandjera East and Otjetjekua cover about 40,000 and 47,000 hectares respectively (Meijs et al., 2014). In total, the areas designated for agricultural purposes amount to about 147,000 hectares, which is about 3% of communal land in north-central Namibia. A detailed analysis of the designation of areas for agricultural purposes is presented in Chapter 7; however, the point for this study is that designation of areas for agricultural purposes forms part of the major processes of territorial and economic restructuring, and is one of the drivers of transformation that is underway in north-central Namibia.

Economic restructuring

Increasing peri-urban areas and commercial centres

In addition to territorial restructuring, north-central Namibia's communal areas are undergoing economic restructuring. Instead of being merely spaces of subsistence agriculture, with people tilling the land and rearing livestock in the rangelands, north-central Namibia is characterised by a diversity of economic activities that are cash and capital-based. In his book, *Traders and Trade in Colonial Ovamboland, 1925-1990*, Dobler (2014) takes us through the economic history of north-central Namibia, from the time the region was a rural, self-reliant society, to today, as a monetised economy realised through trading stores. Starting from a space with a few trading stores, which have grown over time, north-central Namibia is now characterised by peri-urban centres, commercial centres and central business centres of villages, all vibrant with commercial and business enterprises. Along the main arterial roads from Oshivelo, the border point between north-central Namibia and central Namibia, to Ruacana; with branches off at Oniipa to Eenhana; Ondangwa to Oshikango; and at Onhuno to Okongo; from Oshakati to Okalongo and from Oshakati through Okahao to Omakange, a large number of peri-urban and commercial centres dominate the landscape. These centres go beyond changing the spatial territory of north-central Namibia, to reshaping and restructuring the economic landscape in an increasing commercialisation of land use.

Land uses have diversified and intensified, and have undergone commercialisation. Land is increasingly being used to generate cash income. Land uses come with a variety of booming commercial enterprises, in the forms of horticulture, hospitality and tourism ventures, filling stations, private schools and clinics, and retail and wholesale trading stores. These different land uses bring vibrancy and massive investment into communal areas. The diversity of land uses are indications of ingenuity and a spirit of entrepreneurship in communal areas. These changes were structurally inhibited during the apartheid era, when communal land or areas were seen as places for people who were regarded as to be old or sick, and for children and women (also see Werner, 1993), when land use was exclusively geared to self-provisioning and, importantly, when communal areas were labour reservoirs. Transformation that leads to the establishment of commercial centres is triggered by both internal and external factors and actors. Factors include population growth and growth of urban localities; and actors include land users (both rural and urban residents) and the state. Furthermore, transformation manifested through the development of commercial centres stimulates proclamation of local authority areas. Areas that are being proclaimed today emerge from what started as a space with a single cuca shop, increasing to many shops of different scales and purposes, amalgamating into a centre for the village, with people making different kinds of investments. Cuca shops are "small drinking places selling [*o*]*tombo* [a local brew], soft drinks, beer and wine [and basic, essential items needed in rural homesteads] (Dobler, 2014, p. 129). What Becker saw as an "untamed" stream of investments, seemingly of an unpromising nature (2006, p. 32), has become vibrant investments that have transformed the economic space in a significant way. The transformation currently taking place in north-central Namibia's communal areas refute the long-held conventional position that a lack of certain types of property rights, i.e., the freehold type of rights/tenure, inhibits investment in land. Similarly, the conventional worldview of communal land as dead capital is being proven inaccurate. The dynamics we see show that people invest even though they do not have formalised tenure security, and this indicates that they have sufficient confidence in the customary tenure system to make investments.

With commercial centres, what we are witnessing is a complex web of land uses that now form part of the rural economy. The economic restructuring process shows that land is increasingly becoming more than just a means to provide shelter and basic subsistence livelihoods, but is also a means through which investment and accumulation of wealth is realised. Commercialisation of land uses has also led to the commercialisation of land relations. Some traditional authorities have gone as far as reviewing the fees they have long been charging for access to land.

Traditional authorities in north-central Namibia had a common price list for access to land for different uses, for example, a set, once-off price of N$ 600.00 for a crop field and residence. These fees were not customarily regarded as payments, but as *ombadu yekaya,* a token of appreciation. Today, as land uses change, bringing new diversities, new payments have also been introduced, and are regarded as *oofuto* (payments). Table 2.3 shows payments being charged by one of the traditional authorities – Uukwaluudhi Traditional Authority in north-central Namibia – for access to land for different kinds of land use (Uukwaluudhi Traditional Authority, 2016).

Table 2.3: Fees levied for different land uses by Uukwaluudhi Traditional Authority

Payments when a person wants land		
#	Land use	Price N$
1	Lodge	15,000
2	Complex	15,000
3	Service station	15,000
4	Mini market	3,500
5	Flats	3,500
6	Open market	3,500
7	Market	3,500
8	*Ositola*	3,500
9	Bottle store	800
10	Bar	800
11	*Oshini*	800
12	Restaurant	800
13	*Epya*	600
14	*Okakefe*	150
15	Barbershop	800

Note. No. 8 *Ositola* – shop; No. 11 *Oshini* – milling station;
No. 13 *Epya* – landholding and homestead; No. 14 *Okakefe* – café

Commercialisation in north-central Namibia also applies to what has long been understood to be the subsistence crop production sector. Some farmers have turned their crop fields into spaces for generating cash income and have started enterprises through which *omahangu* is commercialised. An example of such an initiative is an enterprise called *Iyaloo Omahangu,* which is generally owned by women who use their *omahangu* for commercial purposes, by turning their production in the village into a commercial product by processing it through milling and then selling it. The main markets for these enterprises are the populations in urban areas as far afield as Windhoek, the capital city of Namibia. Products are sold from different venues, including supermarkets. Enterprises such as those selling *Iyaloo Omahangu* products help to deconstruct the conventional belief that cultivation or crop fields in the communal areas are solely for subsistence purposes. It indicates that what is produced in the crop fields can also participate in commercial markets. Farmers in rural areas can no longer be regarded as mere subsistence producers; they have become commercial producers in their own right.

Restructuring rural livelihood sources

Since 1990, the Central Bureau of Statistics (now called the Namibia Statistics Agency) has undertaken three Namibia Household Income and Expenditure Surveys, in 1993/1994, 2009/2010 and 2015/2016 respectively. The reports reveal a changing and restructuring livelihood base of the Namibian population. In this book, I refer to the rural livelihood bases of the north-central Namibian regions in particular, which used to be predominantly agrarian. The 1993/94 report reveals that an average of 64% of households in the north-central Namibian regions reported subsistence farming as their main source of livelihood (National Planning Commission, 1996). This figure declined to 40.2%, as reported by the 2009/2010 report (Namibia Statistics Agency, 2012). The more recent report, released in 2018, shows that the trend continues to decline, with only 22.5% of the households in

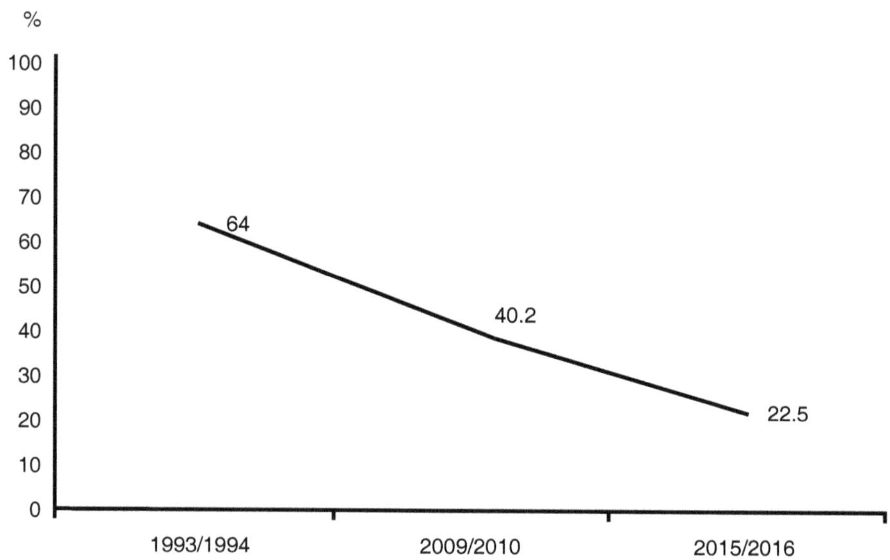

Figure 2.1: Percentage of households indicating subsistence farming as main source of livelihood from 1990 to 2016
Data sources: Namibia Statistics Agency (2012, 2018); Republic of Namibia (1996)

north-central Namibia indicating subsistence farming as the main source of livelihood (Namibia Statistics Agency, 2018). Figure 2.1 shows the declining trend of subsistence farming as the main source of income in north-central Namibia.

There are regional variations in the role of subsistence farming as a main base of livelihood in north-central Namibia. Figure 2.2 illustrates the dynamics at regional level, as revealed by the 2015/2016 Namibia Household Income and Expenditure Survey. Omusati is the dominant region in terms of households indicating subsistence farming as the main source of livelihood, while only 7% of households in Oshana did so. It is worth noting that, of the other regions, Oshana is the most urbanised, a factor that could explain the low percentage of households indicating their dependence on subsistence agriculture for their livelihoods there.

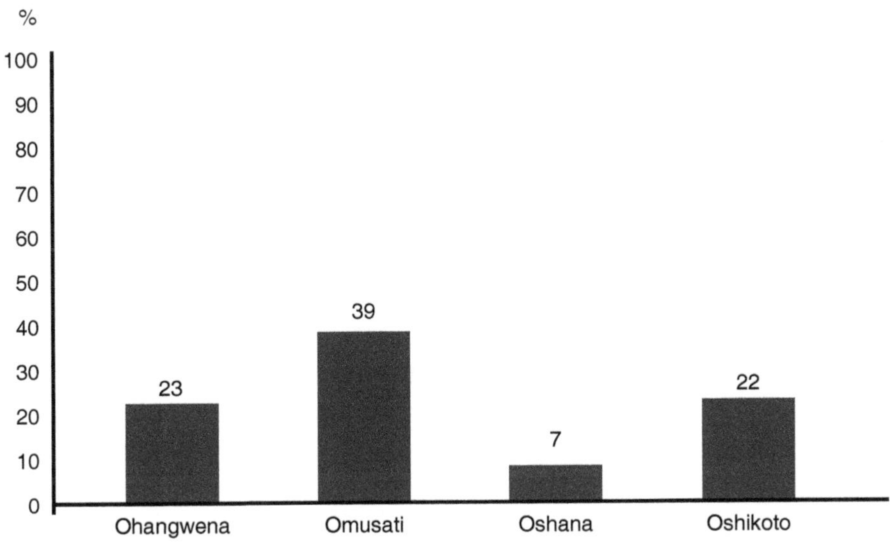

Figure 2.2: Regional disaggregation of households indicating subsistence farming as main source of livelihood
Data sources: Namibia Statistics Agency (2018)

Figures 2.2 and 2.3 show that off-farm income as a source of livelihood is increasingly prevalent. Off-farm income sources may be salaries and wages, pensions, business income, remittances, grants, drought aid, in-kind receipts, or commercial farming sales (Namibia Statistics Agency, 2018). Figure 2.3 compares combined off-farm and subsistence farming activities as sources of livelihoods for households in north-central Namibia.

Iipumbu Shiimi, the former Governor of the Bank of Namibia, is correct in stating that "people are not only sustained by agricultural activities… if they would solely depend on agricultural activities, they would not be able to make ends meet!" (Iipumbu, 2012, p. 8; see also Fig 2.3). Winterfeldt explains that:

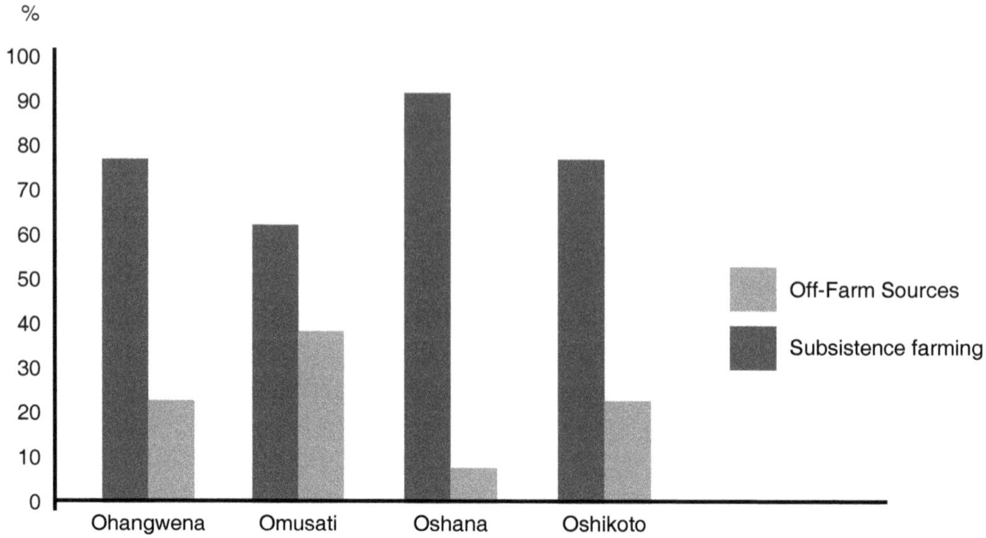

Figure 2.3: Percentage of households with off-farm and subsistence farming as main sources of livelihoods
Data source: Namibia Statistics Agency (2018)

> Centuries old tradition of practising and depending on agrarian economy was and is not left unaffected by the exposure for more than a century to colonial capitalism and post-independence market-economy. What this means is that homesteads can no more be happy islands of traditional self-sufficiency in a sea of commodified consumption. School fees, social events and family celebrations, traditional and religious rites of passage, emergencies, and not least the call of fashionable consumer goods – all require monetary resources that most rural households generally lack (2013, p. 9).

Elsewhere, James Ferguson explains

> In contemporary South Africa... smallholder agriculture, both crop farming and livestock, seems to be on the decline, and in many places in the former 'reserves' it is reported that fewer fields are being cultivated, and cultivated with less intensity, even by those who do have land rights (2013, p. 167).

More recently, De la Hey and Beinart (2016) confirmed this shift away from cultivation in Mbotji, a village on the coast of Eastern Cape in South Africa. They placed this shift in the context of "intensifying environmental pressures, decreasing access to household labour, perceptions of risk, alternative income sources and evolving aspirations" (De la Hey & Beinart, 2016, p. 769). Some scholars consider the diversity of sources of income to be a core component of the de-agrarianisation process that is underway. De-agrarianisation is defined as the "process by which agriculture becomes progressively less central to national economies and to the livelihoods of the people even in rural areas" (Hall et al., 2011, p. 1).

While the traditional rural livelihoods base is being transformed, alternative employment in rural areas, or even in urban areas, is not really available. The Namibia Labour Force Survey 2018 Report indicates that the unemployment rate in Namibia has risen, from 27.5% in 2014 to 33.4% in 2018 (Namibia Statistics Agency, 2019b). The report, furthermore, shows that the unemployment rate remains higher and more pronounced in rural areas, at 33.5% (Namibia Statistics Agency, 2019b). In this context, people, especially the youth, are forced to migrate to urban areas which are not sufficiently equipped to digest the influx of people in terms of providing employment, services, land delivery and housing. For some segments of the rural population, especially medium to large farmers, diversification of livelihoods is "diversification for accumulation" (Bernstein, 2010, p. 107).

Enduring importance of farming

As we have seen above, the process of de-agrarianisation may be underway in north-central Namibia; however, it does not diminish the importance of farming or of land. In fact, as Araghi argues, de-agrarianisation "is not a completed or self-completing process leading to the death of the peasantry. Social classes do not simply end and die; they live and are transformed through social struggles" (2009, p. 138). Farming and land remain at the heart of people's economic and social lives. Many of the participants in this research expressed the sentiment that land was important for their livelihoods. This may be the case even though they use less than two of their 5 hectares of land for agricultural purposes. In fact, as Ferguson argues, for southern Africa at large, "the importance of land, and the desire for it, seems in some ways to loom as large as ever" (2013, p. 167). An internet search about the land issue returns a mammoth number of sources, with headlines from local newspapers such as, "Address land issue" (Haidula, 2015), "Land issue: a problem or crisis" (Nyambali, 2015), "Land problem in Namibia – a time bomb" (*Informante,* 2014). The late Pempelani Mufune, who was a professor in the Department of Sociology at the University of Namibia and an expert on rural sociology, in particular, correctly concluded that it is "impossible to imagine rural livelihoods in Southern Africa without some kinds of access to land" (Mufune, 2011, p. 54).

The paradox of what seems to be de-agrarianisation, on the one hand, and increasing desire for land, on the other hand, can only be explained by taking full cognisance of the fact that land is valuable for different purposes – agricultural use and production is not the only value that people attach to land. Additionally, as Hall et al. assert, "processes working against agriculture... coexist with others that speak to the enduring importance of farming" (2011, p. 1). Socio-cultural expectations still rank owning land, and farming, highly. While statistics over the years show a declining percentage of households depending on subsistence agriculture as the most important source of livelihood, and an increasing number of households living *on* the land but not *off* the land, there are, indeed, poorer households that still live *from* the land. This means the 39% of households in Omusati, 23% in Ohangwena, 22% in Oshikoto and 7% in Oshana, for whom subsistence remains core to their livelihoods, are important. It is important to underscore that the practice of farming involves more than the need for sustenance. It goes beyond meeting the material needs of people; instead, farming is a "customary" activity. People in north-central Namibia refer to farming as part of their culture. Thus, farming goes beyond the need for subsistence – it is also about identity. Access to land is therefore important as a productive resource, a backstop for precarious livelihoods and as a symbol of identity and belonging (Hall et al., 2011). De la Hey and Beinart (2016) report a similar trend for South Africa, where the majority of households still engage in some agricultural activity, and some express a strong cultural motive for doing so.

The cultural expectation for people to till the land and to rear livestock is also entangled with the desire of the state that each household has some form of access to land to ensure food security. Because of the need to ensure food security, government policies and plans emphasise the enduring importance of agriculture and farming, evidenced by the support government provides to agriculture, as an important factor in land relations. Government policies are informed by the past, and also by the international discourses that place agriculture at the heart of poverty reduction (Hall et al., 2011). Land users and the state are important actors in maintaining the importance of agriculture, and they share the same desire to maintain agriculture – the state by means of policies, and land users by maintaining some forms of agricultural production and by "fight[ing] for land even while they absent themselves from the countryside" (Hall et al., 2011, p. 2). The profound transformations we have witnessed, therefore, signify "the changing – rather than declining – significance of rural land" (Hall et al., 2011, p. 5).

The foregoing analysis illustrates important trajectories in communal land relations and land uses: On the land referred to as communal land, people settled and have lived on for many years before the coming of modern states (the colonial and independent states); the agrarian economy is in transition and is being restructured; a process of de-agrarianisation is underway; there is territorial restructuring through the designation of areas for agricultural and conservation purposes; communal land is being alienated for the purposes of local authorities; ever more peri-urban and commercial centres are being established; and land use is being commercialised. New sources of livelihood now complement subsistence agriculture; however, access to land, as part of an overall livelihood strategy, remains important for many reasons other than those that are directly economic.

3

Customary Land Tenure System in Practice

This chapter presents evidence of the way customary land tenure system functions at a micro level. While the focus of the study is on north-central Namibia at large, this chapter takes a closer look at specific areas which I call Ondobe and Okongo.[10] Ondobe area comprises the villages of Ondobe, Omunyekadi, Efidi, Ohengobe and Etope, all of which are in the Ohangwena Region. They fall under the jurisdiction of Oukwanyama Traditional Authority, with the exception of Etope, which falls under the Ondonga Traditional Authority. Okongo area comprises the villages of Onghalulu, Okambali and Onane (see Figure 3.1).

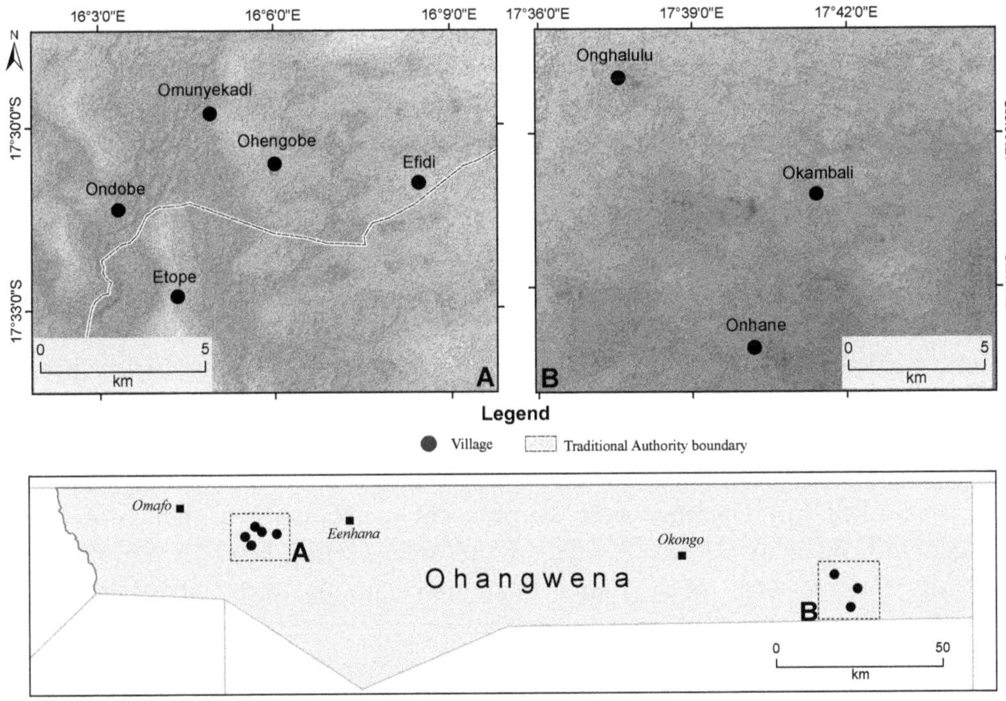

Figure 3.1 Ohangwena Region showing Ondobe area (comprising Ondobe, Omunyekadi, Ohengobe, Efidi and Etope villages) and Okongo area (comprising Onghalulu, Okambali, Onane villages and the individual farms to the east), the specific ethnographic setting for this research.

10 I call these Ondobe and Okongo areas purely for purposes of analysis.

Settling in the area

Ondobe village is located in the Ohangwena Region, in the Eudaneko district, under the jurisdiction of the Oukwanyama Traditional Authority. The village is known for having one of the oldest churches in north-central Namibia, which was established in 1937 under the leadership of Reverend Vilho Mwadikange Kaulinge. Ondobe village, like many other villages in the middle of the Cuvelai floodplain, and especially those located in the east of Ondobe, were founded during the first two decades of the 20th century. These decades were characterised by Portuguese invasion, the terror of colonial warfare, and droughts, which were exacerbated by rinderpest (cattle disease) and raids in the northern floodplain (in Angola). This situation induced mass population flight into the middle floodplain (in Namibia) (Kreike, 2004).

Kreike (2004, p. 58) identifies two major peaks of population flight from the northern floodplain: The first took place in 1915, during the Portuguese invasion; and the second took place between 1926 and 1928, as a result of the transfer of the Neutral Zone to Portuguese control. The Neutral Zone was a stretch of land that "lay between the boundaries claimed by the Portuguese and Germans" (Vigne, 1998, p. 293). People I interviewed singled out the destruction of the Oukwanyama kingship as a major driver of population flight. The Oukwanyama kingship was destroyed after the death of King Mandume ya Ndemufayo, the king of the Ovakwanyama, who died in a "battle against a military expedition dispatched by Pretoria in February 1917" (Hayes, 1993, p. 89). From 1917, for 79 years, Oukwanyama remained without a king or queen, and was ruled by a council of headmen. The kingship was restored only in 1996, when *Ohamba* Cornelius Mwetupunga Shelungu was instated by the council of headmen in Oukwanyama, and confirmed by the government of an independent Namibia (Shiweda, 2011). When their king died, *omalenga* spread out widely and scattered throughout Oukwanyama, both north and south of the *onhaulila* (the Namibian-Angolan border). Most *omalenga* moved out to find their own wilderness areas, which they cleared, and established new villages. Some of the people who fled and *omalenga* were the pioneers and founders of their respective villages. Others, who already resided in the area, consolidated their power by allowing others to settle on their land. In an interview, one of the village headmen in Ondobe area narrated this process as follows:

> After the death of their King *omalenga* became *oovene vedu* [the owners of the land] on which they settled, either as village headmen or *omalenga* controlling districts (interview with village headman, OM75_2015).

Reverend Kaulinge himself was an advisor of King Mandume ya Ndemufayo, and he established Ondobe village. *Tatekulu* Inghepa ya Hedimbi was *elenga* for King

Mandume; he established Omunyekadi village, adjacent to Ondobe village. Villages in the surrounding area, such as Ohengobe and Efidi, were established in the same way. Like many other villages in north-central Namibia, the names of the villages in Ondobe area, including Ondobe itself, are historical repositories that convey the origins of the villages and explain why their pioneers or founders settled there. The names also indicate the significance of events that occurred during the period when people were settling there, thereby creating a link between the inhabitants and their environmental history. Thus, there is more to a name than its being simply a geographic marker on a map. For example, Ondobe village is known as *Ondobe yeno.* The pioneers or founders settled there because there was *ondobe* (a pond of water), which was surrounded by *eno* (thorn trees), hence, the name *Ondobe yeno* (see Figure 3.2 which shows the dried up pond and the remaining thorn tree).

Figure 3.2: The tree from which Ondobe derives its name

The pioneers decided to settle in this spot because there was water. When elders in Ondobe area describe the settlement history of their respective villages, they emphasise that people settled where they found water. They explained in Oshikwanyama language, *omeya oo haa shili ovanhu* (water attracts/pulls people).

As the elders of the villages explained, the pioneers or founders of the villages were followed by *ovapiya vavo* (their "servants"), relatives and acquaintances, some of whom had travelled with the pioneers; others followed later. This settlement history is clear when one traces how people in these villages are connected and related to each other. The majority of the people I interacted with were connected through kinship. Most of them emphasised their connection to the founders of their respective villages. They emphasised that, *ondi li momukunda wa tatekulu* (I am in my great/grandfathers' village), or *ootatekulu ovo va ka po omukunda ou* (our great/grandfathers cleared/founded this village). Here, the reference *tatekulu* is used broadly. It includes both maternal and paternal great/grandfathers, and it also refers to respected men of the family in the matrilineal lines.

In the early days of the villages, population density was low. The oldest members of the villages around Ondobe were born in the 1920s. Those I interviewed remember that, when they were growing up, they could hear hyenas laugh and jackals howl. Households were sparsely distributed. The elders narrated, "there was enough land for everyone – people had big landholdings". At that time, the bravery of a man was measured by the size of his landholding; one of the elders I interviewed stated specifically that, "When men were men like my father, they used to fortify their fences". During that time, the ability to fortify a fence and having a large landholding signified bravery. Still referring to her father, she described his bravery: *Omulumenhu okwa li ha ke ongubu* (the man used to fortify his fence) (interview with landholder, OM91_2015). Population movement from the northern floodplain continued throughout the period 1915–1960, and even later (Kreike, 2004). The border between what was to become Namibia and Angola divided the precolonial Oukwanyama kingdom, the Ovakwanyama people, families and relatives, friends and acquaintances between the two colonial powers – the Portuguese and South African regimes. The continuous movement of people between the northern and middle floodplain during the colonial period, and which we continue to witness today, reflects people's drive to maintain relations, just as much as for economic reasons. Some moves are mere back and forth between the northern and middle floodplains, while others result in permanent settlement in the middle floodplain.

This resettlement, together with internal factors such as increased birth rates of people in the middle floodplain, contributed to population increase, such that people now complain of a shortage of land. Most of the land has been individualised for residences, and commonages are dwindling fast. The villages are now so full that even the headmen complain that there is no more land for allocation. In conversations I had with village headmen and their secretaries, they reported that the only allocations they can make currently are when existing landholders subdivide their landholdings, or when somebody dies, and the landholding has to be reallocated to someone else.

During the time of field research, Ondobe village had about 70 households, and Omunyekadi village had about 200 households, the latter considered to be one of the largest villages. A village in north-central Namibia refers to an area under a headman, comprising several households. A number of villages fall under a district that is led by a senior headman. As described at the beginning of this chapter, the villages of Ondobe, Omunyekadi, Ohengobe and Efidi all fall under Eudaneko district, which comprised 39 villages during the time of field research. During this time, there were 11 districts under Oukwanyama Traditional Authority. All the village headmen in Ondobe area claimed that they were *miipundi yoohe/yoohekulu* (they took over from their fathers' or grandfathers' reigns). The inheritance of villages (headmanship) largely follows both matrilineal and patrilineal lines. Sons, grandsons, even great-grandsons, inherited villages from their fathers, grandfathers or great-grandfathers, and nephews inherited land from their maternal male relatives, whom they refer to as *tatekulu*. It is difficult to trace the beginning of this practice. It is recorded in literature that, in Uukwambi, one of the traditional authorities in north-central Namibia, for example, following the death of *omukwaniilwa* Iipumbu yaShilongo in 1932, the Native Commissioner, Carl Hugo Hahn, appointed four senior headmen and vested in them power to allocate land (Legal Assistance Centre, 1991). When the senior headmen died, these titles were inherited by members of their clans, a practice that continues in that area (Legal Assistance Centre, 1991).

In addition to the village headman, there are village leadership committees, locally known as *elelo lomukunda* (sing.), that comprise *ookapatashu* who, together with headmen, collectively manage village affairs. *Ookapatashu* are important because one of them may represent the village headman and act as the village headman in his absence. Some village headmen are employed in urban areas up to 1,000 km away, and may only come home once a year. In their absence, the *ookapatashu* run the daily affairs of the villages, including allocating land and dealing with land disputes. These positions are largely gendered: there is low representation of women in the leadership of traditional authorities across north-central Namibia. The few women in leadership roles work mostly as secretaries and treasurers. On 14 September 2013, I attended a district meeting of the Eudaneko district, where all 39 villages were represented. The meeting comprised three sections of participants, all seated in a circle: the district members (the villagers), the judges at the main or high table, and the secretaries of the meeting. The main table comprised six judges, of five men and one woman. The secretaries' table comprised mainly women (see Figure 3.3).

Figure 3.3: Eudaneko District Meeting showing the main table at the tree (left) and secretaries' table at the back.

The low representation of women in traditional authorities' governance structures can be explained by the general feminist perspective, which emphasises the subordination and undervaluing of women in the different spheres of life, socially, politically and economically, in most societies (Levit & Verchick, 2006). The practice of appointing women as village headwomen and senior councillors in traditional authorities' structures only started in the mid-1990s, due to political change in Namibia which came with goals of gender equality (Becker, 2007). Today, the underrepresentation continues, despite Ohangwena Region as a whole having the largest number of female-headed households of all regions in Namibia, and the current *ohamba* of Oukwanyama Traditional Authority being a woman: *Meekulu* Martha Mwadinomho ya Christian ya Nelumbu.

Allocating, sharing, and distributing the land

The process of gaining access to land demands that the applicant approach the village headman or *ookapatashu* and indicate a desire to be allocated land for residence and cropping in the village. Ideally, the village headman consults with the *ookapatashu,* and even landholders adjacent to the land being applied for, to ascertain availability, before rejecting the request, or granting approval. Often, this remains an ideal procedure rather than practice; some village headmen approve applicants without due consultation with all the affected parties. In some villages, members have complained and expressed dissatisfaction about their village headmen allocating land near to members' own land, thereby reducing or "using up" the land that existing landholders use as commonage. One other factor taken into consideration in the granting or rejection of applications for land allocation, is disputes over a parcel of land, in the absence of which the parcel of land being applied for may be allocated. Once the application for land has been approved by the village headman, the applicant pays *ombadu yekaya.* The current amount for *ombadu yekaya* is N$ 600.00, or one head of cattle across all the traditional authorities in north-central Namibia (see also Hinz & Namwoonde, 2010).

Ombadu yekaya is a once-off payment to the village headman. Village headmen often stated that the payment of *ombadu yekaya* at land allocation level is a form of cost recovery, for *ombadu yekaya* that headmen, in turn, had paid to senior headmen when the former had become village headmen. Headmen also asserted that they were responsible for many activities in their villages, which they carry out on behalf of various parties, even the government, and for which they are not remunerated. Thus, most village headmen believe *ombadu yekaya* is justified. Some village headmen complained that the amount for *ombadu yekaya* is too low. They referred to other prices that had risen – even the price of matches – but that *ombadu yekaya* remained the same. The current amount of N$ 600.00 was adopted in the early 1990s by the seven traditional authorities in north-central Namibia. Paying *ombadu yekaya* is an element in the legitimation of land rights. When the payment is made, the name of the applicant is registered in the village headman's book by the village secretary, as the legitimate landholder of a particular landholding. By paying *ombadu yekaya,* the applicant is granted legitimacy and rights of exclusion for residential and crop land. Rights of exclusion include rights to "determine who will have access right, and how that right may be transferred" (Schlager & Ostrom, 1992, p. 251). The applicant is, furthermore, granted rights relating to management, namely, the right to "regulate internal use patterns and transform the resource by making improvements" (Schlager & Ostrom, 1992, p. 251). If the landholder dies, the rights revert to the village headman, who will reallocate the rights, often to someone with family ties to the deceased. New land rights holders then have to pay *ombadu yekaya,* so that the rights are registered in their name, or so that the land rights are legitimated to them. Rights to exclude others can be understood to be on a gradation scale. Landholders gain a multiplicity of rights to their respective individualised landholdings; however, they are aware that these are not exclusive or absolute rights. They can only exclude others from the land to a certain extent. Landholdings are still on communal land which local people refer to as *edu laaveshe* (land for all). Other people can still make use of the land, either because a footpath crosses it, or because they need to use the land to connect to the central water pipelines, or because the common rural water point is on their landholding. These rights are not only the result of the Communal Land Reform Act, 2002 (Republic of Namibia, 2002); under the customary system, the communality of land use is evidently identifiable. People in Ondobe area refer to what is locally known as *omalila,* wide paths that have been in existence for many years, which used to connect villages, and even kingdoms, to one another, for example, the path that connected Ondonga to Oukwanyama. People used these *omalila* for various purposes, for instance, to connect to their kin in other villages or kingdoms, to drive cattle from one place to another, and for trading purposes. Some of these *omalila* are now used as village boundaries. In Omandongo, a village in Ondonga Traditional Authority, where the Finnish missionaries first arrived and settled, there is *oshitauwa (elila* in Oshikwanyama) that connected to other mission stations. People make symbolic assertions that their ancestors use these *omalila.* Some of the *omalila* pass through individualised landholdings and, therefore, individual landholders cannot close or block others from using the paths, in other words, no-one can claim absolute rights. As the practice of individualisation of land intensified, some landholders closed off *omalila* by erecting fences around their landholdings, and locking gates and, by doing so, blocking people from crisscrossing their landholdings. When landholders block others from crossing their landholding, symbolic questions are asked: Where does (s)he expect us and/or our ancestors to go through? Does (s)he expect us to detour and perhaps go through her/his homestead to continue our journey? This discussion indicates that landholdings and land uses are connected in complex ways to a wide range of users that include both the living and the dead; people who hold rights legitimated by the village headmen; and people who have access rights as derived from customary conventions. As indicated by several research studies that were conducted between 1920 and 1960 on land relations in Africa, the case above reflects that "a mythical association between ancestors and land... [is] present in belief systems" (Cousins, 2005, p. 417).

Once village headmen have legitimated the rights, rights holders pay what is locally known as *iifendela yedu,* roughly translated as a land tax that goes to the particular traditional authority's fund. The current amount for land tax for customary land right is N$ 20.00, paid annually. Land tax for land used for commercial purposes is higher than that of customary land rights (defined as rights for residential use and cropping). In Ondonga Traditional Authority, for example, the land tax for a small shop is N$ 50.00, while the tax for large farms is N$ 2,000.00. In Ondobe area, the annual land tax for a small shop is N$ 40.00. These sums are increasing, especially for larger businesses. For example, the land tax, or even *ombadu yekaya* for a supermarket, is much higher than that for a small trading store. Additionally, payments by large businesses are not dealt with at the village level, but at the district level. While the payment of *ombadu yekaya* is for legitimation of land rights, the payment of *iifendela yedu* represents the maintenance of this legitimation for land rights. Annually, village headmen collect *iifendela yedu* from their respective villages and submit these to the traditional authorities' head offices, called *ombelewa yoshilongo.* The cash payment for access to land represents a monetised element within the so-called subsistence economy, and is based on customary tenure rights, where land relations, originally or historically, were not mediated by money. Headmen in the villages I studied indicated that, in the far distant past, *ombadu yekaya* could be paid by means of a basket of *omahangu,* or by offering labour to cultivate the crop fields of village headmen. The shift to monetary payment signifies the increasing value attached to land, as well as the intensification of commodification of land relations and land use. This change implies that access to financial means determines access to land. Diversification of land use, beyond residential, cropping and commonage, also means diversification of income sources for the traditional authorities. Diversification applies not only to different land uses, but also to orientation – the introduction of land uses oriented to a market economy or exchange economy – has resulted in the revaluation of *ombadu yekaya* and the land tax. In Ondobe area, there is a vibrant commercial centre called Okahenge, located in Omunyekadi village. Different kinds of business activities take place at Okahenge, including open markets, which local people call *omatala,* where people sell meat, vegetables, *vetkoek* (fat cake, a type of deep-fried dough), second-hand clothing, seeds or grains such as *omahangu,* and beans. At Okahenge, there are also small or large liquor trading shops, bars, supermarkets, a car filling station, motor vehicle repair businesses, car wash businesses, tailoring businesses, government services like the post office, and many shops owned by Chinese business owners. Okahenge is expanding so fast that the village headman and inhabitants in the surrounding areas speculate that the area will soon be proclaimed as a local authority area.

The prospect of a local authority area being proclaimed causes different reactions. Some people welcome it as a form of development, while others hope it does not materialise. Those who have the latter view refer to what they call losses, which are linked to the proclamation of local authority areas: loss of customary land rights, change in the traditional practice of land use, commercialisation of land relations, and reduced landholdings. Their reactions ranged from, "I cannot live in a town, where will I cultivate as old as I am, how can I live in a town, how will I survive?" to, "When a town is proclaimed, it means our daily livelihoods will change from depending on our land to depending on Shoprite for our everyday needs" (interview with landholder, OM63_2015). Management and exclusion rights are placed in a hierarchy of rights in relation to land in communal areas. At the upper level of this hierarchy is the state, which holds communal land in trusteeship, followed by traditional authorities, to which administration of and access to land is entrusted and, on the lower levels of the hierarchy, are the landholders and users in whom land is entrusted as a possession. We should differentiate within the category of landholders and users: Landholders have management and exclusion rights ascribed and legitimated to them by the village headmen. Landholders may not necessarily be the land users. Land users may be the landholders, but they may also be people who derive benefits from the land through various social relations access mechanisms. Thus, differentiating between landholders and land users allows us to appreciate that there are different mechanisms of access to land: formal, rights-based access mechanisms, and access mechanisms that are based on social relations. The rights-based mechanism is one of the many access mechanisms or relationships that enable people to benefit from land and land-based resources. Some people are landholders and use their land; others are landholders and do not necessarily use their land; others are only land users, and not necessarily landholders. Such differences are not readily observable or obvious. Often, what meets the eye is not what is happening in practice in terms of relations to a particular landholding. This means that someone can be seen to be living and farming on a landholding, leading to an assumption that that person had been granted the land rights of that particular landholding; however, this may not be the case, as the land rights may belong to someone else. Therefore, what exists is a complex constellation of parallel mechanisms and social arrangements that shape benefit flows. Ribot and Peluso (2003) provide a useful conceptualisation of access by differentiating between rights-based access mechanisms, and structural and relational access mechanisms. Rights-based access mechanisms are sanctioned by law, custom or convention, and they are granted, sanctioned and legitimated by the socio-political authority (Ribot & Peluso, 2003, p. 161). In the case of north-central Namibia, traditional authorities are one of the socio-political authorities. People who benefit from land through rights-based access mechanisms "assert their sanctioned rights... to control access" – they have gained access control (Ribot & Peluso, 2003, p. 162). Access control is defined as "the *ability* to mediate others' access" (Ribot & Peluso, 2003, p. 158). Through access control, other access mechanisms come into play – these are relational access mechanisms. Relational access mechanisms are mediated through social relations, kin relations and social identities. We observe them in the form of land users who are not landholders, or whose names are not registered in the books of the village headmen, but who derive benefits from land. We observe them in the form of land users who live on the lands of their kin, or who have a piece of land that was subdivided from that of their kin and who have not been granted land rights legitimated by village headmen. We observe them in the form of landholders who have multiple landholdings and benefit through rights-based mechanisms, though they do not necessarily derive benefits from all their landholdings. The examples below show these different variants at play in Ondobe area:

Case 3.1

Meekulu Mkwaneuma,[1] *Efidi Village, Ohangwena Region*

Meekulu Mkwaneuma is 90 years old. She lives on a 36 hectare land parcel – the largest land parcel in the five villages included in this study. The average size of land parcels in the villages around Ondobe is between 3 and 5 hectares. The land belongs to her *tatekulu,* who lives in Omuthiya with his family, about 200 km from Efidi village. *Meekulu* Mkwaneuma has been living on this land for many years (she cannot remember how long, but stated that it is more than 10 years). She stated repeatedly, "It is not my land, the land belongs to *tatekulu".* She lives with her three grandchildren (two children of her son, who lives in Walvis Bay, and one of her late daughter). Her son has not been home in years; she hopes he will visit. He never contacts them, neither does he send money to his mother (*meekulu* Mkwaneuma). *Meekulu* Mkwaneuma stated that she planned to request him to return home via a radio announcement. Her only source of monetary income is the state pension of N$ 600,[2] and N$ 250 for one of the grandchildren, who is an orphan and receives state support under Orphans and Vulnerable Children grants. Another source of livelihood is the land on which she lives and where she is able to produce *omahangu.* When I talked to *Meekulu* Mkwaneuma, she stated that the neighbours usually complain that "her" land parcel is too big, and that she is not cultivating it all, nor does she have any livestock to keep on it. In my observation, the part that is cultivated is less than 2 hectares, and judging by the size of her granary, the output is not substantial. To people claiming that "her" land is big, she responds that it is not her land, she is just living on it; it is not her name recorded in the books of the village headman, but her *tatekulu's* name. "The land is not yet registered with the land board", she explained. If it were to be registered, she emphasised, it cannot be registered in her name, since the land is not hers. She is just using it – irrespective of the fact that she has lived on this land for more than 10 years and that her *tatekulu* lives elsewhere, with his family.

1 All names used are pseudonyms.

2 This interview took place before the old-age pension was increased. It has since increased to N$ 1,350.

Case 3.2

Meme Mkwanangobe, Ondobe Village, Ohangwena Region

Meme Mkwanangobe lives in Ondobe village. She is in her early 40s. She lives with her three children on a small landholding of less than 2 hectares, on which she has her homestead and crop field. At first glance, this seemed to be an independent landholding, but during our conversation it transpired that the land is not actually hers, but a part of her maternal uncle's land. She is permitted to use it because she does not have land of her own. She has only rights of use. Her uncle's homestead is less than a kilometre away, in the same perimeter boundary, in addition to another three homesteads, which belong to her uncle's sons who, unlike her, have rights to their subdivided parcels. This means their names are registered in the books of the village headman. These sons lived with their father, and when they married, they received their subdivided parts. The original total size of the entire land was 36 hectares. *Meme* Mkwanangobe is not sure whether this arrangement is permanent. "Maybe it is permanent, but I am not sure. However, my uncle is also old. If he passes tomorrow, I do not have any claim to this land, because my name is not registered in the village headman's books. He just subdivided this part for me to use, an arrangement between us. In that case, the land will just go to the wife and the children, because that is what the law says."

The vignettes above are among many that exemplify the social relations-based mechanisms of access to land. They signify that kinship relations are central to access to land. Similarly, they show how individuals are related to one another through land. Matriliniarity is central in access to land. Maternal uncles are important, especially for women, in providing access to land. These vignettes also show that land is embedded in the economy of sharing and of (re)distribution, often based on the principle of reciprocity. The obligations that are attached to the practice of sharing and (re)distribution are clear to the people involved, though not defined on paper. The rights are clear: You may use the land, you may till the land, and the produce is for your own use. When it comes to alienation, you have no rights. In the first case described above, the participant claimed that her neighbours complain that she has a big landholding, and she should give up some of it. In response to these complaints, she said, "If they want parts of the land, they should talk to the owner. I am not the owner; I have just been given use of the land". For many people, the unspoken obligation or reciprocity is to keep the social space alive in the village, while the children of the landholder are growing up, or for the holder of the rights to return when they retire from their salaried jobs in urban areas, or in times of crisis. A physical presence is a requirement by custom; if the land is not cultivated for three consecutive years, it will be re-allocated to other people. In my own family, elders in the family are constantly urging people in whose names landholdings are registered to show some form of presence, which could be through cultivation. The elders often express the fear that, "If this land is not cultivated next year, the village headman will re-allocate it to other people". In 2020, the landholding in question was re-allocated to other people, justified by the village headman because the land had not been used for three consecutive years. In Ondobe area, I have, furthermore, observed landholdings being held for the purposes of keeping them socially alive. A study participant stated that

> I was just selected to come live on this land so that we can keep it in the family. The deceased was not married and did not have children. All the siblings have landholdings of their own. There was no immediate person to inherit the land, so they called me to come in just so that the family keeps the land (interview with land user_OM41_2015).

The practice of sharing and (re)distributing benefits, that is found in north-central Namibia as in other southern African rural areas, is a "vital part of many poor Southern Africans' livelihoods" (Ferguson, 2013, p. 166). In other words, "successful livelihood strategies for the rural poor hinge crucially on the distributive [sharing] dynamics" (Ferguson, 2013, p. 177). Landholders "expect the same object [in this case, land] to return eventually" (Widlok, 2016, p. 23). The focus and practice of sharing and (re)distribution should, therefore, be understood as "extending the circle of people who can enjoy the benefits of the shared resource" (Widlok, 2016, p. 24). The practice involves sharing functions on the basis of kinship and solidarity amongst people, and establishes or maintains hierarchies and classes of landless who are land users, and landholders who are not necessarily land users. Certain users will remain landless, at least in formal terms, or in terms of mechanisms that are rights-based. Relational mechanisms of access to land operate on the basis of arrangements between landholders and land users.

These social relations-based mechanisms of access to land indicate that land plays an important role in the creation and maintenance of relations between people, and that relations between people are an important means of access to land. Thus, social relations are important parts of people's livelihoods, especially for the landless and, in customary tenure systems in particular, in the context of inequalities regarding access to land and characterised by gender inequities, where women have no land rights and have, in the past, accessed land through male affines. It is often women who benefit from social relations-based access mechanisms. Widlok (2016, p. 24, citing Bird-David, 2005, p. 207, and Belk, 2010, p. 724), explains this type of sharing in the context of a non-egocentric theory for sharing; it is about "entangled identities", "joined lives" or "extended self". All these access mechanisms have long operated and remain in the realm of customary tenure systems controlled by the customary authorities. There is neither modern statutory involvement, nor recognition or protection relating to the land, transferring land, and inheriting land.

Relating to the land, transferring land, and inheriting land

Households are the effective units of landholding and land use; they are effective units of production and consumption. Members of each household relate to land and each other in different ways. When asked what land means to people, responses offer rich histories of people's backgrounds and lives, and rich histories of the landholdings themselves – how they were first settled, who settled there first, and how land has been transferred over generations to the current landholders and land users. People in villages often assert, *oku li mepya la* [name of person], (he/she is on the land of [name of person]), in most cases, referring to someone who has died. These histories are linked to the histories of the villages (see Section 3.1), such that *oku li mepya li li momukunda wahe/wahekulu* (he/she is on a landholding of his/her *tatekulu).* In mapping how people relate to land, the following settings were identified in Ondobe area.

The area contains household units comprising a husband, wife, their children, and their kin, of which the husband is often the head of the household and the land rights holder. That is, land relations are organised around affinal relations (marriage and children). The wife and the other family members are secondary rights holders, who justify their rights to the land on the basis of their relationship to the head of the household, who is the husband. Other household units comprise a mother with her children; she is the head of the household and the land rights holder, having inherited this land from her husband. The children are secondary rights holders who claim their rights to this land on the basis of this land having been their father's land, which now belongs to their mother. The land users justify their claims to the land on the basis of both affinal and matrifocal relations. These kinds of land relations emerged in the 1950s, among the modernising elites, who started organising land relations around affinal relations. The modernising elites are village members who "owed their status, more to their school education, their formal-sector profession or their political leadership which they sought to provide in the modern state than to any traditional legitimacy" (Dobler, 2014, p. xiii). They were the first who "stood in conflict with the 'old' elites of village headmen" (Dobler, 2014, p. xiii). They were also the first to question and move away from the 'old' ways of relating to land and transferring land – from matrilineal to affinal relationships.

In other cases, the mother may be the head of the household, but not necessarily the land rights holder. In such cases, the land rights are in the name of one of her children, typically a male child, who inherited the land rights from his father and was entrusted by the father with the responsibility of taking care of his mother and siblings. The responsibility of taking care of others, locally referred to as *a tekule vakwawo,* is a form of social vesting, meaning the land is actually vested in this individual on behalf of others for collective benefits. Other researchers refer to this form of vesting or individual in whose name the land is vested, a trustee (see, for example, Peters, 2020). In 1965, Max Gluckman referred to these social arrangements as nested systems (cited by Peters, 2020). Vesting in this context does not involve the "full complement of power over land that is possible, i.e. private property" (Cousins, 2005, p. 425). I conceptualise land relations of this type as domestic group relations that emanate from affinal relations. There are also units comprising elderly and middle-aged women, who live with their children and grandchildren, sisters, and their nephews and nieces; in this case, the elderly or middle-aged women hold the land rights. A married nephew may live in the household with his wife and children; however, the rights are not held in his name, because this land is linked to the maternal grandmother, and many other family members who may or may not have their own households, all claim rights to this land. In other words, this landholding is reserved for all family members from one root, the grandmother/great grandmother. These kinds of landholdings are held on the basis of matrilineal descent relations, the clan, for example, *epya olo olo va kwaluvala* (that landholding is for the *Ovakwaluvala* clan). These cases are in line with findings by Peters in Malawi, which "run counter to the notion that women's land rights are always secondary and 'fragile'" (2010, p. 180). The findings from Malawi show a deliberate practice of keeping land rights in the name of one woman, as a buffer against losing the land rights. Matrilineal land tenure "provides considerable scope for women to obtain and secure land" (Peters, 2010b, p. 180). The long-held customary setup dictates that a landholding can be in the name of a male relative even though that particular male relative is married, with the assurance that, even if he dies, the land rights/landholding would not be inherited by the wife, but would pass along the matrilineal line. This practice has changed, with state laws now emphasising the protection of widows' rights. Findings from the field indicate that keeping the maternal land in the name of one of the women, and not the married nephew, is important. Below, I present one of the cases that explains how this relation manifests itself.

Case 3.3

Tatekulu Haimbili (now deceased) had a landholding in Efidi village. When he died, he was in his early 70s. He had inherited the landholding from his father. As such, his siblings and his siblings' children also have claims to this land, though more symbolically – they often refer to it as "our father's land". He was legally married to *Meekulu* Mkwaanyoka with whom he had five children, who are all adults with their own children. He married a second wife by customary law, and fathered nine children with her. He separated the households for the two wives: one household, for the first wife, is in the Efidi area, and that of the second wife is in a village in *ofuka*. Upon his retirement from a job he had held in Windhoek, he married a third wife, a civil servant who lived in one of the towns in north-central Namibia. He had no children with the third wife. His legal wife (the first wife) died in 2010. In 2014, he legally married his third wife, who then took up physical presence at the residence in Efidi village, the residence where the husband lived with the children of his first wife. *Tatekulu* Haimbili died in 2017. The question in the family was, who was to inherit the land? According to statute, the legal wife should inherit the land. However, the family was divided into two opposing opinions of whom should inherit the land. Some members of the extended family felt that the third wife should inherit the land, as it was provided for by the land law (*oveta yomadu*), while other members of the extended family felt that the land should be inherited by the children. The latter group added that the third wife did not even have children with the deceased. The late *tatekulu* Haimbili's children also asserted their claims; they did not support the idea that the third wife should inherit the land. They emphasised that they would not have a problem if the second wife inherited the land. Their opinion was that the third wife had spent too little time with their father to justify her inheriting the land. However, the final decision of the family was that the third wife would inherit the land *e va tekule* (to take care of the children of the first wife). In this case, *e va tekule* is not meant literally, as these are adult children, but it emphasises the vesting principle. The children who are aggrieved by the decision still maintain that, perhaps, the last option should have been to subdivide the land between the children and their stepmother (the third wife). They are afraid that, because the new wife lacks a long attachment to the land, she may not value it, and may sell the land. They also asked what would happen if she were to marry again?

What this case shows is that patrilineal and matrilineal relations which define access to land are affected by new state laws on land rights (which will be discussed further in Chapter 6). For matrilineal cases, like that described above, the argument put forward is that "without intending to do so... statutory land policy runs the risk of threatening those very rights" (Peters, 2010b, p. 180).

There are household units comprising siblings (both male and female) and where the land rights are held in the name of one of the male siblings. The land may have been inherited from the parents and, often, the extended family chose a male sibling in accordance with the saying, *opo a tekule vakwawo*, which refers to the vesting practice. Having the land rights in the name of one of the male siblings only means that the rights are vested in him in trust for the well-being of other siblings – it does not denote ownership. In such a scenario, rights are not vested in female siblings, because the question is always, what will happen when she marries? The usual practice is that, upon marrying, a woman moves to live with the family of her husband and thereafter the married couple will find land of their own. The general risk inherent in one of the male siblings inheriting the land, in this case, is that when the male sibling marries, the wife's claims to that land take precedence, especially when the husband dies. In such cases, other siblings' claims to the land are precarious. Cases like these have led to subdivision of landholdings to provide for the security of all involved, the security of the wife, and also the security of the other siblings. However, this solution is only possible when the parties involved are flexible; in some cases, it has led to contestations that have turned into disputes, sometimes, "converting kin to strangers" and becoming "central to the division of matrilineal families" (Peters, 2010a, p. 155). In other cases (as exemplified by the vignettes of *Meekulu* Mkwaneuma reported above), elderly or middle-aged women who live with their children or grandchildren do not have any land rights in their own names, but live on landholdings belonging to their kin, often their maternal uncles, who live elsewhere with their wives and children. In this scenario, rights to the land can be derived either from their relation to the landowner, or, one degree removed, from the need for the women to act as guardians for the dependents of the landowner. Landowners often keep landholdings as a form of land banking for their sons, for when they are adults. In the meantime, female relatives often serve as caretakers of the land. They are permitted to derive benefits from it, but do not have formal rights over it.

In other household units, siblings and cousins live together in a holding that was left by the father/uncle, who may have gone to establish another household in the *ofuka* areas. He left the land under the leadership of one of the male children, who is vested with the responsibility to take care of the others. These kinds of land relations operate on domestic group relations. Below, I present the example of Omunyekadi village, which functions on the basis of domestic group relations.

Case 3.4

Ndilokelwa is a middle-aged woman who has lived in Omunyekadi village since 1996 (for 17 years, at the time of fieldwork in 2013). She had been living with her maternal uncle, her mother's brother, until 2000, when her uncle moved further east in Okongo area, where he obtained a new landholding. He relinquished his land rights to his son (Ndilokelwa's cousin) *a lele vakwawo* (to lead others). The son married and the couple have *omuhandjo* (a part of the main homestead designated for their use, including their own cooking place). Ndilokelwa and other members of the household live on another part of the homestead. This means that in the household there are two cooking places (*omapata avali*): one for Ndilokelwa and other family members (six in total: her four children and two cousins), and one for her cousin and his wife. Even the landholding is divided into two, one for Ndilokelwa and one for her cousin and his wife. This division was, however, not official – meaning the division into two separate landholdings is not registered in the books of the village headman; it is merely an agreement between Ndilokelwa and her cousin. Ndilokelwa's cousin, his wife and their children live in Windhoek, and they only return to the village for Christmas holidays and a few occasions during the year. Ndilokelwa takes care of the homestead, and even helps to cultivate her cousin's portion of the land. Ndilokelwa asked her cousin to legitimate the agreement with the village headman. However, this request resulted in conflict between the two, to the extent that her cousin wanted to evict her. In July 2013, her cousin gave her an ultimatum, to find a new place by December 2013. For Ndilokelwa, this was a not a good outcome, as she had lived on that land, and in that house for a long time. She was worried about where she would find a place. She indicated that an aunt of hers, in another village, offered to accommodate her on one of her lands in Omunyekadi. This may seem a relief, however, she had fears that she would still be living on someone else's land, and would never hold land of her own, just as it was with her cousin.

In some cases, social relations-based mechanisms of access to land carry security, in others, as is shown by the case above, it causes insecurity for some land users. In one of the household units I studied, a young adult male lived on the land he had inherited from his stepfather. The stepfather had biological children, but appointed the stepson to take over the land. The stepfather's first wife had left the husband many years ago, and he married a new wife who already had a son. The couple did not have children. The second wife died first, and, in his old age, he was taken care of by his stepson. Before he died, he confided in one of the village's elders that his stepson should inherit his land when he died. However, the first wife and the children from the first marriage have a claim to this land, because it was their father's and her husband's land.

All these descriptions reflect the complexity of land relations, not only in Ondobe area, but in the entire north-central Namibia. The argument that emanates from the cases is that land relations are social relations. Landholdings may have clear spatial boundaries. Within these boundaries, however, landholdings comprise units with complex relations between people and land. Land relations and tenure systems in north-central Namibia are socially embedded, and have a distinctive character, as is found in many other African rural settings (Cousins, 2007). Landholders and land users exploit these social relations concerning land to justify their claims to land. What we observe are bundles of rights, interests, and claims to land. Using the rights-based mechanisms of access to land provides a narrow understanding of how people relate to land. Rights-based mechanisms of access to land should be understood as one of the many mechanisms by which people are able to derive benefits from land. Different people have different claims on the same landholding, and though claims are not necessarily competing, competition arises when claims come under threat, land users asserting their claims when their security faces imminent threat. On the same holding, someone will claim, "it is my land, I inherited it from my husband"; some others will claim, "it is our land, we inherited it from our father"; some will claim, "it is our land, we inherited it from our uncle"; and, beyond the household, people will claim, "we also have rights to the land, as the original owner was our grandfather".

Hierarchies between these claims seem to be absent in the relations within the household. Hierarchies arise at the level of legitimation of land rights. Legitimation is done on a single name – starting at the traditional authorities and the state level (state level will be discussed in Chapter 6). The main conclusion of this section is to recognise that access to land and land use transcend right-based mechanisms; mechanisms based on social relations are equally central, perhaps even more important, as they reflect equity in access to land, equity being understood as broad-based distribution of benefits, in this case, access to land. As complex as they may be, these relations reflect the economy of sharing, a social arrangement "enabling access to what is valuable through a bundle of social practices of responding demands" (Widlok, 2016, p. 78). These kinds of systems of sharing landholdings "form an 'invisible' or 'hidden' structure of social support" (Peters, 2020, p. 72).

Dividing landholdings, multiple landholdings, banking the land

Over the past couple of decades, the average size of landholdings in Ondobe area has declined markedly. Many landholders have subdivided their landholdings to cater for the needs of their adult children and kin, or to trade a part of their land rights to other, unrelated people. Land users in Ondobe area refer to specific landholdings as follows: "All that was one land, it was divided to accommodate all those households". Most of the subdivisions are done for residential purposes, which reduces the size of land available for crop production. What used to be a single holding, today often consists of three to five independent landholdings, which are registered with the village headmen. Land "owners" indicate to village headmen that they are giving up part of their landholdings to their kin and doing so means the arrangement becomes formal and has to be formalised and/or legitimated by the headmen. Once legitimised by the village headmen, and by payment of *ombadu yekaya* by the new occupant, the land ceases to be part of the original landholding. Other subdivisions remain informal, that is, informal arrangements between the landholder and the occupant, because the landholder does not wish to relinquish the rights.

The process of subdivision is intertwined with a different dynamic: the practice of having multiple landholdings in different areas. A household can have one piece of land in Ondobe area for residential purposes and some crop production, a parcel in Okahenge for a small shop, and landholdings – *onhele yoilonga,* land for work – in *ofuka* areas for extensive farming purposes, in particular, livestock farming. The landholding(s) in *ofuka* is where the cattle are kept and, increasingly, where crops are produced. The land in the Ondobe area is "home": this is where people feel they belong, where they were born, where their ancestors originate, where their most important social relations are and, consequently, where not only they themselves, but also their children, should have land for purposes of social identity. As Brankamp (2013) explains, territory and collective identity are intertwined; this drives the subdivision of landholdings to accommodate young adults. If they need land for farming, young adults can find it in *ofuka* areas. Farming in *ofuka* areas, which may be more than 100 kilometres away from their residence, requires some form of financial means, to which not all farmers have access. Thus, the customary tenure systems and land relations are underpinned by social differentiation: not all farmers have multiple landholdings, and not all farmers have land in *ofuka* areas. Some have multiple landholdings, in Ondobe area and in *ofuka* areas, and in the latter, some may have multiple landholdings. Today, most of the land in *ofuka* areas is individualised, and the *ofuka* is not the open area it was in the past; hence, these landholdings refer to individualised holdings, which are often fenced, and used by a household.

The practice of multiple landholdings is linked to so-called land banking. Farmers argue that, since land is becoming scarce in *ofuka* areas, too, they would like to reserve landholdings there for their children, for when they are adults. Therefore, having multiple landholdings does not only serve present needs, but aims to serve the needs of the future, to reproduce family relations and stabilise them over generations. Land relations cut across multiple timeframes – the past, the present and the future. While wealth in a bank account and in formal properties represents generational wealth that children in other societies or contexts can inherit, the generational wealth of north-central Namibia, as in many other rural contexts, is bound to the land and in livestock.

Working the land

Farmers start working the land around September, with the process called *oku dima omafita,* which involves digging out the stubs of *omahangu* of the previous season, cutting all the small shrubs in the field, collecting them into heaps throughout the crop fields, and then burning them. This is done to prepare the crop fields for the upcoming cultivation season. NGOs and officials working on projects funded by international organisations such the UN, have trained some farmers in conservation agriculture and encouraged them to leave the soil intact, for better yields. The farmers who have been trained have become trainers of trainers (ToTs), and train other farmers to use conservation agriculture approaches. The trainers of trainers organise meetings in their villages and at constituency level to sensitise other farmers about conservation agriculture just before the cultivation season starts. I observed that only a few farmers were applying conservation agriculture methods – the majority of farmers continue to use traditional farming methods. Around the same time, farmers with livestock start applying manure to their crop fields. Farmers who have cattle keep some of the cattle (in addition to goats and donkeys) in Ondobe area, and those who have access to *ofuka* areas, keep most of their cattle there.

There are two important observations in this regard. The first is that farmers in north-central Namibia, like many other agro-pastoralists in the arid lands of Africa, are known to have "highly mobile lifestyles and to use natural resources widely and sparsely" (Fujioka, 2010, p. 129). For north-central Namibia, this has been the case for the cattle economy in particular. The second is that this pattern of using resources has been affected by the enclosure of local frontiers (Fujioka, 2010). In north-central Namibia, land in the *ofuka* areas has been enclosed since the 1970s. Therefore, my emphasis on farmers who have access to land in *ofuka* areas denotes this differentiated access to resources.

After the harvest, and once the resources locally available, that is, the remains or crop residues on the fields, have been exhausted, some farmers drive some of their cattle from the cattle posts to Ondobe area, and back. The livestock available "at home" in Ondobe area generate manure which is used to fertilise the crop fields. Late in the afternoons, after school, children can be observed scattering manure in the crop fields. Men mend and fix the perimeter boundary fences, to prevent livestock from invading crop fields. Men who own oxen and ploughs prepare their tools for ploughing. Women work the homesteads, preparing seeds and visiting their neighbours and kin to exchange seeds in the case of shortages. This division of activities reflects the deeply-rooted gender roles of men and women in north-central Namibia. At the open markets in towns, peri-urban areas or commercial centres, such as Okahenge, traders can be observed selling a variety of seeds for *omahangu,* sorghum, maize, beans, groundnuts and watermelon, with buyers lining up to make sure they are prepared for the coming season. Government agricultural extension services at constituency level provide seed and fertiliser to the farmers at subsidised rates. Pensioners wait eagerly for the announcement of pension days, to ensure that they have money to rent tractors, owned by the state, through agricultural extension centres, or by wealthy members in their villages, for ploughing. As indicated in Chapter 2, rural north-central Namibia is not homogeneous, but is marked by social differentiation. Wealthy members of villages have invested in activities "ancillary to farming, like crop trading and processing, rural retail trade and transport… renting out draught animals and tractors" (Bernstein, 2010, p. 106). Some people own milling stations at commercial centres, where *omahangu* is processed into flour. Some own tractors that are used to plough the fields. During this period, this class of farmers or land users (through their employees) ensure that their tractors are in working order for the upcoming season. The sound of tractors roaring in the village is common. This excitement means the planting season is imminent. What we refer to as the subsistence agricultural economy does not maintain itself, nor does it exist in isolation, as is often assumed. Subsistence agriculture is linked to the wage and exchange economy. Farmers who are not working, people without access to cash income through pensions, and others with kin in the urban areas, remind their kin of the imminent planting season and request them to send money for ploughing. The linkage to the wage and exchange economy is one of the indications that farming in north-central Namibia is not so traditional, not so peasant-like, not subsistence, nor is it confined to rural relations. The production or farming processes that we call peasant take place through contributions from elsewhere: contributions from the capitalist exchange economy, and from far-off places, from the urban places. Henry Bernstein argues that farming households that we often term subsistence are, instead,

> integrated in capitalist commodity relations, they are subject to the dynamics and compulsions of commodification, which are *internalised* in their relations and practices... [Their] production [is] funded from wages, which are also used to buy food when own-account farming is inadequate to supply household needs, whether on a regular basis or in bad harvest years (Bernstein, 2010, p. 103-104).

Through all the activities that take place in preparation for the upcoming cultivation season, farmers observe the signs that promise or forecast good rains or a bad year: the types of birds flying around, the trees and other signs. As I walked through the villages of Ondobe and Omunyekadi with my research assistant, he pointed to certain trees that promise good rains. Andy Botelle, in his report titled *A History of Marula Use in North-Central Namibia*, cites research participants indicating that marula trees can predict the weather. His participants, for example, reported that

> some people, the older farmers mostly, study each of their marula trees carefully. They say the marula trees tell them the future; 'this one is behaving as if drought is likely'... this one is telling the *Efundja* [floods] will come" (Botelle, 2001, p. 15).

The signs did not look promising for the upcoming cultivation season during September 2013 when I was in the field. In addition to local people forecasting rain using their own methods, government meteorological services, too, transmit radio messages with forecasts for rain. In general, the rains start around October/ November, taking full hold between December and March. In cases of late, sporadic, or below-average rain, people in farming villages and towns alike are consumed by worry and hope. Once good rains start, farmers begin to plough and sow their crop fields. A few weeks after ploughing and seeding, and after follow-up showers, the crop fields stand in their lushest green of *omahangu,* sorghum, maize and beans. The *iishana* and the commonage are also at their greenest, delighting livestock farmers (see Figures 3.4 and 3.5).

Farmers get busy in their crop fields. Village discussions during this time centre on rains and the crop fields. Delight is replaced by worry and despair in the case of poor rains. On the radio, the constituencies' councillors encourage farmers to start ploughing their land, to visit agricultural extension centres to register for tractors and to collect fertilisers and seed subsidised by government. Similarly, village headmen announce on the radio that the cultivation season has begun, and livestock farmers should start herding their stock to prevent damage on other farmers' crop fields. In the afternoons, after school, or for some, instead of school, young boys can be observed herding goats and cattle in the nearby commonages. This grazing takes place on land that is not settled, and on the *oshana* areas found

Figure 3.4: A crop field in Ondobe area with rows of *omahangu* at an early stage (4 weeks).

Figure 3.5: Pond in Ondobe area. Farmers in communal areas use these kinds of common water sources for different household chores.

within villages. Some farmers have relatively large landholdings, which comprise crop fields and homesteads, and also what is known locally as *ekove*, land within one's perimeter boundary, often on the periphery, which is not cultivated and is used as grazing grounds. During the cultivation season, the grazing grounds in *omakove* are used exclusively by the household that holds the land. During the off-season, some farmers permit their neighbours' livestock to graze there, while others fence off their landholdings to prevent grazing access by other farmers. The *oshana* in the villages are often open only to the members of the respective villages. Livestock farmers seldom crisscross between villages unless there is permission or arrangements with village headmen and members of the respective villages. Even within individual villages, the *oshana* in the different sections of villages are often open and used as grazing by farmers who reside in those particular sections. This practice is not inflexible; farmers can access grazing grounds other than those in their own villages, or sections of their villages. As indicated above, most farmers keep only a few cattle and some farmers have none, even in Ondobe area. Most farmers reported that their cattle were in *ofuka* areas, either because they had landholdings there, or because they had entrusted their cattle to their kin who have landholdings in *ofuka*. Some farmers reported having cattle as far away as Oshimholo, in Angola.

Among the cattle at home in Ondobe area, are oxen. Farmers have been using and some still use oxen to plough crop fields. Because of the dwindling commonage in the area and the permanent establishment of villages in *ofuka* areas, where farmers also have crop fields, the long-held practice of seasonal migration of cattle is dying out. More often, today, cattle are kept in *ofuka* areas. Besides, cattle ownership is marked by social differentiation; not all households have cattle. This differentiation relates to wealth, and to gender. Cattle are predominantly owned by men. Furthermore, many of the young men who were responsible for ploughing have migrated to urban areas and no longer work the fields. Consequently, the use of oxen to plough is declining, although it is still observed in some villages. Some farmers plough using donkeys; other households use tractors. Using a tractor costs between N$ 350 and N$ 600 per hectare, and is paid for with pension money and/or subsidised by income from wage employment and business activities, depending on the economic status of people in the household. Participants in this research often referred to their kin in urban areas who send them money for ploughing the land. The government, through the Ministry of Agriculture, Water and Forestry (now Ministry of Agriculture, Water and Land Reform) and its programme for extension services provides subsidies for tractors for farmers who are registered with the extension services. The Ministry also provides improved seeds and fertilisers to farmers at subsidised rates, and technical support for conservation agriculture. All this support, together with the work of the farmers themselves, aims to promote and contribute to the continuation of agriculture, not only in Ondobe area, but also in other parts of north-central Namibia and other communal areas in general. During January to mid-March, farmers are normally weeding; they harvest in May to June, and thresh, sift, and store the produce from June to July. Weeding takes place before planting, especially by poorer farmers who do not have access to financial resources, cannot afford to pay for a tractor, and do not own oxen or donkeys. Thus, they weed with hoes to prepare the land for seeding. Reciprocal relationships do exist, and farmers who do not own oxen or donkeys are assisted by those who do, in return for grazing grounds on their fields after harvest, or in exchange for money. After planting, the second stage of weeding takes place, to remove the weeds that grew after the rain, and to clear the weeds from the fields.

In addition to cultivation, the rainy season involves other activities. One particular activity that stands out relates to marula fruit. Marula fruits are significant in many ways: they provide *oshinwa* (juice), *omaongo* (wine), *omaadi eengongo* (oil), and the outer shell of the seeds can be burned as fuel for fire, just like wood. The process of extracting marula and consuming *omaongo,* in particular, involve processes that build and strengthen social relations, and involve redistribution. The extraction process is a role confined to women, who gather in groups of two to five neighbours, including young girls who share the labour and enjoy the interaction. The juice is squeezed from the marula fruit and left to ferment into *omaongo.* The juice from the marula fruit often goes to the household which owns the tree. The neighbours take the seeds and flesh, from which they make *oshinwa,* a refreshing drink. When the seeds have dried, the women extract the kernels from which to make oil. The neighbours also receive some *omaongo* from the household which owns the tree, in appreciation of their company in the marula processing. Figure 3.6 shows women extracting marula juice in Omunyekadi village. A co-researcher and I joined in the work.

Omaongo is often, although not exclusively, consumed by senior male members of households, who invite their peers to enjoy the festivities. A part of *omaongo* is sent to urban areas, for other members of the extended household to consume or sell. If the household head lives in an urban area, he, in particular, has to be sent *omaongo* from home.

Thus, both the extraction process and the consumption are redistribution processes in their own right. Not all households have marula trees on their land. A more deliberate process of redistribution takes place when households without marula trees are allocated trees by their neighbours, friends or kin. I often accompanied one of the research participants, who had been given a marula tree by her neighbours. She has full rights to this tree; she decided when to collect the fruit, and she called on neighbours to help to process the fruit for *omaongo.* The *omaongo* extracted belongs to her household, not to the household on whose landholding the

Figure 3.6: Women squeezing juice from a pile of marula in Omunyekadi Village.
In the foreground and close to my co-researcher are the skins from the marula fruit, and in the buckets are the fleshy marula seeds. The small buckets contain the juice squeezed from the fruit.

tree is growing. This is one of the many examples of the access arrangements that exist. It means that someone can hold the rights to land, but other people can derive benefits from the land, even benefits that are extended to land-based resources. Furthermore, this is support for the contention that the production of "agricultural goods is really only one of many, many ways in which land is used" (Ferguson, 2013, p. 166). Uses such as these are "best understood as part of processes of distribution that are a vital part of many poor Southern Africans' livelihoods" (Ferguson, 2013, p. 166); they should be understood within the context of the economy of sharing.

The rainy season is characterised by delicacies. These include the leafy green vegetable *Cleome gynandra*, locally known as *ombidi/omboga* when it is fresh and *evanda/ekaka* when it is moulded and dried, which is handy during the dry season. *Ombidi* is harvested from crop fields. Fresh fruits available during the season are *eembe* (*Berchemia discolor*), *eenghwiyu* (*Ficus sycomorus*), *eenyandi* (*Diospyros mespiliformis*), and the makalani palm nut *eendunga* (*Hyphaene petersiana*).

During years of above-average rain, and the years of *efundja* (flood), "a variety of fish are delivered to the region" (Mendelsohn et al., 2000, p. 13). *Efundja* years are

1. Traditional and modern fences. Landholders often start off with traditional fences, and once they acquire financial resources, they put up modern fences. Photograph: Author

2. The author enthusiastically explaining her project to a farmer in Ondobe area. Photographer: Laura Wiedmann

3. People gathered outside Oihole Shrine in southern Angola waiting for the Angolan delegation from Luanda and Ondjiva to officially open the centenary commemoration of Mandume's death. The portrait shows Mandume ya Ndemufayo, the Ovakwanyama King. The same celebration takes place in Oukwanyama in Namibia. Photograph: Napandulwe Shiweda

4. Information banners about land rights registration displayed at the land office in Eenhana, Ohangwena Region. The government has made concerted efforts to raise awareness on the importance and processes of communal land rights registration. Photograph: Author

5. Cattle in *ofuka* area. The dense forest that characterises *ofuka* areas is evident in the background. Photograph: Author

6. A woman farmer threshing *omahangu* with a tractor in *ofuka* area. Photograph: Author

7. A pond of water fenced within a customary landholding in Ondobe area. Photograph: Author

8. A homestead in Ondobe area with chickens and a dog (middleground, right).
Photograph: Author

9. A granary locally called *eshisha* where people store *omahangu* grain. Having sufficient grain in the granary is important for household food security. In the picture is a small portable solar panel (below right) to charge cellular phones often in the absence of conventional electricity. Photograph: Author

10. A fence cordoning off a customary landholding on communal land. Fencing customary landholdings is permitted on communal land to protect crops. What is not permitted are fences that cordon off communal land such as pasture or common water sources. Photograph: Author

11. A *Berchemia discolor (Omuve)* tree creating shade for the midday hours in Ondobe area. Photograph: Author

12. Typical narrow corridor allowing movement of people and cattle from one area to another, between fenced off communal land which previously could be used by everyone.
Photograph: Jill Kinahan

13a (above) and 13b (below): Individualised and fenced off landholdings with better rangeland conditions. Outside the fences, the public or common resources are depleted. There is still commonage grass in summer, but all of it is gone by the time the dry season comes.
Photographs: John Mendelsohn

14. An older woman working in her field. Elderly women in rural areas are not only household keepers, but also keepers of fields and villages. They are often the active adults in rural homes, in most cases the youth having left to live in towns. In the absence of an active labour force, elderly women take responsibility for producing the home grown food, which forms part of the safety net protecting the poor in communal areas. Photograph: John Mendelsohn

15. An aerial view of a village adjacent to Ondangwa Town, showing landholdings, households and some forest cover. Photograph: John Mendelsohn

described as when "water from the upper part of the catchment in Angola drains slowly southwards" into the middle floodplain (Van der Waal, 1991, p. 201). The "fish caught in the *oshanas* provide households with a temporary supplement of protein... some are sold in markets" (Mendelsohn et al., 2000, p. 13). My field research from 2013 to 2017 coincided with several drought years that swept across Namibia. Rains came late and very sporadically, and were below average, thereby exacerbating already semi-arid conditions. Therefore, working on the land was difficult and yields were affected severely – some people did not harvest anything. In 2014 and 2015, a state of emergency was declared by the president. The drought affected mainly people who depend on the land and on farming for their livelihoods. Like other farmers across Namibia, farmers in Ondobe area harvested low yields from their agricultural production in the years between 2013 and 2017. The government expanded its drought-aid distribution programme, but many households had to rely on pensions and social support for orphans and vulnerable children.

Even when not faced by drought, people still supplement their earnings and even the production of crops from farming, with incomes from elsewhere. They need money to buy all the other items required by households. Funds come from different sources: pensions, business activities, wage employment, selling parts of

Figure 3.7: The pension grants distribution point in Ondobe, showing traders under gazebos and the shade of the tree, and in the open commercialising a variety of products.

landholdings, remittances by urban members of the extended household, and, in exceptional circumstances, sale of livestock. While farming remains important to many people, it is not sufficient to cater for all the needs people have in rural areas. Instead of producing a surplus, farming is often even subsidised by off-farm income.

Farming in *ofuka* areas

This section briefly explores farming in *ofuka* areas. The landholdings discussed below do not necessarily represent landholdings belonging to farmers of Ondobe area; these landholders may have come from other villages, or even other parts of north-central Namibia. The common denominator for these farmers is that they all came from *oshilongo* areas to the villages of *Onghalulu, Okambali* and *Onane,* and some individualised landholdings in the eastern part of Okongo, in the region of Ohangwena. These are also areas where registration of rights of leasehold for agricultural purposes takes place (more details on this in Chapter 7). The dynamics around land use in *ofuka* areas are observably different from those in *oshilongo* areas. Firstly, the *ofuka* areas remain predominantly a male-dominated environment. Secondly, farmers are largely preoccupied with cattle, although crop production has also been introduced. Early in the morning, or in the late afternoon, farmers take the livestock to water points which are boreholes either drilled by the government, or privately, on individualised farms. The boreholes run on diesel power, and the farmers share the cost of diesel. Farmers who are too far from the boreholes dig *omifima* (ponds), which they use and maintain collectively.

The villages of *Onghalulu, Okambali* and *Onane* were established in the early 1970s. The founders of these villages came from *oshilongo* in the middle floodplain, some even from the western areas of north-central Namibia. The primary reason people came to these areas was lack of grazing in their areas of origin as a result of population increase. Research participants often stated that *oimuna oyo ye tu e ta mofuka or ouhupilo woimuna* (it is the livestock that brought us into the wilderness, or we came here because of our livestock's survival). The old cattle posts had always existed in *ofuka* where there was enough water, but expansion of and permanent settlement in the *ofuka* areas was driven by newly built infrastructure, especially boreholes provided by the apartheid government for its project to modernise rural agriculture. Farmers describe these areas as having bountiful grazing for their cattle. Commonage in *oshilongo* began to dwindle fast due to population growth which entailed increasingly individualised landholdings created by clearing of commonages for residential and crop production purposes. Thus, farmers found alternative areas for grazing in the further eastern part of the floodplain. As the war of liberation for Namibia's independence escalated through the 1970s and 1980s, people deserted *ofuka* areas (particularly the village of *Onghalulu*) and moved back into the *oshilongo* areas, where there was better protection. They only returned to the villages after independence in 1990. People resettled in these villages from 1994. The farmers who came first, or the pioneers, became the village headmen. Their kin followed, some by physically moving there, others by entrusting the pioneers with their livestock. The *ofuka* areas started as cattle posts, where only herdsmen came to take care of the cattle. The herdsmen had to bring food from *oshilongo* areas. As years went by, and water infrastructure improved, herdsmen started cultivating the land in the proximity of where they grazed their cattle. The areas started changing, from purely cattle-posts, to what was called *omaumbo-hambo,* cattle-post households. According to Aawambo conventions, a place transforms from a cattle post (*ohambo*) into a fully-fledged household through cultivation, which is women's domain. However, these transformations are gradual, and cultivation starts without the presence of women. These kinds of households were called cattle-post households because of the absence of women, as custom dictates that a cattle post is a space exclusive to men. Women do not visit cattle posts. As time passed, the cattle-post households became fully-fledged households. Women started moving to the *ofuka* areas when people started crop fields, which were conceived as women's domain. Today, former cattle-post areas have become permanent villages, with people having individualised landholdings for residential purposes and cropping (relatively larger than those in *oshilongo* areas) and sharing the commonages with others in the village.

In 2000, the villages of *Onghalulu, Okambali* and *Onane* consisted of about 52 households collectively. This number increased to just over 100 in 2012 and to 185 in 2015 (Nghitevelekwa, 2015). Despite the fact that crop production has made inroads into the *ofuka* areas, livestock keeping remains significant. The area to the east of these villages, up to the border with Kavango West Region, has a different structure and comprises large, individualised farming units. Here, there are farms with ranging in size between 100 hectares and in excess of 4,000 hectares. Farmers in these areas access land through various mechanisms. Some landholders have their rights legitimated by the traditional authority, while others let their land to users who farm it, either for themselves or for the landholder. Some farmers settled in these areas before independence, others came after independence. The landholders have accommodated other farmers from their villages – relatives, friends, or acquaintances – either by giving them sections of their farms, by keeping their cattle, or by being entrusted with relatives' cattle. In a single farm, there may be between five and 10 other farmers, who have all been in the area for many years. Similarly, in a single cattle kraal, one may find cattle that do not belong to the landholder. Social-relations based mechanisms of access to land are not confined to the crop sector, instead, they are evidently manifest in the livestock sector.

When not tilling the land

Work on the land is not a full day's, or a year-round activity. In a year, the work on the land is confined to the period between September and June/July (the agricultural season). The other months are the dry season. During the agricultural season, there are times allocated to working on the land, which adhere to the rising of the sun and the course of the day. Most households work in their crop fields in the early morning hours, some starting as early as 4:00, to around 11:00 or 12:00. Household members then take a rest, after which some, depending on the period in the agricultural calendar, return to the field to till. Essentially, the late afternoons and early evenings belong to another set of activities related to the small businesses in what can be termed the villages' central business districts, locally called *uundingosho:* a place comprising cuca shops and medium-sized trading stores.

Trading stores have their roots in the years 1939 or 1940, when the first trading store was opened in north-central Namibia, a forerunner of the astonishing business boom of the 1950s (Dobler, 2014). Trading stores in north-central Namibia boomed: by 1974, there were 1,388 licensed and 6,075 unlicensed shops. These numbers have continued to increase in post-independent Namibia. Some trading stores have, furthermore, attracted the establishment of other kinds of business, including big supermarkets, Chinese-run stores, and open markets such that these places have grown into commercial or peri-urban centres. Other centres have remained small, with only a few cuca shops in the village. The cuca shops offer the villagers a range of products, such as sugar, salt, matches and candles, (the basics needed by households) and the traditional brews of beer, commercial beer, soft drinks and other necessities. Villager members themselves, either men or women, own the cuca shops which make marginal profits. Commercial centres offer more than this, including government services, such as postal services. Cuca shops boast colourful and rather theatrical names. Through these names, the owners reflect the influence of places they have lived, for example, a store may be called Katutura, after the township in Windhoek. Some reflect the names of football teams supported by the owners, such as Manchester United or Liverpool. Some stores are named after television shows or films the owners have watched, such as the Latino *telemundos*, for example, My Three Sisters. Others refer to world events, for example, after the election of Barack Obama as president of America, cuca shop owners named their stores Obama; other shops are called Twitter or Facebook.

This is a clear indication that the people in north-central Namibia regarded by most as peasants have been integrated into the globalised world. The impacts of globalisation can be seen not only in cuca shop names, but also in some of the products they sell, for example, biscuits from Brazil and the globalised Coca Cola. Shops that have electricity may also have TV, and broadcast, live, soccer matches played in Europe. The opportunity to watch television attracts young adults to the commercial centres. Frequenting cuca shops for entertainment is sometimes frowned upon, especially during the agricultural season. In fact, village leadership, and even the constituency councillors, often make radio announcements to encourage farmers to focus on their crop fields. During the planting season, the hours of operation of cuca shops are regulated, especially to ensure they open only at 12:00.

The information presented in this chapter provides a basis for understanding the way long-held rights to land work in Ondobe area and in other parts of north-central Namibia. To justify these rights, landholders and land users often refer to the histories of their respective villages and landholdings. They assert their claims to land and justify their land rights using their relationships to the founders of the villages and to their kin who cleared the land they live on. The rights to their land are transgenerational rights.

This chapter also provides a basis for understanding the different social relationships, mechanisms and arrangements that enable people's access to land, and that shape benefit flows, including arrangement of transfer and sharing that are crucial for people's livelihoods. Access to land functions on the basis of the economy of sharing and (re)distribution. Land claims are based on membership of a descent group, such as a clan or lineage, either patrilineal, matrilineal or cognatic (Peters, 2020, pp. 71–72). The social relationships that shape benefit flows vary, and may be based on matrilineal, patrilineal, matrifocal, domestic group and affinal relationships. Some relationships, such as matrilineal relationships, have defined access to land for many years; however, new social relationships have come into play such as affinal relationships, which originated in the 1950s and 1960s, pioneered by modernising elites. Access to land through affinal relationships does not necessarily involve socio-political authority, at least not at the negotiation stage, though it may be involved at the legitimation stage. Socio-political authorities are primarily involved in the rights-based access mechanisms. For many land users, access comes through group membership, rather than from allocation by authorities. While other types of relationships have come into play, matrilineage remains one of the primary social relationships through which access to land is gained.

While affinal relationships are increasing in importance, whether they play a role depends on the history of a particular landholding: whether it has been passed along the matrilineal, or even patrilineal lines. This means that, if the landholding has a history of being passed on according to matrilineal or patrilineal relationships, granting access to land based on affinal relationships does not proceed without contestation, which sometimes leads to disputes and conflicts. To counter loss of matrilineal or patrilineal land (*edu lofamili*), people resort to subdividing landholdings. Subdivision leads to land fragmentation, though it represents egalitarian distribution and equity in access to land, including both gender and generational equity. Patrilineal relationships also shape access to land. Members justify their land claims on the land having been inherited in their father's lineage.

Other landholdings are held in accordance with domestic group relations. Domestic group relationships, a term used in kinship studies, signify "a social group occupying or centred in a dwelling house, living (and usually eating) together and characteristically exercising corporate control over family property" (Keesing, 1975, p. 149). Domestic group relations function according to the vesting principle, or by exercising corporate control of land. Relations can be a mix of affinal relations, and matrilineal or patrilineal relations that provide access to land. For example, some members would refer to the land as having belonged to their fathers, others as having belonged to their maternal uncles, and others even as their paternal uncles'. Domestic group relationships around land, the vesting principle, and the arrangement of corporate control of land exclude individualisation. Many people depend on and have claims to the same land, and each person draws on different bundles of social relationships. In the same way, different social relationships define access to land. Mechanisms of access to land are not only rights-based, depending on that function of legitimated rights that involve socio-political authorities, access to land is socially embedded.

This chapter further shows that not everyone is a landholder, and landholders are not necessarily land users, especially in agricultural terms. Landholders are defined as the people whose names are registered in the village headmen's books. This definition provides a basis for understanding the complexity of sharing arrangements that exist, arrangements that ensure access to land for the landless. Access to land is organised around the economy of sharing, of which the principle of reciprocity is part, but not necessarily the primary element. Although reciprocity is part of the arrangements, the economy of sharing that underpins land relations is important for people's livelihoods. If it were not for the economy of sharing, some people's livelihoods would be in a severely precarious state. Peters (2020, p. 72) fittingly states that "these intricate social relations are absolutely central to the lives of the vast majority of African people for everyday efforts to achieve a decent livelihood".

The economy of sharing land involves obligations. The exercise of any right within the mechanism of sharing land through social relations "is limited to obligations and counterbalanced by others' rights and privileges" (Cousins, 2005, p. 417). The obligations involved relate to keeping the social space in the village alive and active. Widlok (2016) explains that sharing is one of the [re]distributive practices. The way land is distributed and accessed directly "affect[s] the ways the social relationships make up our lives" (Widlok, 2016, p. xv). The economy of sharing is not a new phenomenon: it is a human cultural heritage that emanates from the past, that we live with today, and that defines future access to resources. This phenomenon is evidenced in land banking. The conclusion of this exposition is captured by Cousins (2005, p. 425), who states that

> in Africa, land rights tend to be attached to membership of a unit of production, are specific to a resource management or production function or groups' functions, and are tied to and maintained through active participation in the process of production and reproduction at particular levels of social organisation.

Without a doubt, these kinds of relations result in social differentiation and class formation which is not necessarily linked to production terms, but to access terms. Landholders and people who are not landholders both often state, "This is my uncle's land".

The foregoing details about the lives of the rural population of Ondobe area, who live on communal land, provide a foundation that raises questions to be addressed in subsequent chapters; they provide insight into how communal land reform fits into the customary land tenure system, what kinds of transformation have been brought about, and how these are accepted and internalised in society.

4
Emerging Land Markets

During the course of the fieldwork for this study, one of the research participants developed a keen interest in the research. He followed me as I visited landholders, and even took part in the discussions I had with other participants. As we crisscrossed the villages in Ondobe area, my research assistant described the histories of the different landholdings – how the landholdings had been transferred and exchanged between various landholders. In one of the discussions, he explained that a certain landholding had been inherited by a descendant of the previous landholder, and that the new landholder subdivided the landholding into smallholdings, for which he received money. The original landholding was about four hectares, and the subdivided and alienated parts were 300 and 500 square metres in size, which the landholder exchanged for N$ 2,000, and N$ 3,500 respectively. The price for land allocation (landholding for the use of residence and crop fields) in these villages, and in other parts of north-central Namibia is N$ 600.00, as set collectively by the eight traditional authorities (Ondonga Traditional Authority, 2014). It was therefore astonishing to hear what my research assistant recounted. In our discussion, he stated that these transactions were between the landholder and the new occupants (the buyers). The village headman or the village leadership was not involved until the new occupants (buyers) paid *ombadu yekaya* of N$ 600.00 for their respective holdings to be registered in the village books and, ultimately, for their rights to be legitimated by the traditional authority.

Throughout my research in Ondobe area, until early 2015, I believed this was an isolated case, or even anecdotal evidence. I did not encounter similar cases, nor did I follow this up further; I considered it to be an anomalous case. My thinking replicated the long-held and stereotypical "assumption that underlies the non-market 'ideal type' communal tenure model that has historically dominated policy thinking in Africa" (Chimhowu & Woodhouse, 2010, p. 385). My belief was unshaken until 2016, when I participated in a study titled *An Inquiry of Land Markets in Namibia's Communal Areas*. This study was commissioned by the then Ministry of Land Reform, through its Programme for Communal Land Development (PCLD). The objectives of the study were to inquire into the existence of land markets in Namibia's communal areas, to gain an understanding of their extent, how they functioned, and the actors involved, that is, both sellers and buyers, and to reflect on policy options. The study involved all the regions, except /Khomas Region, where there is no communal land. The findings of the study indicated that, of all 13 regions in Namibia, the greatest number of emerging market-based transactions to gain access to land were observed in the four regions of north-central Namibia (Mendelsohn & Nghitevelekwa, 2016). Land markets are defined as "transfers of land [rights] marked by payments of market exchange values" (Chimhowu & Woodhouse, 2005, p. 397).

Considering this definition, and the findings of the above-mentioned study, the seemingly isolated case recounted by the research assistant in Ondobe area actually forms part of wider market-based transactions relating to access to land that are emerging in north-central Namibia.

Nature, extent, and hotspots of land markets in communal areas

The conclusion of the study that investigated land markets in Namibia's communal areas was that land in communal areas is widely traded (Mendelsohn & Nghitevelekwa, 2016). Through trading, sellers relinquish rights over their landholdings to the buyers (Mendelsohn & Nghitevelekwa, 2016, p. 9). One of the participants in the 2016 study stated convincingly that the sales of land are taking place "on top of the roof" (interview with landholder_OMA56_2016), meaning that the demand is very high. A member of one of the traditional authorities considered emerging land markets as problematic. With reference to the areas where the practice is the most active, the traditional authority member stated that it is proving difficult to control. A regional-level official at the then Ministry of Land Reform shared similar information, namely, that the land markets were developed, and, reflecting on the future, that they were here to stay: There is no way to stop them, but there is need to control them. These findings were complemented by observations during my field research. A B1 highway from central Namibia to north-central Namibia, demarcations of plots are observable on landholdings a few kilometres after Oshivelo. The ordinary traveller is unlikely to notice. Land markets are disguised and are only observable if one has a keen interest in the changing landscape.

The number of demarcations of plots increases as one approaches the town of Omuthiya, which is the administrative centre of Oshikoto Region. A few kilometres after Omuthiya, the market is well developed, with identifiably active areas forming a residential enclave which resembles a town, although it is on village land. One of the participants of the study, an active seller, proudly stated that when this residential area was "integrated into the boundaries of the expanding townland, this will be the Klein Windhoek of Omuthiya town" (interview with landholder, OMA56_2016). Klein Windhoek is a suburb in Windhoek where the elite reside. In 2016, these residential developments were limited to the southern side of the Omuthiya–Ondangwa road. Every time I travelled to north-central Namibia, whether after a few weeks or months, I observed changes in the landscape. In 2018, I noticed that the residential developments were also taking place on the northern side of the road. Most crop fields around the area have been demarcated into small plots that are for sale. In this area, a plot of 35 by 35 metres (1,225 m^2) costs about N$ 30,000. Some crop fields on the northern side of the road have been divided into two by the railway line between the south and Oshikango, a town on the Namibian/ Angola border. Landholders have partitioned parcels to the south of the railway line for sale.

Between Omuthiya and Ondangwa, a stretch of about 70 kilometres, isolated demarcations can be seen, which increase in number as one approaches Oniipa, a recently proclaimed town council. The 30 kilometre stretch between Ondangwa and Oshakati represents the most active area of market-based transactions that provide access to land. A member of the Ondonga Traditional Authority reports about this area that "sales of communal lands are a problem that our traditional authority is facing. The most abuse is taking place in villages between Ondangwa and Oshakati" (interview with member of traditional authority, OTA72_2016). Between Ondangwa and Oshikango – a stretch of 60 kilometres – land markets are thriving too, particularly in the areas close to Ongha, a village that is about to be proclaimed as a local authority area. Ongha itself is a commercial centre that straddles the main road from Ondangwa to Oshikango. Here, the land market is well developed, as it is in the villages surrounding it. Between Onhuno and Okongo, hotspots of the land market can be found in areas around commercial centres: Okahenge area close to Ondobe, in the villages just before and after Eenhana, and in the villages just before and after Okongo. Most of the hotspots listed above are conceptualised as peri-urban areas. This finding affirms the argument of Chimhowu and Woodhouse (2005) that vernacular land markets are most active in Africa's peri-urban areas, which offer lucrative opportunities for customary rights holders. Until 2018, most of the land sales were along the arterial roads. Since then, land sales have become entrenched in villages as far as 5 km or even more away from the arterial roads. Further away from the roads, the sizes of land parcels are bigger and, therefore, the prices are higher. In the villages surrounding Omuthiya town, land parcels of 1.5 hectare are sold for N$ 90,000. Smaller plots of 30 by 30 m can also be found, and are sold at N$ 20,000.

Participants or actors in land markets include landholders, speculators, agents, and even members of the traditional authorities. Landholders sell rights to parts of their landholdings; speculators seek out people who wish to sell their rights, and agents involve people in the know who have heard of people selling their rights, and can direct potential buyers to sellers. Below, three case studies exemplify the character and drivers of the land market, as explained by participants in the 2016 study.

Case 4.1: Seller

I am 56 years old. I acquired this landholding 12 years ago. I have a certificate for my land. My land is big. It is 12 hectares. I was using this land for my homestead and crop field. However, I was not making much from the land in terms of the produce, so I thought hard on how I can use my land efficiently. Therefore, I decided to subdivide my land into small plots for sale. The buyers use these plots for residential purposes. These plots are in demand, because the Omuthiya town is the regional centre for government services, and many government officials were relocated here when the offices moved from Tsumeb. Thus, my buyers are mostly civil servants working for government. People want to live near town services, but do not want to pay for rates and taxes charged in towns. Therefore, they find relief in communal areas and villages close to towns. For me, I decided to take on that opportunity. I know that the town is expanding and will soon reach this place. By the time the town's boundary reaches here, I would already have reaped benefits from my land. Because I know, the compensation they give is low. I intend to demarcate roads on the land. I have already put in a transformer, which I bought together with some plot owners. There is water supply. I even plan to give it a name. This is going to be the Klein Windhoek of the rapidly expanding town, Omuthiya. It is purely a residential area. I got permission for this use from the senior headman, though not from the village headman – the village headman is against it because he says I cannot sell land, but I know that it is just because the money is not going to him. In addition to that, I have my certificate, which certifies that this is my land, therefore I can do anything I choose to with this land. I pay the individual subdivisions' *ombadu yekaya* (N$ 600) into the bank account of the traditional authority. There are no agreements between me and the buyers. However, a certain lawyer advised me to get an affidavit from the court. I am in the process of getting that. The court will be the mediator in the transactions, so that the buyers may feel at peace with their land. Through the sales of these plots, I have managed to buy three farms [still in north-central Namibia] and many cattle, and I have good infrastructures at these farms, and I employ other people. I employ 12 people through my businesses (extract from Mendelsohn & Nghitevelekwa, 2016, p. 13).

Case 4.2: Seller

I inherited this land from my parents. I started selling plots in my land in 2010. My son bumped someone's car and was required to pay $90,000. My son only had part of the money, so I had to add to what he had. That is how I started selling off my rights over parts of my landholding. In addition, I have to pay university fees for my other children. I generate this money from these sales. I have sold 15 parcels of this land, for N$ 15,000 each. Before I started to sell, I went to the headman where I got permission to sell. I pay N$ 600 to the headman for each of the plots I sell and pay the annual land tax (*iifendela yedu)* of N$ 20. I have all the papers for the parcels I sold. I am not the only one selling land here. I am surrounded by others who sell their land too. One of my neighbours inherited the land from her husband. The husband initially got the land from his brother. When the widow started selling off rights over parts of the landholding and making money, the brother-in-law all of a sudden wanted his land back. Even the stepchildren wanted part of the land. The problem now is that most of the land is sold and I am sure she does not have the money. Now the woman is scared that people will say she should pay back the money she earned from the sales (extract from Mendelsohn & Nghitevelekwa, 2016, p. 18).

Case 4.3: Buyer turned seller

She bought the land, which was once someone's landholding. She bought it for N$ 15,000 in 2011. Now she wants to subdivide it into two and sell one part for N$ 15,000 in order to recover her money. She is building a private school and will use the money for that purpose. The land is about 1,000 square metres. She stated that open plots in Ongha are no longer available; most of those available now are being sold by people who are reselling their plots. People subdivided their *omahangu* fields into plots and sold them. People buy land in Ongha because it will soon become a town. Most people buy plots in Ongha for residential and business purposes. Businesses in towns such as Ondangwa are saturated; therefore, business people flock to emerging areas, places such as Ongha. Business is starting to boom there, and because of the need, land is in demand (extract from Mendelsohn & Nghitevelekwa, 2016, p. 9).

The emerging land markets, or market transactions to gain access to land, are one of the major transformations underway in north-central Namibia. The extracts above represent just a few of many cases involving landholders. The land market is a transformation on its own, which results from many other transformations, or many other drivers. The argument is that, as many other transformations take place, landholders in communal areas are not idle, nor are they silent victims of these transformations. As the extracts above show, landholders participate in the sale of land rights as a result of many factors: they wish to utilise opportunities, protect themselves against the proclamations and expansion of townlands, increase the returns of their landholdings in light of low agricultural productivity, and overcome distressing circumstances. Overall, they participate in the ongoing process of commodification of land use. As shown in Chapter 2, north-central Namibia is inundated with proclamations and expansions of local authority areas, in the forms of settlement areas, village and town councils. Landholders on communal land in the proximity of townlands sell rights to parts of their landholdings and take advantage of the land demand that arises from the expansion of townlands. In **Case 1,** the landholder indicated that, while people may work in towns, they may not necessarily want to live within the town boundaries. Similarly, people may wish to use the services that towns offer, but still do not necessarily wish to live within the town. They do not wish to pay monthly municipal rates and taxes. This is the perspective of the buyers; on the part of the seller, the argument is that "government pressure for appropriation of customary land for urban housing is a factor prompting... [sellers] to 'cut their losses' and sell land rather than wait for lower levels of compensation following state appropriation" (Chimhowu & Woodhouse, 2005, p. 397). In Chapter 2, I explained how land uses in communal areas are increasingly becoming commodified and commercialised. A greater variety of different commercial enterprises are arising in communal areas. All these dynamics fuel market-based transactions relating to access to land. Those at the forefront of commercialising land uses speculate on the availability of land, while the landholders capitalise on this demand.

Urban and rural land questions: two sides of one coin

Urban and rural land questions are proving to be two sides of one coin. Affordability of land in Namibia's biggest urban centres, such as Windhoek, has become a serious problem, to the extent that the situation is widely described as "in crisis" (Delgado & Lühl, 2016, p. 3). In recent years, high prices for urban housing have been recorded, and the trend continues. Social movements have emerged to challenge the status quo. The land question has traditionally been discussed in relation to agriculture; currently, the land question has turned urban. In 2012, Namibia was ranked "fourth [in the world] with highest annual increase in house prices" (First National Bank Namibia, 2012, p. 1), after Brazil in third place, Dubai in second place and Hong Kong in first place. The housing market "available in the country [was] out of reach for the vast majority" (Delgado & Lühl, 2016, p. 3). From about 2014 through to 2016, to afford a property worth N$ 800,000, the average property price, a potential buyer had to earn a monthly salary of at least N$ 24,000. Yet the Labour Force Survey of 2014 showed that only 4% of the Namibian population earned more than N$ 10,000 per month. The majority, that is, 89% of the Namibian population at the time, was categorised as ultra-low-income earners, who earned less than N$ 5,000 per month. This means house prices were out of reach for the majority; out of reach for the middle class, and definitely out of reach for ultra-low income earners. More recently, the Labour Force Survey for 2018 revealed that the national average wage was N$ 7,935 per month (Namibia Statistics Agency, 2019b), while the national average housing price was 1.1 million, which still reflects inequalities in access to affordable housing.

Unaffordability of housing in urban centres is linked to land delivery. There is an acute shortage of serviced land in urban centres. The slow rate of land delivery resulted in a mismatch between the supply and demand of serviced land and, thus, housing. The price of serviced land in urban areas is exorbitant. For example, in 2014, the City of Windhoek auctioned plots in one of the residential areas, the majority of the plots being sold for over N$ 900,000. The highest price realised was more than N$ 1 million, and the lowest price was N$ 850,000 (*The Namibian,* 2014). Over the past 10 years or so, land delivery declined but the trend indicated that land delivery slowly began picking up from 2018 (First National Bank Namibia, 2018).

The unavailability of urban land is, furthermore, linked to a bigger problem, which is the skewed distribution of land in the country and the slow pace at which government acquires land for redistribution. The farms surrounding urban centres, such as Windhoek, are being turned into residential estates through private housing development initiatives, thereby perpetuating traditional elitist land ownership in urban areas. This does not address land delivery and urban housing challenges. One of the reasons why urban dwellers seek refuge in rural areas, on communal land, is the land and housing crisis in urban centres. Among the buyers of land in communal areas for residential purposes are people who work in urban centres in north-central Namibia, or even urban dwellers from as far away as Windhoek. Buying a hectare of land on communal land for between N$ 15,000 and N$ 70,000 is more affordable than buying a plot of 400 square metres in an urban setting for more than N$ 800,000. The dynamics of land and housing delivery in urban centres, not only Windhoek, but other urban areas too, is one of the drivers of emerging land markets in communal areas.

The process is visible in the sheer number of housing developments taking place along the main roads of north-central Namibia: there are large investments in housing, and investments in services such as electricity and water supply. Land markets in communal areas are not only changing the face of customary land tenure, but also the face of rural landscapes. Rural areas are no longer islands of traditional ways of life with traditional homesteads and huts. The many transformations taking place in rural areas are blurring the divide between rural and urban in terms of investment and appearance. Rural dwellers, particularly those in the proximity of sprawling urban centres, respond to the increasing demand for land by demarcating lands once used for cropping into small plots for sale.

The disguised nature of land markets in communal areas

Land market transactions have increased to the extent that even transactions between kin relations are increasingly monetised. Some of the research participants in the 2016 study on emerging land markets in the communal areas asserted that, "Nowadays no one can give you land free anymore, in most cases there is always money involved, whether it is your brother or uncle". This is an indication that land relations in communal areas are increasingly becoming commoditised, land value is being pushed up, and social relations concerning land are undergoing transformation.

The growing formation of land markets in rural areas of Africa has been met with scepticism concerning whether they constitute classical land markets (Peters, 2013b). In Namibia too, some government officials have registered their scepticism about whether what is taking place in rural areas is mere illegal transfer of land rights, rather than an active market. Peters (2013b) argues that this scepticism can be explained by the fact that "most of the transfers remain defined by, or are 'embedded' in, social relations" (Peters, 2013b, p. 552). My research supports this approach: transactions are disguised by social relations. Traditional authorities report that, when sellers and buyers come to legitimate the land rights that have been exchanged, they often state, "I am giving part of my land to my nephew", or "I am giving part of my land to my friend". Most of these transactions are swept under the carpet. What is certain is that the emerging market-based transactions in land are broadening the mechanisms that provide access to land. The implications are that access to customary land is increasingly a function of buying power, i.e., it disadvantages poorer members of society. Traditional authorities and social-relations based mechanisms are no longer the only actors or avenues through which land can be accessed, because private transactions are increasingly becoming a means to access land.

Polarised views on land markets in communal areas

Trading in land rights in communal areas is legally prohibited. In Namibia, like in many other African countries, legally recognised markets in land exist only in freehold areas. The government, through the Communal Land Reform Act,

2002 (Republic of Namibia, 2002), adopts a protectionist approach to communal land. Prohibiting land trading originates from the intention that communal land should provide a safety net or means of security for the rural poor. This prohibition protects landholders who would dispose of land rights in ways that would leave them poorer if their land rights were tradable. Therefore, on a formal and legal level, land rights holders in communal areas are protected from the forces of the market. This policy principle is part of the polarised debate between "those seeking poverty reduction through land markets and those who seek to protect the poor from losing their land to the forces of the market" (Chimhowu & Woodhouse, 2005, p. 408). Land markets are broadly characterised by inequalities, as access is increasingly determined by access to financial means, which not many people have access to. Only wage earners, businesspersons, and the like are likely to afford land. Even for wage earners, salaries are generally so low that their income is not sufficient. Allowing market-based transactions to access land in communal areas is a form of exclusion, which will have negative impacts, especially on poorer communal land users, in the form of creating landlessness and therefore destitution, but also in the form of affordability: as the demand increases, prices are also pushed up. Therefore, there are merits concerning the state adopting a protectionist approach to communal land. Although trading in land is legally prohibited, registered, and formal estate agents publicly advertise properties for sale in communal areas – the practice is an open secret.

As reported elsewhere, land markets in Africa have proliferated (Colin & Woodhouse, 2010, p. 4). What this chapter has shown is that market-based transactions to access land have also made inroads into north-central Namibia's communal land. The long-held assumption that customary tenure is immune to market forces has been proven invalid. Access to land is changing, from being underpinned only by social relations and socio-politico authority, to also being subject to market forces. Landholders are exchanging their rights for money. The important question to ponder is no longer whether there are land markets in Namibia's communal areas, but how to respond to them. Would it be better to regulate these markets, should they be prohibited, or should they be left to continue unregulated? If we decide to regulate them, how do we regulate them without leaving people landless and destitute? Who are the winners and who are the losers in any of the choices? Chimhowu and Woodhouse (2005) argue that "recognition of specific characteristics of 'vernacular land markets' – market-based transfers of land under customary tenure – is essential if state policies are to succeed in promoting the interests of the poor". For Namibia, what kinds of reforms are needed regarding these dynamics, to protect the interests of the poor? While debates regarding whether to allow land markets are polarised, what is clear right now is that this issue demands immediate policy and legal direction.

5

Institutions and Processes in Tenure Reform

Although the Communal Land Reform Act was passed in 2002, the process of communal land reform effectively began after the Act came into force in March 2003. Key to communal land reform is tenure reform and providing security of land tenure in communal areas. After the promulgation of the Communal Land Reform Act, the then Ministry of Land Reform began putting in place the required institutions and processes that are instrumental for tenure reform and for bringing about security of land tenure.

Land tenure in north-central Namibia's communal areas, as in many other parts of the country, has been defined through customary systems of traditional authorities. The rules of control, access, use and transfer of land, and the associated responsibilities and restraints, have long been defined and derived from customary law and social practices, often instituted without written records. Land tenure in the communal areas has been outside the realm of statutory institutions and laws. Communal land reform, through its component of tenure reform, therefore, provides statutory and legal recognition of customarily derived land rights. Recognition of land rights is done through the process of land rights registration. Land rights registration in communal areas differentiates the different types of land rights, which correspond with different land uses. The different types of land rights registered for communal land are customary land rights, rights of leasehold for general commercial enterprise, rights of leasehold for agricultural purposes, and occupational land rights. Occupational land rights are granted for land uses to provide public services, and to public institutions, such as government ministries, agencies and offices, education, health, social, sports, religious and other institutions, such as NGOs and community-based organisations which provide public services, and for community projects (Republic of Namibia, 2013).[11] An analysis of customary land rights, rights of leasehold for general commercial enterprises, and rights of leasehold for agricultural purposes will be discussed separately in Chapters 6 and 7, respectively. This chapter focuses on institutions and processes involved in tenure reform.

11 Communal Land Reform Amendment Act No. 13 of 2013.

Communal land boards

Communal land boards are established under the Communal Land Reform Act, 2002 (Republic of Namibia, 2002), and are established in all regions which have communal land. As new institutions in land administration, their role is to provide statutory recognition and ratification of customary land rights. Furthermore, they grant rights of leasehold for agricultural purposes, rights of leasehold for general commercial purposes, and occupational land rights. While communal land boards provide statutory recognition and ratify customary land rights, these rights remain under direct management of traditional authorities. For example, it is still traditional authorities who can cancel or make amendments to these rights, which will then be ratified by the communal land board. The rights of leasehold for agricultural purposes and the rights of leasehold for general commercial purposes are under the management of communal land boards. Communal land boards are also involved in dealing with land-related disputes that emanate from the villages, a function that arises through appeals. The establishment of communal land boards has led to a duality of institutional structures for administering communal land: land boards and the traditional authorities. In countries such as Botswana, traditional authorities lost their functional power over land administration, including land allocation, when communal land boards were established. In Namibia, communal land boards work in parallel with traditional authorities, each with their respective functions and mandates, as defined in the Communal Land Reform Act, 2002 (Republic of Namibia, 2002).

As discussed in Chapter 1, during the formulation of the Communal Land Reform Act (Republic of Namibia, 2002), there were contestations regarding the establishment of the communal land boards. Traditional authorities were uncomfortable about the establishment of the land boards, arguing that the boards would take over traditional authorities' long-held function of land administration in communal areas. The draft Bill of the Communal Land Reform Act initially followed the Botswana version regarding the functions of communal land boards, which would have removed the powers of traditional authorities regarding land administration. After the 1996 Consultative Conference on Communal Land Administration, the Namibian Government changed course, and defined and confirmed the roles of traditional authorities regarding land administration in the law by clearly differentiating them from the roles of the proposed communal land boards. While the differentiated roles and functions of communal land boards and the traditional authorities are clear in the Act, some traditional authorities are still threatened by the existence of communal land boards. For example, during my field research, some traditional authorities called through local newspapers for communal land boards to be dissolved. Their justification was that communal land boards obstructed the functions of traditional authorities. Despite these contestations, the institution of communal land boards has promoted accountability in land administration, in that traditional authorities no longer have the last and absolute say in land-related matters.

Composition of communal land boards

Communal land boards comprise members drawn from a wide range of backgrounds who represent various institutions and interests. The boards are composed of representatives of traditional authorities of each region. If a region has more than one traditional authority within its boundary, then its land board will comprise representatives from those respective traditional authorities. For example, in the Ohangwena Region, some communal land areas fall under the jurisdiction of Oukwanyama, and others under the Ondonga traditional authorities. Accordingly, both Ondonga and Oukwanyama traditional authorities are represented on the Ohangwena Communal Land Board, each representing its traditional authority's interests. The role of the traditional authorities' representatives is not only to represent the interests of their respective institutions, but also to offer advice and to guide processes of tenure reform. For example, the representatives of traditional authorities are essential for confirming the legitimacy of consent letters provided in the land rights registration applications, and to communicate changes in the traditional authorities, for example, changes at village or district levels.

Representatives of the Ministry of Environment, Forestry and Tourism, and the Ministry of Agriculture, Water and Land Reform also serve on communal land boards. The representative of the Ministry of Environment, Forestry and Tourism is pertinent because they represent the interests of the Ministry; for example, when the board has to decide on a land right for land uses that require an environmental impact assessment, this representative provides the necessary guidance for the decision-making process. Similarly, the representative of the Ministry of Agriculture, Water and Land Reform provides guidance on matters related to agriculture and water. The two ministries' representatives play roles related to providing sectoral guidance to avoid granting competing and conflicting land rights. The representative of the Ministry of Agriculture, Water and Land Reform knows which areas may not be granted certain types of land rights, possibly because a water source has been found there. In 2012, an aquifer was discovered in the Ohangwena Region which was estimated to be able to supply water to northern Namibia for 400 years. Concerns arose that unauthorised and uncontrolled drilling of boreholes at individual level could threaten the potential of this aquifer. As a result, the former president placed a moratorium on land allocation and granting of land rights in that specific area, especially for land uses that involved drilling for underground water. The representative of the Ministry of Agriculture, Water and Land Reform, therefore, played a crucial role in advising the communal land board on this matter. Similarly, the representative of the Ministry of Environment, Forestry and Tourism may advise communal land boards that certain kinds of rights cannot be granted in a certain area if it is a conservation area. The representatives of community-based conservation areas of each region complement the roles of the two ministries. If a region has community-based conservation areas, either a communal conservancy or community forest, then these bodies are represented. For example, in Ohangwena Region, the Okongo Conservancy and Okongo Community Forest are both represented on the Ohangwena Communal Land Board. A representative of the regional council, often the chief regional officer, represents the developmental interests of the region, and a member represents the regional farmers' union.

The Communal Land Reform Act, 2002 (Republic of Namibia, 2002) has reserved a quota of four women for membership of communal land boards. Two of the women are to represent the interests of farming communities in the region, and two serve as women with expertise on the functions of the board. I, for example, served on the Ohangwena Communal Land Board from 2015 to 2017, in the capacity of a woman with expertise on the functions of the board. Setting a reserved quota for women to serve on the communal land boards is a deliberate effort by government to improve gender equality across all its governance structures. While other representatives or members of the communal land boards are appointed by their respective institutions, the gender quota representation is advertised in local newspapers (as of 2015). Having a gender quota for communal land boards is regarded as important, as traditional authorities who have a primary role in land administration, are, sadly, patriarchal institutions. Communal land as a public resource cannot be left in the hands of men alone. Having a gender quota for communal land boards falls within the radical movement called ecofeminism. The ecofeminist approach requires that institutions which govern a public resource cannot be solely dominated by men, thereby marginalising women when it comes to representation. If it were not for the quota system, the probability is that communal land boards, just like the institutions of traditional authorities, would mostly, if not exclusively, be run by men.

The former Ministry of Land Reform was represented by the deputy director, who is the senior official of the Ministry in each region. The Ministry, furthermore, acts as the secretariat for communal land boards. As the secretariat, the Ministry is responsible for providing application forms for land rights registration to the traditional authorities, and collecting applications from them; leading the mapping and verification process of land rights applied for; displaying applications; receiving complaints, dispute letters, and communications from villages; preparing agendas for communal land board meetings; calling, organising and hosting communal land board meetings; printing land rights certificates; delivering the certificates to traditional authorities; communicating with traditional authorities on the land rights that were not ratified and the justifications; and organising investigation committee field missions.

This diverse representation on communal land boards helps to emphasise the diversity of interests in communal land. Using the example of north-central Namibia, communal land comprises different actors with different interests in land. There are different uses of land within the designation communal land. The stakeholders include the state, traditional authorities and land users in their respective differentiations: farmers, business people, different social groups, including women in their different designations, and stakeholders from community conservation areas. The diverse representation on communal land boards, therefore, functions to ensure that all the different interests are included.

At the start of their tenure, communal land boards organise introductory meetings with the respective traditional authorities whose communal areas they will serve during their term. For example, when the board I served on started its three-year tenure in 2015, we visited the Oukwanyama Traditional Authority to introduce ourselves as members of the Ohangwena Communal Land Board. The introduction was done during a monthly meeting that was attended by all the senior traditional councillors, the senior leadership of the traditional authority, including the *Ohamba* herself, and her advisors. The emphasis of the meeting was that the two institutions should work together, and that the traditional authority should communicate the procedures relating to consent for land rights applications. Through the meeting, the traditional authority communicated which consent letters were legitimate, to avoid fraudulent activities. Overall, this meeting was important for informing the traditional authority about the members of the communal land board.

Some members of the traditional authority asked, "This land board comprises only young adults, where are the elders?" For the 2015-2017 tenure of the communal land boards, the then Ministry of Land Reform limited the ages of the appointments to, at most, 65 years. The majority of the members of the Ohangwena Communal Land Board for this term were aged between 30 and 40, with a few just over 60 years. Land administration has long been confined to men, who have been mostly middle-aged to elderly. The motivation for the question by some members of the traditional authority was actually whether these young people would be able to make decisions on land, which is regarded as a complex socio-cultural matter.

Traditional authorities

Traditional authorities remain core institutions in communal land administration. The primary roles and mandate, as provided for by the Communal Land Reform Act, 2002 (Republic of Namibia, 2002), is to manage customary land rights, and to allocate and cancel land rights in communal areas. They retain the function of land allocation.

Land rights application

The process of registering and formalising land rights requires several steps and involves the land boards and traditional authorities in their hierarchical structures. On paper, the process starts with the identification and allocation of land in a village by the headman. In practice, this step is often complete, as it takes place within the realm of customary system, and the village headman would already have allocated the land. Wily explains that tenurial reforms "simply recognise customarily-obtained land [rights] as fully legally tenured 'as is', in whichever form and with whatever characteristics they currently possess" (2000, p. 2). The fact that the state recognises customarily obtained land rights as fully legal tenure 'as is' can present challenges. Peters (2004), for example, refers to processes of exclusion, deepening social divisions and class formation within customary systems of landholdings. Chapter 4 showed how the different mechanisms of access to land reveal these particular processes: processes of social differentiation regarding access to land, with some people being landholders, and not necessarily land users. Therefore, registering and formally recognising customarily obtained land rights represents providing legality to exclusion, social division, and differentiation, because in some cases, the process is characterised by inequalities and inequities.

The registration process starts with the step of landholders completing application forms and submitting them to their respective village headmen. The applicants are required to pay an up-front application fee of N$ 25.00 and to attach the receipt to the application forms. In addition to the receipt for payment, the village headmen need to attach letters of consent, proving that the applicants' claims to land are valid and that applicants have been granted or allocated rights to use the land for which they are applying. From this step on, different traditional authorities have different procedures. Ondonga Traditional Authority, for example, requires applicants to take their applications in person to the local traditional authority's office, referred to as *ombelewa yelelo* or *ombelewa yoshilongo*. The *ombelewa yelelo* then prepares letters of consent, which indicate that the traditional authority does not oppose the granting of the land rights applied for by the applicants. For Oukwanyama Traditional Authority, the village headmen collect all the applications from their respective villages, which they submit to their traditional authority's office in Ohangwena. The traditional authority's office validates all the applications received and stamps the consent letters from the respective village headmen and the applications forms. The stamp of the traditional authority represents permission for the applications by the highest level of traditional authority. These checks show the robustness of the process, especially in ensuring that the land rights applied for are legitimated by the traditional authorities in their hierarchical structures and, ultimately, that there is legitimacy in the rights applied for.

Technical officials of what was called the Ministry of Land Reform at the time collect the application forms from the traditional authorities' offices. The officials then visit the respective villages to map and verify the landholdings of the rights applied for. The mapping and verification process takes place in the presence of village headmen, the respective landholders and, sometimes, their neighbours, who collectively confirm the boundaries of the landholdings. In some cases, there may be disputes over boundaries between neighbours. In such cases, the mapping and verification team do not proceed until such disputes have been resolved by the customary system. Counterclaims are often addressed during the mapping and verification process, some are contested at the traditional authority level, and even up to the land boards through appeals, but until the counterclaims are resolved, the landholdings in question cannot be registered. During field research, I came across landholdings that had not been registered yet, although most landholdings in those specific villages were registered. The reason given by the research participants was that registration was being held up by disputes over boundaries. Thus, the approach of delaying registration of land subject to disputes works to prevent giving legal recognition of tenure where counter or conflicting claims to landholdings exist.

After the mapping and verification process, the Ministry displays all the lists of applicants and the details of the land rights applied for, at its offices. The applications are displayed for seven days to enable objection, in the absence of which the process continues to the next level. During my visits to Ohangwena Region for field research and, ultimately, as a member of the communal land board, I observed very few objections. Most objections had already been lodged during the mapping and verification process, and are usually addressed before applications are displayed. Nevertheless, displaying land rights applications remains an important step, especially in the context of differentiated access mechanisms and the absence of some landholders from communal areas. The process of displaying applications circumvents double ratification of land rights, ratification of overlapping land rights, and ratification of rights on landholdings with competing land claims.

During my tenure as a member of the Ohangwena Communal Land Board, I observed one of the objections. It was lodged by a landholder, a senior politician based in an urban area some distance away, who had given his kin a part of his landholding to use because she did not have land of her own. This woman had lived on this land since the mid-1990s. Of interest was the fact that the landholder was also the village headman, in spite of being in full-time employment at a distant urban area, and was thus represented by *kapatashu* in the daily administration of the village, including land allocation and even granting consent letters for land rights recognition. The woman applied for land rights, and was granted consent by the *kapatashu;* the application was then validated and consented to by the traditional authority's office. When the applications from that particular village were displayed at the Ministry's offices, and upon realising the woman was applying for land rights, the landholder objected. The landholder clarified in a letter to the land board that the land had been given to the woman for use and not to own. Widlok (2016) describes this as a type of sharing which involves someone providing a share of a valuable resource with the expectation that it is to be returned eventually. The application was removed from the registration roll based on counter and competing claims.

Fundamental to this case is not only the necessity of preventing the ratification of counter and competing claims to land, but the question of who benefits from secured land rights: landholders or land users? As explained in Chapter 3, landholders are not necessarily land users, and land users are not necessarily landholders. This case, one of many, provides evidence of the need for and importance of distinguishing between landholders and land users. Chapter 6 further expands on this. However, the essence is that these kinds of cases call for a reconsideration of the model to grant security of tenure that is equitable and that considers the difference between land users and landholders.

Once applications have been displayed for seven days, the Ministry, as the secretariat, convenes a communal land board meeting to ratify the land rights applications – a process that works to legally recognise land rights.

Land rights ratification

Communal land boards meet on a quarterly basis, but extraordinary meetings may be called if there are pending issues that cannot be dealt with in ordinary meetings, for example, if the board is behind on its annual targets for land rights ratification. During their sitting, the secretariat presents land board members with the land rights applications for ratification. Applications are differentiated between customary land rights, rights of leasehold for commercial enterprises, rights of leasehold for agricultural purposes, and occupational land rights. The applications are differentiated further according to traditional authorities (e.g. for Ohangwena Region, between Ondonga and Oukwanyama Traditional Authorities). Depending on the agenda, the meeting may take between one and two full days. A typical land board agenda comprises up to 2,000 customary land rights applications to be ratified, and fewer, up to 10, rights of leasehold. There are seldom applications for occupational land rights, possibly because institutions have not been sensitised enough to register their land rights. The agenda also contains discussion points: letters of complaint, dispute letters/cases from different villages, communications from the Ministry's central office and so on. The agenda may also comprise hearings and disputes that have been escalated to the land boards through appeals, after failure by traditional authorities to resolve them to the satisfaction of the aggrieved parties. All members or institutional representatives mentioned above sit around a table and discuss the agenda items. As part of the ratification process, the members examine all the important requirements for each application before ratifying it. These requirements relate to whether the applications were done on the correct forms; whether the sizes of land are within the set limits; whether the forms are signed by the applicants; whether the applicants are Namibian citizens, and whether there are consent letters according to the procedure of the respective traditional authorities. Some of these requirements are described below.

Letters of consent

The letter of consent is the first requirement that land board members scrutinise when they ratify land rights. Letters of consent show that landholders have been granted permission or authorisation to occupy or hold land in a village. The roles of the land boards and traditional authorities in the land rights registration process are interlinked; however, each institution has its own mandate, as defined by the Communal Land Reform Act, 2002 (Republic of Namibia, 2002). Traditional authorities allocate land rights, and land boards ratify these allocations and rights. Allocations of either existing or new land rights by traditional authorities have no legal effect until the allocations have been ratified by land boards. Equally, land boards cannot ratify applications for customary land rights, unless there are letters of consent by traditional authorities. Thus, all the land rights applications submitted to land boards must be accompanied by letters of consent or recommendation by the respective traditional authorities, represented by village headmen and must be accompanied by consent from traditional authorities' main offices. The duality of institutional authorities has brought about better accountability and transparency in customary land rights administration. In the past, decisions of traditional authorities were final, and there was no possibility of further appeal (Legal Assistance Centre, 1991, p. 79). The fact that the decisions of traditional authorities in land administration are no longer final, and have no legal effect unless ratified by land boards, is an indication that any possible injustice within the customary system can be brought to the land boards for redress. As Quan (2000) explains, there is no longer absolute control by traditional authorities. Furthermore, letters of consent are important because in cases of disputes related to land rights, traditional authorities serve as witnesses in adjudicating the disputes.

Sizes of landholdings

Concerning the registration of land rights, the Communal Land Reform Act, 2002 (Republic of Namibia, 2002) provides regulations regarding the sizes of the landholdings for which rights are applied. Regulations relate to the jurisdiction of communal land boards in terms of the decision-making powers. From the beginning of the registration process in 2003, the limit for land rights' ratification within the jurisdiction of the land board's decision-making powers was 20 hectares for customary land rights. For rights of leasehold, the regulations set a maximum size of 50 hectares and/or 10 years for which the rights could be held. Applications exceeding these prescribed limits must be submitted to the Minister of Land Reform, who must grant approval before the land boards can ratify these rights. During the time of field research, and especially in the first years of the registration process, the Ohangwena Communal Land Board received many applications for existing customary land rights that exceeded the 20 hectare limit for ratification. This meant that many applications were directed to the central office of the then Ministry of Land Reform in Windhoek, for the minister to grant approval before ratification by the land board.

From the start, the Ministry set timelines for the completion of the registration process for all land rights. The first deadline was 2006, which was extended to end of March 2009, then extended to 2012, then to 2014. In 2014, the ministry set an indefinite deadline, "until further notice" (Thiem, 2014, p. 34). These deadlines were extended because of failure to meet the targets set for registration (Thiem, 2014). Many reasons can be given for this inability to reach targets, of which the size limit of 20 hectares for customary land rights is one of the contributing factors. While the size limit relates to the jurisdictional powers of the land boards and the minister, some landholders understood 20 hectares to be the maximum allowable limit of land for customary land rights. Therefore, some landholders were discouraged from applying and opted not to do so, believing that the size of their landholdings were beyond the limit and, therefore, parts would be alienated and reallocated to others. For landholdings exceeding 20 hectares, applicants must provide a motivational letter explaining why they would like to maintain their rights. While some landowners opted not to apply for land rights, those who understood the requirement of the motivational letters applied for land rights and included their motivational letters; others subdivided their landholdings to accommodate the 20 hectare limitation. Those who did not understand the requirement avoided registration.

The various strategies that landholders adopt concerning the registration process demonstrates that the process is an interactive one between landholders and state regulations. The perception that landholders are passive recipients of state directives and changes is somewhat misguided, primarily because it fails to acknowledge the agency of landholders in processes pertaining to issues of transformation. In most of the motivations provided, landholders cited the need to bank land for their children for the future, and that land users depend on the land for their livelihoods, as justification for retaining land in excess of 20 hectares. Others responded by subdividing their landholdings for their children and registering subdivisions with village headmen before they launched their applications. Overall, the issue of size affected the progress of the registration process because some landowners were deterred from applying by fear, while others applied, motivating their applications. For those who applied, the process then entailed obtaining approval for their applications from the minister, which prolonged the process and, therefore, prevented targets being met. The consequences of this are, for example, that if the land board is required to ratify 500 customary land rights applications in one sitting, 100 applications may be for land above the size limit, and therefore have to be escalated to the minister for approval. This means that these 100 applications will be ratified only at subsequent meetings, thus, the target that was set for that specific sitting cannot be achieved. In 2015, to ease the process, the Ministry increased the size limit to 50 hectares for customary land rights and 100 hectares for rights of leasehold. As a result, fewer applications had to be escalated to the minister, as most of them are usually within 50 hectares. These changes indicate that the process is flexible enough to accommodate future changes.

Although this flexibility could be seen from a positive angle, it may also be seen as counterproductive. This applies particularly to amendments that do not involve public consultation and participation. For example, the amendment to increase the size limit for land to be ratified by communal land boards from 20 to 50 hectares for customary land rights and from 50 to 100 hectares for rights of leasehold, has fundamental implications. While the limit relates mainly to jurisdictional powers of the communal land boards and the minister, it is fundamental regarding the egalitarian distribution of land. The issue of the size of the land unit was one of the controversial points during the formulation of the Communal Land Reform Act, 2002 (Republic of Namibia, 2002). The Ministry's decision to change the size was purely to reduce the number of applications referred to the minister for approval before ratification and, thus, to increase the rate of land rights registration. However, this decision has negative ramifications in terms of egalitarian distribution of land and, in particular, exacerbates the demand for and scarcity of land available for allocation. Having landholders with 50 hectares of landholdings, while others have nothing, does not indicate equity in access to land.

Nationality of applicants

Confirming that an applicant is a Namibian citizen is an important requirement in the ratification process, thus, land board members refer to national identity documents that are attached as proof. The Communal Land Reform Act, 2002 (Republic of Namibia, 2002) prohibits access to customary land rights by foreign nationals. Foreign nationals may be granted rights of leasehold on communal land, which the minister has to approve before the right is ratified by the communal land board. Prohibiting foreign nationals from being granted customary land rights is proof of the protectionist approach of the state to communal land and, in particular, customary land rights. Communal land and, in particular, customary land rights, provide a safety net for the rural poor. It is a means through which people derive their livelihoods. It is a buffer zone that even people in urban areas can fall back on when they lose their jobs or retire.

Types of land rights and uses of land

The Communal Land Reform Act, 2002 (Republic of Namibia, 2002) provides rights for specific land uses: residential, cultivation or common grazing, which can be practised under customary or leasehold rights. The distinguishing feature between these rights is, primarily, the objectives of land-based production: subsistence or commercial. For example, applications for land uses geared to subsistence are granted customary land rights, while land uses geared to commercialisation are granted rights of leasehold. Through this distinction, communal land reform recognises different land uses, and each receives a particular form of protection and duration of tenure.

When all the requirements have been met, the land boards cause the rights applied for to be registered and land rights certificates to be issued. The registration process ultimately represents the formalisation of land rights that have been acquired and held through customary tenure systems, in the realm of statutory laws. The process leads to the parallel existence of customary land rights under both customary and statutory systems through a card from the traditional authority and a certificate from the land board.

Status of land rights registration

Since 2003, the Ministry of Land Reform has identified 245,000 existing land rights for registration countrywide (Ministry of Land Reform, 2018) of which 152,000 or 62% are in the regions of north-central Namibia (Thiem, 2014). In the initial days of registration, the process was slow (Thiem, 2014). Some of my research participants confirmed this slow pace, indicating that they had submitted their applications in 2005 or 2006, and received their certificates only in 2012, while some were still waiting for their certificates in 2018. During 2017, the Ohangwena Communal Land Board was still ratifying land rights for applications submitted between 2009 and 2012. The registration process gained momentum in 2009 (Thiem, 2014). By 2014, when communal land reform had been implemented for a decade, an average of 64% of landholdings had been digitised for registration, though only 36% of the digitised landholdings had been registered (Thiem, 2014). By March 2017, 88% of the landholdings were reported as digitised. During the Second National Land Conference in 2018, the Ministry of Land Reform reported that of the target of 245,000 land rights nationally, a total of 119,227 (49%) were registered (Ministry of Land Reform, 2018). The majority (99%) of these are customary land rights; rights of leasehold account for only 1%. The Ministry of Land Reform's regional offices reported that Ohangwena had recorded about 23,830 (64%); Omusati had recorded about 34,570 (71%); Oshana had recorded about 16,036 (78%); and Oshikoto had recorded about 12,298 (43%) land rights, which have been registered and approved by communal land boards. These add up to about 86,734 land rights that have been registered in north-central Namibia, which represents 73% of the countrywide record. While there are still some milestones to reach, the 59% (out of the set target of 152,000) land rights registered in north-central Namibia is notable. It means that these landholders on communal land have secured land rights, not only in the customary system, but have also obtained statutory recognition.

Dealing with land disputes and conflicts

As indicated in the preceding sections, a typical agenda of a land board meeting does not only involve the ratification of land rights, it also includes discussion points emanating from the field, including land disputes and conflicts. A land conflict is defined as

> A social fact in which at least two parties are involved, the roots of which are interests over the property rights to land: the right to use the land, to manage the land, to generate an income from the land, to exclude others from the land, to transfer it and the right to compensation for it. A land conflict, therefore, can be understood as a misuse, restriction or dispute over property rights to land (Wehrmann, 2008, p. 9).

Land conflicts start as land disputes, where "incompatible interests/goals and perceptions/values" between more than one party emerge (Brankamp, 2013, p. 15). Land disputes in north-central Namibia are a result of the complexities that are inherent in household structures, in the different mechanisms of access to land, and in the varied and sometimes competing interests and claims over land. Disputes I observed in field related to the following:

1. Boundary disputes between neighbouring land users. In this case, the role of the headmen is that of mediator, because they allocate the land and set the boundaries. Within the context of communal land reform, these disputes are relatively easy to resolve, especially if the landholding is registered. The certificate includes a map that shows the boundaries of the different landholdings.

2. Boundary disputes between neighbouring villages, or even traditional authorities. These disputes are addressed at the level of village headmen or senior headmen, or the higher office of the traditional authority. Each headman or traditional authority protects the territorial interests of their respective villages and traditional authority area. Communal land boards often receive letters from the villages about these kinds of disputes; however, these kinds of disputes fall outside the mandate of the land boards and are therefore referred back to the traditional authorities. In these cases, the role of representatives of the traditional authorities on the land boards come into play, as they advise on the correct procedures.
3. Disputes about illegal fencing between land users and, sometimes, village headmen in specific villages. Villagers oppose landholders who are fencing land, particularly the commonage. In some cases, village headmen are in conflict with landholders who have fenced land illegally. Typically, these disputes arise when a landholder is allocated a specific landholding, with specific boundaries, but the landholder extends the boundaries without the permission of the village headmen. This disadvantages other communal land users who have interests in the fenced land, because they use it as commonage, or to reach water resources. Disputes about illegal fencing do not only arise between the land users, and do not only involve village headmen – they could go as far as involving the government. The government's involvement is in the context of the new legal prohibition against fencing on communal land, as provided for in the Communal Land Reform Act (Republic of Namibia, 2002).
4. Disputes can arise between land users over double allocations, when village headmen allocate the same land parcel to two people. This is common in peri-urban areas. These disputes involve conflicting claims to a single parcel of land.
5. Disputes over illegal eviction from land, including eviction of widows from land that they once shared and lived on with their deceased husbands.
6. Uncertainty about the validity of claims to land can cause disputes. Landholders assert claims to landholdings, but village headmen dispute it, having allocated the land to someone else.

Some landholders take their dispute cases directly to communal land boards, without having gone through the structures of the traditional authorities. Some take their dispute cases directly to their lawyers, who then take up the cases with the relevant communal land board. The land boards then receive letters from lawyers representing their clients. Some claimants exhaust their cases within the traditional authority structures, where they are sometimes resolved. If they are not resolved, the aggrieved parties appeal to the Minister of Land Reform, and cases end up having to be adjudicated by communal land boards. These dynamics are captured by the concept and practice of institution shopping, or forum shopping, which is a practice "whereby people seeking a judgement will try different options, to see which institution is more likely to rule in their favour" (Toulmin, 2008, p. 13). Institution shopping or forum shopping is common in contexts where there is a duality of institutions and laws.

The procedure to address disputes should, however, be through traditional authorities. This means that issues have to be addressed according to the hierarchical structure of the traditional authority, starting at the village level. If disputes are not resolved at that level, they are taken to the district level, and if not resolved there, they can be taken to the traditional authority main office. Only after the traditional authority main office has failed to resolve the dispute, should the land/rights holder appeal to the Minister of Land Reform, who will then refer the case to the communal land board. In these cases, a communal land board will establish an investigation committee (using the provision of Section 37 of the Communal Land Reform Act), the members of which will visit the site to investigate the case. The committee will report to the land board, which will call a hearing and invite the aggrieved parties and their witnesses, as well as other parties and traditional authorities as witnesses. Only if disputes are not resolved at the level of communal land boards, may aggrieved parties appeal to the land tribunal. This procedure appeal works to prevent or counter institutional or forum shopping, which may be abused by people hoping to circumvent the law.

My findings show that, in some cases, a decision to approach the communal land board directly, without exhausting the traditional authority structures, is not a matter of forum shopping, but a matter of having no voice at the traditional authority. In some cases, the landholders are aggrieved by the traditional authorities themselves and, therefore, believe that there will be no justice if their cases are addressed to the same institution (also see Werner, 2008). For example, in a case relating to illegal eviction, a widow was evicted from the land with the village headmen siding with the family of her deceased husband. It turned out that the headman had already reallocated the land to someone else (who was the family of her deceased husband's preferred inheritor). She reported the case to the communal land board, however, she was sent back to report her case to the village headman and told that, only if she received no redress there, could she proceed to the next level in the traditional authority hierarchy. However, to proceed to the next level of the traditional authority, she needed a letter from the village headman who was party to her eviction. Such cases present dilemmas for aggrieved parties and, therefore, approaching communal land boards directly may prevent further vulnerability and should not be seen as forum shopping.

I introduced the communal land reform process by focusing on the institutions and processes at play in its implementation. Communal land boards were instituted to recognise and ratify land rights that were allocated by traditional authorities. The institutions of communal land boards work to ensure that land administration is integrated in a statutory governance system, and that the majority of land rights holders have statutory recognition. The presence of communal land boards means that traditional authorities are no longer the only institutions involved in land administration; in fact, the decisions they make, especially in terms of land rights allocation, are not final and legal until they have been ratified by the boards. On the other hand, the continuing role of traditional authorities reflects the embeddedness of land administration in social systems. In reality, the two institutions need each other to complete processes that involve checks and balances, thereby ensuring some level of transparency and accountability.

Similarly, positive changes in the justice system are reflected by the fact that, if parties involved in land-related disputes are not satisfied by the decisions at the traditional authority level, they can appeal. The system allows specific processes to be followed, in that someone cannot lodge a dispute without exhausting the first levels. I argue that this system prevents what is called forum shopping in cases where people attempt to abuse the system. However, the system could also be counterproductive when someone is aggrieved by the traditional authorities themselves, as it may be unproductive to raise their issues addressed there.

In general, the duality of the institutions involved in administration of communal land reflects positive developments. However, this can only be maintained if each institution continues to function within its jurisdiction, that it has the capacity needed, and that its decisions are firm and in the interests of the poor.

6
Registration of Customary Land Rights

Issuing customary land rights certificates

After customary land rights certificates have been issued and printed, the secretariat of the communal land board, i.e., the land reform regional offices, submit these certificates to the traditional authorities' offices, from where they are collected by the respective village headmen and distributed to landholders. I will present this process as it takes place at the village level, by sharing my experiences and observations from attending village meetings in one of the villages in Ondobe area.

It was 3 August 2013, a windy and chilly morning. Members of one of the villages in Ondobe area gathered, one by one, for a village meeting organised by the village leadership. The village had not met for a while as over the past months the farmers had been busy with their crop fields. They had just finished harvesting, sifting, and storing their produce. While the village members were gathering, the leadership held a preparatory meeting in the homestead of one of the elders, in whose field the meetings had always taken place. The previous week, the village secretary had announced the meeting on the radio, and had urged every household to be represented at the meeting, not by children, but by adults. The villagers responded to the announcement and the meeting was well attended, with most of the households in the village represented (Figure 6.1). The meeting's agenda was packed: disputes between neighbours, and a dispute relating to an accusation of poisoning at the nearby commercial centre; the opening hours of commercial centres in the village; disputes over land inheritance; land rights certificates; deadlines of payments of *iifendela yedu* (land tax) for the year; reminders for the payments of *ombadu yekaya* by the new landholders who had inherited lands; and a discussion regarding a Pentecostal church in the village, which was operating on one of the landholders' land. The preparatory meeting, which I also observed, was about how to deal with the issue of the Pentecostal church in the village. The main meeting or gathering also served to celebrate what is locally referred to as *Oshipe* (thanksgiving). The cultivation season had just ended and, as a customary practice, the farmers gathered to celebrate *Oshipe*. Some were dressed in their beautiful, colourful traditional attire (Figure 6.2). I, too, took part in these celebrations, dressed in my own traditional attire. We sang, danced, and ululated. The event was magnificent, and I could not separate the researcher from the local in me.

Figure 6.1: The well-attended village meeting session

Figure 6.2: Members of the village in traditional dress celebrating *Oshipe*

I observed that the agenda point the members dwelled on longest was that on the Pentecostal church. One of the members had erected a tent on his landholding from where he operated a Pentecostal church. In the villages in Ondobe area, and north-central Namibia at large, Lutheran, Catholic and Anglican denominations are predominant, which people refer to as "our traditional churches". Some members of this village worshipped at the Anglican Church located in the village, and others worshipped at the Lutheran church, located in the adjacent village, Ondobe. In recent years, north-central Namibia, and the rest of Namibia, has experienced an increase in the number of Pentecostal churches, which have not been welcomed by all. Some people argue that the new churches "confuse people", "entice people from their traditional churches", are "after money", and have come to "disturb peace". Young adults have been most vulnerable to the allure of the Pentecostal churches and, therefore, most parents, leaders of "traditional churches" and the authorities oppose the Pentecostal churches and warn young people to avoid falling prey to them. In this context, the member of this village who was operating a Pentecostal church was doing so to the dismay of many other village members, including the village leadership. The village leadership brought this issue to be discussed in the village meeting and asked the members to make a collective decision about whether this landholder should be permitted to continue his church activities on his landholding in the village. The discussion was structured around two questions: One, may he operate his church activities on his landholding, and two, may he operate his church activities in the village? The members did not agree to either. Members opposing church activities in the village based their justifications on the fact that they already had two churches, that is, Lutheran and Anglican, in the area, and therefore did not need another new church. Arguments of members who opposed church activities on the man's customary land emphasised the type of land rights that the landholder had over the land, that is, customary land rights. They argued that customary land rights mean that the landholder has rights only for residential and farming activities. "Those are the only uses that can take place on that land", one member of the village leadership said. "If you need to use the land for church activities, then you need to change your rights with the land office in Eenhana", another member of the village leadership charged. The village headman ended the interventions from the main table, by stating that

> with that you have to launch another application with the land board in Eenhana in order to change your rights from customary land rights to rights that allow you to practise church activities, or even to rights of leasehold, because you are collecting a lot of money from the members – it is a business operation (notes from village meeting_OM_2015).

These assertions reveal that stakeholders in communal land use the regulations of the Communal Land Reform Act (Republic of Namibia, 2002) to justify their claims or to support their arguments. In this case, the villagers used the regulations to support their interests, using them to lend force to their point that they did not want the Pentecostal church in their village. People use regulations to enforce their interests. The landholder in question left the meeting immediately on hearing the outcome, informing everyone loudly, "You do not want to allow me to have my church here, on my landholding, see you at the land office (*kombelewa yomadu),* it is my landholding, you cannot prescribe what I do on my land, Namibia is a democratic country" (notes from village meeting_OM_2015). Often, when landholders or land users refer to the land office, or *ombelewa yomadu,* they are referring to communal land boards; they often fail to distinguish between the two bodies (communal land boards and the land reform office). The response of a member of the village leadership, who had been trained on the Communal Land Reform Act, 2002 (Republic of Namibia, 2002) and how to interpret it, was, "See you at the land office". He knew that, based on customary land rights granted for residential and farming purposes, the meeting's decision was correct and that they had a case.

As Hall et al. (2011, p. 16) explain, "land [use] regulation is meant to encourage [and/or maintain] certain kinds of behaviour and discourage others". In Namibia, the government instituted regulations for using land for which customary land rights are granted, to ensure that households have access to land for crop production, which continues to be essential for subsistence or for basic food security at household level. Government further uses these regulations to ensure security of shelter. Although subsistence agriculture's contribution to livelihoods is declining and other sources of income have become more important, its importance endures. Thus, through communal land reform, the government secures customary land rights to maintain subsistence farming. Customary land rights are a form of zoning the kinds of land rights granted to land users and land uses. This zoning is important, and it is a form of protection of what is fundamental, namely, farming at the level of households.

This argument addresses an important question raised by Nancy Fraser (1996, p. 35) in the context of ensuring recognition of "which people need what kind of recognition". It is important to permit recognition of distinctiveness in land rights. Actors at the social practice level not only welcome this recognition and security, but also mobilise the powers inherent in regulations as tools for local-level decision-making, for enforcing prohibitions, and as justifiable basis to exclude other uses. Similar cases of village headmen in the area I studied using the regulation of use, refer to landholders opening trading stores on their customary landholdings. Trading stores are for commercial purposes, and landholders are encouraged to acquire land at commercial centres where they obtain rights of leasehold for general enterprises. However, while this expectation is clear in the regulations, it is not strictly enforced. People who are excluded or whose land uses are excluded through these regulations, such as the landholder operating the Pentecostal church, oppose these local decisions and, ultimately, resist the regulations. For example, what the landholder operating the Pentecostal church resisted is the very regulation established by the state and implemented by the communal land boards, to which he intended to appeal.

The assertion by the landholder that "you cannot prescribe what I do on my land" raises fundamental points about the implications of communal land reform, and the materiality of land rights registration. To start with, the regulations that provide for the recognition of land rights are inherently a form of land-use planning aimed at eliminating overlapping and conflicting land uses, and to encourage and promote certain kinds of behaviours. For landholders, it is important to recognise and secure the rights to residence and rights to a crop field, because they serve as safety nets and are the basis of a minimum level of subsistence for the majority of landholders and land users in communal areas. On the part of government, this kind of protection is important, as it ensures that shelter is guaranteed, as is food security at household level. Through regulation, other uses or users of land are excluded. As Hall et al. (2011, p. 8) assert, exclusion "is a necessary feature of every type of land use and tenurial arrangement". Regulation is a form of protection; thus, protecting customary land rights means keeping these off-limits for predatory users and external forces, including market threats. It prevents predatory users from accessing land that has been set aside to provide minimum subsistence. Regulation is one of the powers of exclusion that defines conditions of land use and protects certain kinds of land uses; without regulation, these land uses might be at risk. Thus, in this context, regulation as a power of exclusion is viewed in a positive light.

The meeting in the village in Ondobe area proceeded with other matters of the day. One of these was the distribution of land rights certificates that had recently been received from the traditional authority office and the communal land board. The village secretary called out the names of the landholders whose certificates were ready. She distributed some of the certificates, but informed others they first had to settle their outstanding *iifendela yedu* before they could receive their certificates. She informed landholders who had inherited lands, but who had not yet paid *ombadu yekaya* and who therefore could not apply for their land rights certificates, that forms were available. In these cases, the lands were still in the names of the deceased, and to change this, and to receive applications for land rights registration, the inheritors needed first to pay *ombadu yekaya*. Of course, landholders are free to fetch the applications forms directly from the land reform's regional office. However, in these circumstances, the catch would be the consent letters from the village headman who would not co-operate before these landholders had settled their *ombadu yekaya*. Landholders from other villages, and even other traditional authorities, did the same: village headmen did not hand over the certificates or application forms before landholders had paid and given their *iifendela yedu* or *ombadu yekaya,* respectively.

These elements of land rights legitimation under the customary system are proving to create powers of exclusion from the statutory recognition of land rights. As communal land is vested in the state for the benefit of the people living there, the state has failed to provide guidelines and procedures on how these payments should operate. Arrangements are left to traditional authorities to determine. Some village headmen have been reported to have misused this vacuum to overcharge people, or even, in this case, to deny people access to statutorily recognised land rights. While traditional authorities in north-central Namibia have collectively determined a price of N$ 600.00 for customary land rights, some landholders stated that they were required to pay more than that to some members of the traditional authorities. These are understood to be dealings between village headmen and applicants who want land, and offer the headman a price. This implies that access to land is determined by access to financial resources. In the absence of regulation, this is bound to be misused, as has been reported here. Local media reported that the president asserted that "tribal (sic) leaders are supposed to be financially sustained by their subjects" (Shinovene, 2017). These days, *ombadu yekaya* and the *iifendela yedu* are the main means by which traditional authorities raise income. This assertion provides a sense of legitimation for these payments for communal land, which is contrary to Section 42 of the Communal Land Reform Act (Republic of Namibia, 2002) which prohibits traditional authorities from charging for customary land allocations.

Hall et al. (2011) argue that legitimations are never unopposed. In Namibia, the Communal Land Reform Act, 2002 (Republic of Namibia, 2002) does not have the necessary legal provisions for aggrieved landholders to oppose these unacceptable practices by the traditional authorities, for instance, if a village headman refuses to give a letter of consent. The provision to oppose legitimation only applies to granting rights of leasehold, in which case the Communal Land Reform Act, 2002 makes provision for the communal land boards to intervene by submitting the matter to an arbitrator for decision, who may then grant consent in the place of the traditional authority if the arbiter is satisfied that the traditional authority is withholding consent unreasonably (Republic of Namibia, 2002, p. 19). However, this does not apply to customary land rights: there are no legal provisions for the communal land boards to intervene in the case of exclusion from applying for customary land rights. The only provision is that the Act provides for publication of customary land rights allocations, to enable people to raise objections, as provided for in Section 22.

Surety for life and lifetime security

Customary land rights "endure for the natural life of the person to whom it is allocated, unless the right is relinquished by the holder thereof", as per the Communal Land Reform Act, 2002 (Republic of Namibia, 2002, p. 13). In principle, this represents surety for life and/or lifetime security. Tenure security is measured by using the duration of rights as the yardstick. In this case, tenure security is not measured according to the type of rights or by using the binaries of freehold vs customary or private vs communal property, but by the longevity of someone's rights. The longevity is not only dependent on the rights holders' willingness to relinquish the rights, but also the fact that, despite people having customary land rights, the land still belongs to the state. Communal land is vested in the state to promote the socio-economic development of the people living on communal land. Land rights on communal land are multi-layered. There are bundles of rights and bundles of rights holders, with the state being the executive owner. The promised socio-economic development or socio-economic benefits come in different ways. These ways include proclamation or extension of local authority areas on land that was once communal land, and construction of road or rail networks, public schools or health facilities, agricultural projects, and electrical substations and transmission lines on communal land or land on which people once had customary land rights. These projects often involve alienating and appropriating land for which landholders had been granted customary land rights, for land uses deemed important in the public interest. Land uses for public interests are often promoted in the name of bringing about employment, socio-economic benefits and poverty reduction. In addition to land alienated for government-led "development", land may also be given to foreign nationals termed investors through rights of leasehold for projects promising employment, direct foreign investment, and poverty reduction. Therefore, tenure security through customary land rights has limits. It is relative security, as the state can, at any time, alienate and appropriate land for purposes it deems are in the interests of bringing about socio-economic development. Therefore, the longevity of tenure has to be measured in relative terms.

Gender equity

In the absence of land alienation or appropriation by the state or relinquishing of land rights at the will of the landholder, the rights holder's security is, indeed, for a lifetime. Upon the death of rights holders, such rights revert to the traditional authorities for reallocation. What this means in practical terms, is that when the landholder was alive, his/her rights were registered in the village headman's book, and he/she may have received certificates from the communal land board. After the landholder's death, the family decides who should inherit the land, or the deceased may have left instructions for whom should inherit the land, or Section 26 of the Communal Land Reform Act applies as it contains specific provisions as to who inherits the land (Republic of Namibia, 2002). Traditional authorities legitimate rights for the new landholder after the decision on inheritance has been made within family structures. The most acclaimed benefit emanating from communal land reform is the recognition, protection and security of women's rights to land, in particular, widows' rights to inherit land from their deceased husbands, and the way it ensures that women have to access land in their own right.

Before independence, customary tenure systems were marred by injustice against women, especially widows, with regard to access to land, rights to land and inheritance of land. Women have been marginal concerning access to land and rights over land. Women could not own and had no rights over land. They could only access land or derive benefits from land through a male affine, their access to land always being mediated through male relations (Becker, 1997). This was the case despite women making up the majority of agricultural producers in communal areas. Upon the death of their husbands, widows were evicted from the lands they had shared with their husbands. The husbands' families grabbed the land. A change in the marital status of women due to the death of their husbands represented loss of everything, including their dignity (Shapi et al., 2017). All in all, women's tenurial access to land was often insecure and alienable (Becker, 1997).

An elderly man in Ondobe area narrated how his mother was chased from the land when her husband died. He was a young man working on farms near Outjo, a town in central Namibia. One day, he received a letter from home, informing him that his father had died. He could not travel home to mourn his father because he still had some months to go before his contract was completed. Once his contract ended, he went home, where he found that things had changed. His mother had already been chased from the land which then belonged to his paternal uncle. His mother had returned to her family. In those days, this practice was customary; therefore, the son went on with his life, and lived with his uncle until he married. On land rights registration, he commented:

> I am happy with the land rights registration because I know when I die, my wife and children are protected and secured. I know that they will take over this land and nobody can come to state otherwise. The law now protects them. My wife is 88 years old, where would she go at that age if she were to be evicted from this land, where would she start even? (interview with landholder, OM90_2013)

Since independence in 1990, the government has pursued the goal of gender equality. The eviction of widows from the land they had lived on with their husbands was one of the first issues addressed in the newly independent Namibia. Traditional authorities, as custodians of customary laws, were required by the government to repeal all the customary practices that contradicted the Constitution and state laws, including the practice of widows' eviction. The participants of the 1991 National Conference on Land Reform and the Land Question, for example, resolved that "women should have the right to own the land they cultivate and to inherit and bequeath land and fixed asset" (Republic of Namibia, 1991b). Subsequently, the protection of widows' rights found a central place in the Communal Land Reform Act, 2002. Section 26 (2) makes provision for the reallocation of land rights to the surviving spouse, the surviving spouse being the first point of reference for inheriting land (Republic of Namibia, 2002). Women, in general, can now also access land in their own right, and they can have land registered in their own names.

In 2016, I participated in a research project on women's land use, access to land and land rights. The respondents were asked to reflect on the benefits of the Communal Land Reform Act, 2002 in relation to gender equity (Shapi et al., 2017). The majority of the respondents associated communal land reform and, in particular, the registration of land rights, with improvements in women's access to land. They indicated that the benefits the Communal Land Reform Act, 2002 had brought include that, by law, widows can no longer be evicted from the land; women and men are now equal in terms of access to land; women have the same right to approach the traditional authority for land; women can have land in their own right and in their own names; women no longer depend on men to access land; women, regardless of their marital status, can have access to land, and daughters can now inherit land from their fathers (Shapi et al., 2017). In total, 39% of female respondents indicated that they own the land they live on, of which more than 70% indicated that they had obtained this land through inheritance from their late husbands. In communal land reform terms, this reflects gender equity realised through the protection and recognition of widows' land rights in statutory law. The provision does not merely consist of a section of an act, but there are clear regulations in place about which awareness has been raised. These awareness campaigns reach out to the public particularly through radio to ensure that women know their rights. Traditional authorities who control access to land and legitimate customary land rights are also trained. These legal provisions operate at practice level and people interact with them in a myriad of ways. In some instances, widows inherit the land in its entirety. In other instances, widows retain only parts of their landholdings, while other parts are subdivided and allocated to other members of the household. The latter usually occurs in cases where there are stepchildren in the household, and where disputes are possible. It also occurs in cases of landholdings that are linked to complex generational histories, landholdings that have been passed on from generation to generation, and which have remained in the same lineage for generations. One of the participants in the research explained that, "When a widow inherits land that has remained in my family for many generations, we break the history". This practice reflects the importance of descent-based customary landholding. In countries such as Malawi, it has been shown that ignoring descent-based customary landholding has resulted in disinheriting other women (Peters, 2020). In north-central Namibia, this is avoided by the family, together with the traditional authority, deciding how to subdivide the landholdings – one part for the widow and the other for one of the family members – in order to maintain connection to the land and provide for the widow. This shows that gender equity can be ensured without creating generational inequities. People who have related to particular landholdings for a long time because of their generational history benefit, and the widow also benefits through the protection of the state.

In other cases, the rights are not technically in the name of the widow, but vested in one of the children, often child, either male or female, who is entrusted with the responsibility of taking care of the mother. In these cases, the mother remains the head of the household, but is not the land rights holder. In such cases, the social protection of the widow lies in the social convention of vesting, and the legal rights are held in the name of one of the children. In cases where the widow's claim to land is under threat despite the legal rights not being in her name, the social convention of vesting is used by the communal land board to support her claim. While gender equity in land inheritance is evident and there are, indeed, legal provisions that guarantee women's access to land, there are still some pockets of inequity in existence. Women are still evicted from their husbands' lands. This is particularly common among women who were married through customary law, and particularly if they did not have children with the deceased. In some instances, even if they are aware of their rights, some women do not fight for these rights. They do know that, if their lands are grabbed, they can bring their cases to the *ombelewa yomadu* (land office), as it is called. However, the women do not do so, because of the customary belief that *edu iha li kondjelwa* (you cannot fight for land). They ask how you can fight for land if you will be buried there. If you fight for land now, it is the same as wishing to die. In the case of widows, mothers tell their children, *kaana kange, oto kondjele edu ove omo to yi* (my child, you are fighting for land knowing that you are going there). This attitude reveals that land is linked to symbolic beliefs, and reference to such beliefs indicate how strongly embedded customary systems are, despite statutory interventions to protect women's rights.

Addressing these inequities is a difficult task, as they result from beliefs; the question remains, how can land be delinked from such beliefs? Land is embedded in a social system, which raises questions about the limits of land reform to address unequal access to and inheritance of land which results from patriarchal and inhibitory customary beliefs. Women's access to land directly from the traditional authorities represents another challenge for achieving gender equity. In the research I participated in in 2016, we asked a question about the number of women holding land rights obtained from traditional authorities (Shapi et al., 2017). Only 15% indicated that they held such rights. Many women pointed out that some traditional authorities, especially at village level, are still hesitant to allocate land to women in the absence of a male figure, especially if that woman is married. Many headmen still ask where the husband is, saying, "You are asking for land, are you running away from your husband?". This statement is usually made by elderly village headmen. One of the research participants noted that elderly village headmen are still attuned to the old culture; they have not assimilated the provisions of statutory law. Thus, land inheritance remains the main mechanism through which women become landholders and land rights holders. Of course, not all women are widows, which means even female siblings can now inherit land from their parents. Peters (2020) explains that, if we are to

> understand gendered relations around land, one cannot make headway using the homogenous term 'women' because distinctions *among* women turn on kinship, descent and marriage – there are critical differences for women in the status of daughter or sister as contrasted with wife or widow (p. 73).

From the beginning of registration process, land rights could only be registered in an individual's name. For example, when spouses applied for land rights registration, these rights were registered in the names of their husbands. When husbands died, wives had to reapply for the rights to be registered in their names, even if they were the legitimate heirs. This meant that they had to restart the process: obtaining legitimation from village headmen, paying *ombadu yekaya,* getting consent letters from village headmen, and then getting the communal land board to ratify these applications. Amendments have been made, so that the registration makes provision for the registration of land rights in the name of a group, and family, individual and/or judicial entity. There is a provision for spouses to apply for land rights jointly, which means the names of both the husband and wife can appear on the certificate, and they can hold the land rights jointly. The new amendment holds the potential to spare widows from having to repay the land that they occupied with their husbands. These amendments are an acknowledgement of equality between men and women, having the potential to recognise women on an equal footing with men but how it plays out in reality is another question. While the registration process makes provision for the husband and wife to register their land jointly, customary beliefs may compromise its positive impact. On radio shows that are presented to sensitise people about the registration process and, in particular, women's rights to land, male callers expressed the opinion that the idea of joint registration will take a long time to be accepted socially. The idea that the husband is the head of the household and the land belongs to the husband is widespread. The assertion is, therefore, that because the land belongs to the husband, the certificate should be in his name. Some women reported comments such as the following: "If I register the land in my name, my in-laws would think that I want my husband dead" or "I cannot register the land on my name, my husband is still alive". It is accepted widely that registering the land in the name of the wife as opposed to the husband, and/or joint registration is a result of "fear of diminished authority [of the husband]" (Peters, 2020, p. 73). In other countries, it has been shown, however, that fearing diminishing authority is only part of the picture. In Tanzania, for example, Peters (2020, p. 73) reported that "when men, instructed to include wives' names on land titles... [had] the worry that 'the land would go to the family of the wife if the husband died first and not to his children'".

The discussion above shows that the registration process takes place within complex customary tenure systems that are marked by beliefs which hinder full social acceptance of several provisions. These systems entail socially embedded beliefs that in the end undermine broad-based benefits from land registration and/or broad-based social equity. Customary systems form the social fabric of societies, and without restructuring the systems in the case of injustice, certain provisions will remain just that, provisions. Land itself is embedded in the social system, not merely as a means of production. In addressing these concerns, we have to acknowledge the heterogeneity of issues relating to women's access to land. The approach that is often taken treats women's access to land as a homogeneous topic, and implies that women face a homogenous problem. What will be useful here is to unpack the different forms of *mis*recognition that exist in terms of women's access to land: is it widow eviction, is it beliefs that oppose fighting for land, or is it beliefs that the land belongs to the husband? Rather than treating cases as examples of simple gender inequity, we should unpack what these gender inequities entail. Doing so will enable us to propose targeted remedies. It is an indisputable fact that the Communal Land Reform Act, 2002 (Republic of Namibia, 2002) has brought about positive effects in terms of women's access to land. However, many women still face several social obstacles. The communal land legislation has not been able to change a system of beliefs and practices which still disadvantages women.

Land rights registration amidst diverse mechanisms of access to land

Registration of customary land rights takes place within complex customary situations characterised not by one mechanism of access to land, but a variety of mechanisms: rights-based and social-relations based access mechanisms. Chapter 5 showed that land relations in north-central Namibia are made up of bundles of claims and interests in land such that in a single landholding, different people may have different claims, interests, and rights. These bundles of claims, interests and rights may have originated in the past, are extant in the present and are foreseen to live on in the future. The land may belong to more than the individual in the present, belonging also to a group past, present, and yet to come (Meinzen-Dick & Mwangi, 2008, p. 37). I identified the following land claims: it is my land that was allocated to me by the traditional authority; it is my husband's land; it is our father's land; it is my land, I inherited it from my husband; it is our land I/we inherited it from our parents; it used to be my/our maternal/paternal grandfather's land; it is my/our land, I/we inherited it from my/our mother's land; it used to be my/our maternal/paternal grandmother's land; it is our maternal uncle's land, and yet more others. As shown in these testimonies, interests and claims over land are derived from social relationships and memberships, relationships that are central to people's livelihoods, social relations, and ecological functions (Meinzen-Dick & Mwangi, 2008, pp. 36, 37).

The registration of land rights has introduced statutory law as another layer on which claims are based or from which they are derived. Thus, in addition to rights derived from social relationships, and rights derived from traditional authorities, landholders now also claim rights derived from statutory law. Landholders claim, "This land was my grandfather's, it was legitimated to me by the village headman and the land rights certificate is on my name". This represents multiple sources of legitimation. When the registration process began in 2003, the focus was on recognising rights-based mechanisms of access to land, that is, rights as legitimated by traditional authorities. The focus was on recognising the rights of landholders – the rights of the individuals – by identifying a landholding and linking it to an individual rights holder. Landholders are people whose names are registered in the books of village headmen. Thus, from the beginning, registration led to individualisation of land rights, while, in the customary system, land rights are held in collectivities. The statutory process confines land rights to individuals. In a context of diversified relationships through which land users access land through different mechanisms and/or relationships, reducing or collapsing land rights to individuals means the benefits of security are not broadly distributed. The security provided is exclusionary; it is provided only to people who relate to land through rights-based access mechanisms, and it excludes those who benefit through social-relations based access mechanisms. Security of tenure is based on a model that favours individualisation of rights, without consideration of the web of relationships that underpins land relations. Toulmin and Quan argue that "registration inevitably introduces [simplifications] into a complex and dynamic set of practices" (2000, p. 207). Meinzen-Dick and Mwangi (2008, p. 38) claim that registration of land rights, or the formalisation of land rights, leads to cutting a web of interests over land,

and creating more exclusive forms of rights to the resource. This process "results in exclusion of holders of secondary rights", rights that are often held by women (Amanor, 2008, p. 14). Secondary rights are derived from primary rights and are sometimes called delegated use rights (Moyo et al., 2015). These delegated use rights are observed within the context of social-relations based mechanisms of access to land. Registration collapses all rights within individuals, to the disadvantage of the distinct, multiple claims by other users, such as women, youths, seasonal users, and others (Meinzen-Dick & Mwangi, 2008). In the process of land rights registration, only landholders' rights are registered, which exacerbates social differentiation that already exists in the customary tenure system. As explained in previous chapters, landholders are not always the land users and the land users are not always landholders. This implies a landscape made up of land users and landholders; sometimes these are held in one person, in other cases they are held in different persons. People establish these informal sharing relations which, under the economy of sharing, creates a hidden social support system. Focusing on landholders as the sole beneficiaries of statutorily recognised and secured land rights means excluding land users. Not recognising arrangements of social support systems disrupts "landholding entitlements, which form the central note of 'hidden structure', [and is also] a disruption to responsibility, obligation, and interdependence" (Peters, 2020, p. 72).

Namibia's communal land reform is flexible to allow for amendments. Recent amendments on the Communal Land Reform Act have made provision for customary land rights registration in the name of a group, family, individual and/or judicial entity. This means groups in their respective compositions can apply for land rights in collectivities. The option to register land rights in groups counters the simplification inherent in many registration processes. For land users who relate to land collectively, their rights can be recognised collectively by the state. Siblings can jointly register land which they inherited from their parents, as a group. Extended families relating to land and to each other over land through matrilineal and patrilineal relations and domestic groups can jointly register land as collectivities. During my tenure as a member of the Ohangwena Communal Land Board, I did not come across applications for registering customary land rights in group names, as the possibility was still new. However, when this option is implemented fully, it will broaden the benefits of land rights registration. The model of customary land rights as group rights could learn from the model that is implemented in the designated areas for small-scale commercial farming (see Chapter 7), where landholders are granted rights of leasehold which also legally protect other farmers who are using land.

Excluding other customary uses of land

Cropping and residential use are but some uses of land in north-central Namibia's communal areas, as is using land for grazing livestock, or commonage. The Communal Land Reform Act, 2002 (Republic of Namibia, 2002) is largely silent on the protection of commonage, which is an important resource for the communal livestock farmers. There are no particular protected rights to commonage, except for commonage in the areas designated for agricultural purposes. Designated areas become individualised, leased land, removed from commonage under the jurisdiction of the traditional authorities. The majority of farmers who are outside the designated areas are excluded from statutory recognition of their land rights to commonages. Commonages have been and continue to be threatened by many processes, particularly land concentration, and medium to large-scale enclosure of communal land. Since the 1960s, significant appropriation of communal land has taken place in north-central Namibia, largely because of the discourse on modernisation of agriculture. At independence, the pace of land appropriation increased due to the vacuum created by the absence of a legal framework governing communal land (Werner, 2015). The promulgation and implementation of the Communal Land Reform Act, 2002 (Republic of Namibia, 2002) did not bring relief in the form of protection of commonages. They remain unprotected and small livestock farmers remain without secure tenure in terms of livestock rearing. Individualisation of commonages has created inequities in access to grazing areas, as has communal land reform, because it keeps commonages outside the realm of statutory law. The only commonages protected in Namibia are those in designated areas that are leased to individual and groups of farmers. Replicating the leasing of land to groups of farmers in other parts of communal areas could bring about greater advantages for farmers who do not benefit from small-scale commercial farms. The uses of commonages are indeed customary uses and should, therefore, be recognised as such.

This chapter showed that communal land reform has improved social equity in that landholders in the communal areas have had their land rights legally recognised and secured by the state. This argument seems valid until one asks the question: Who benefits from recognition of land rights? Asking a question that focuses on the "who" is important for mapping social equity at different levels. This chapter revealed that, from the beginning, communal land reform has led to individualisation of land rights. In a landscape comprising different mechanisms of access to land, different ways in which people relate to land, and the designations of landholder and land user not always being held in one individual, linking a landholding to an individual landholder does not promote social equity. Identifying a landholding and linking it to an individual landholder through legal recognition reproduces inequities in land relations and adds another layer to social differentiation, that of people whose rights to land are legally recognised. The analysis showed, furthermore, how communal land reform has been designed to be flexible, and what this flexibility entails. Through this flexibility, the process has been amended to include provisions recognising land rights on the level of individuals, groups, legal and other entities. This new approach presents potential for social equity: benefits from recognition of land rights by the state may be broadly distributed. Findings also show that communal land reform is mostly positively attributed to gender equity. The analysis identified land uses and, therefore, also land users who are excluded from the recognition of land rights, that is, livestock farmers who use commonage. Lack of legal protection of commonages by the state perpetuates inequities and exclusion of this segment of society, and land uses that are customary.

7
Registration of Rights of Leasehold

Rights of leasehold for general business enterprises

The government recognises that land uses in communal areas are becoming increasingly commercialised. Land uses extend beyond residence, crop production and livestock rearing and, accordingly, land rights granted on communal land are beyond customary land rights. Communal land reform differentiates the different kinds of rights granted for different land uses. While customary land rights are granted for land uses geared for residence and to provide minimum subsistence, rights of leasehold for general business enterprises are granted for land uses geared for commercial activities. A brief survey of enterprises for which rights of leasehold have been granted in one of the regions in north-central Namibia included the following categories of business enterprises: food and beverage, liquor and groceries, hospitality, entertainment, clothing, construction and infrastructure, tailoring, fuel supply, car dealership, electronic and electrical appliances, hairdressing, telecommunication and ICT services, grain milling, financial and commerce, and animal husbandry.

Rights of leasehold for general business enterprises are subject to restrictions in terms of the number of years of the leasehold, or size of the land. Communal land boards can only grant rights of leasehold up to 10 years, and not exceeding 100 hectares; if the duration and/or size exceed these stipulations, the Minister responsible for land reform must grant approval before the communal land boards can ratify the applications. There are many differences between rights of leasehold and customary land rights. Unlike customary land rights, land uses for which rights of leasehold are granted are not predefined in the Communal Land Reform Act, 2002 (Republic of Namibia, 2002). For customary land rights, landholders must submit applications with the traditional authorities, while applications for rights of leasehold are submitted directly to communal land boards. The power to grant rights of leasehold is vested in the communal land boards. Traditional authorities provide letters of consent for allocations. In relation to customary land rights, traditional authorities are involved in managing the rights, which include cancellation or transfer of these rights. However, regarding rights of leasehold, traditional authorities' roles end at the provision of letters of consent for applications. Thereafter, management of rights is in the hands of communal land boards. Leaseholders pay annual lease fees to communal land boards. The lease fees are determined by the size of the land, and not by the uses of the land. For example, a telecommunications company may pay lower lease fees, because it needs less land for its tower, while an upcoming businessperson may pay more for his car wash business, or brick-making business, because these need more land. This means the lease fees are not determined by the returns of a particular business, but by the size of the land required.

Land uses on communal land have diversified beyond residence and farming. Diverse land uses represent the entrepreneurial initiative of the land users on communal land. Rights of leasehold were introduced "in a bid to encourage more investment in land and hence accelerate economic development" (Werner & Bayer, 2016, p. 1). In the literature, having private and freehold tenure is viewed as an incentive for investment in land. The findings of this study reject the long-held assumption that private titled tenure is the only incentive to investment in land, while customary tenure is inhibitory and provides no incentives for rights holders to invest in their properties. Some landholders mobilise funding from different sources (or with collateral obtained elsewhere than communal land) in order to invest in an activity in communal areas. For example, establishing a fuel station, a lodge or other business all require massive investments, which are made without necessarily having private titled tenure. In these cases, it is investment that attracts the need for security, and not the other way around. As investment increases, the demand for more secured tenure increases.

Rights of leasehold for agricultural purposes

> *Epangelo ole ya komalelo opashiwana noshiwana ta li pula apa pu na mhundja nokadila, hapu tukuluka ndiba, ashike kapeshi apa pena omundilo hau shakalwapo* (The government approached traditional authorities and the public asking for areas where duiker and birds are, where a rabbit suddenly appears, but not where there is a fire that is burning).

This extract is from an interview I had with one of the village headman of a village east of Okongo, where the government has designated an area for agricultural purposes. The designated area is formally known as Ohangwena Small Scale Commercial Farms or sometimes Okongo Designated Area. Symbolically, areas where duiker and birds are, where a rabbit suddenly appears, where a fire is not burning, represent areas that are not populated, or which have low population densities. These areas are also referred to as unutilised and/or underutilised land. In this extract, the research participant describes the process of designating the area in Ohangwena Region (Okongo Designated Area), and others in other regions, for agricultural purposes. The Okongo Designated Area is not in close proximity to the actual Okongo village council, being situated about 50 km to the east of it. The name might have resulted from the traditional reference of the area to the far east of Ohangwena Region as Okongo. The designated area itself is divided into two: Okongo East and Okongo West.

The starting point

Since the early 1990s, through the land reform programme, the government has emphasised the need to develop underutilised areas on communal land into small-scale commercial farming units. The underlying objective was to integrate communal farmers into the commercial agricultural economy. This vision was institutionalised or formalised in 1997, when Cabinet approved the Small-Scale Commercial Farms Development Project. In this context, small-scale farms do not mean the conventional smallholder farms where production is subsistence-oriented, but farms where production is market-oriented, but which have not yet developed into a fully-fledged commercial farm. In 2000, the ministry manded for land reform commissioned a fact-finding mission, "which estimated that 5 million hectares of land were unutilised and/or under-utilised in the regions of Omusati, Ohangwena, Oshikoto, Kavango, Caprivi and Otjozondjupa/Omaheke" (Republic of Namibia, 2012, p. 5).

The fact-finding mission recommended that government demarcate, survey, and develop the identified areas into small-scale farming units of 2,500 hectares each, to be leased to farmers with a particular focus on cattle farming (Republic of Namibia, 2012). Small-scale commercial farming was to focus largely on the production of livestock, in particular cattle, which are viewed as capital investment, with a long-term aim to generate income through a cattle economy (Winterfeldt, 2013). The development of small-scale commercial farming and/or the promotion of commercially-oriented farming is contextualised within the broader programme of rural development, upliftment of the welfare of inhabitants of communal areas, and the incorporation of the rural economy into the market-oriented economy. The goal is to shift communal farmers from being subsistence-oriented producers to market-oriented producers. This constitutes a revival of the modernisation narratives of the 1960s (see Werner, 2015); however, it is also a reflection of a drive to move communal farming beyond subsistence-oriented production to participate in commercial agricultural production.

Operationalising the small-scale commercial farming concept

The project was operationalised in 2003, when the ministry mandated for land reform started developing small-scale commercial farming units in some of the identified regions, what was then Caprivi, now Zambezi, Ohangwena, and what was

Kavango, now divided into Kavango East and West. The development was limited to surveying and gazetting farms. The first areas were gazetted in 2007 for small-scale commercial farming units.

As Figure 7.1 shows, in Ohangwena Region, the proposed small-scale commercial farming units were to be developed in areas east of Okongo. Okongo Designated Area was to be developed into 24 equal units of 2,500 hectares each. Implementation started in 2006 with support from the German Government through Kreditanstalt für Wiederaufbau (KfW), under the Programme for Communal Land Development (PLCD), and the Namibian government, through the Targeted Intervention Programme for Employment and Economic Growth (TIPEG) (Meijs et al., 2014; Republic of Namibia, 2015). Since then, the designated areas in Zambezi, Ohangwena and Kavango regions mentioned above have been gazetted, and infrastructural support provided in the form of boreholes.

From 2000, when the areas were identified, until 2006, when full implementation started, the reality on the ground changed profoundly. The populations in the target areas increased, and villages expanded. In 2000, when the Okongo areas were identified as potential sites for small-scale commercial farming, the fact-finding mission recorded 52 households; by 2008, the households had increased to 100 (Republic of Namibia, 2012). Many areas that had once been used as commonage had been appropriated as individualised and fenced-off farms (Republic of Namibia, 2012, p. 8). New people had settled in the area, and the population had increased to the extent that the area could no longer be described as underutilised. Hence, the proposed 24 farming units could not have been feasible unless people were moved.

Farmers in the area often asserted that they settled or were allocated land in these areas before "development" came, that is, before the designation process. Some farmers claimed to have settled or to have been allocated land in these areas between the late 1980s and the mid-1990s, when the area was still largely *ofuka*. The farmers use time periods to assert and defend their claims to land rights and, thereby, to benefit from small-scale commercial farming projects. These assertions

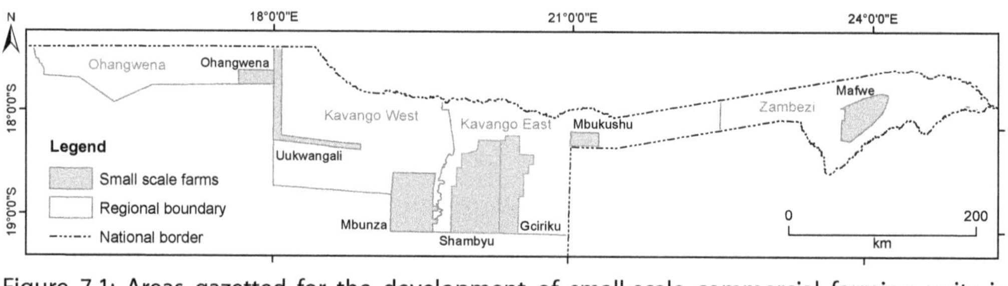

Figure 7.1: Areas gazetted for the development of small-scale commercial farming units in northern Namibia, 2007

are important, because one of the requirements for benefiting from the programme was that landholders or land users had to have been in the area, or had to be existing land users.

These dynamics provide answers to some of the questions asked at the starting point. These questions revolved around reconstructing the events leading up to the communal land reform, and land rights registration: What changes could be observed in the run-up to the registration process? Could changes in land allocation and reallocation, and land-use patterns be observed in the run-up to land rights registration? What implications did these changes have for land distribution, and the registration process itself? These questions were aimed at reconstructing historical developments over the preceding five years before the operationalisation of the communal land reform process.

While some farmers indicated that they had settled in these areas from the late 1980s to the mid-1990s, the increase in population in the area between 2000 and 2008 reflects that landholders had, indeed, appropriated landholdings and settled in these areas in anticipation of the upcoming small-scale commercial farms. The same trend may be observed in areas that are currently being developed. After learning that areas will be developed into small-scale commercial farming units, farmers flock to the areas and appropriate land through fencing to assert their interests. The interesting analysis is, then, how these dynamics have affected the registration process, or how the registration process proceeded in light of the changing reality.

For the government, it would have been too costly, both politically and financially, to implement the proposal for the 24 farming units proposed in 2003 (Republic of Namibia, 2012). Thus, dynamics on the ground readjusted the proposal of developing small-scale commercial farms, from the 24 farming units proposed, to recognising the existing conditions. For Okongo Designated Area, through the PLCD, the government initiated local-level participatory planning workshops to find a way forward on the development of small scale commercial farming units. The local-level participatory planning approach provided a platform for local land users and supporting institutions to discuss possible solutions concerning overlapping land uses; to identify conflicts involving land tenure and different access rights; to select beneficiaries; formulate rules on the use of infrastructure, and to define their own development plans in line with available resources (Meijs et al., 2014).

Throughout and after the local-level participatory planning process, the government developed the small-scale commercial farms according to prevailing social practices and the preferences of local residents (Meijs et al., 2014). The operationalisation of the process recognised the existing conditions on the ground. The 24 initially proposed farming units were not implemented; instead, small-scale commercial farms were developed by taking the actual reality on the ground into consideration. This meant that the existing, individual farming units were to become the small-scale farming units, which would be supported through infrastructural development. Recognising existing conditions on the ground can be said to deliver equitable benefits. Firstly, if the government had followed through with the model for 24 farming units, there would not have been an egalitarian distribution of land. The critical questions to ask are who would have benefited from these farming units, and what selection criteria would have been used? The 24 farming units of 2,500 hectares each would have benefited only 24 individual farmers. The emerging reality would have been that 60,000 hectares of communal land would have benefited 24 individual farmers and implementing the proposal would have carried no broad-based benefits. Following existing conditions carried more equitable benefits, in that the programme now has more than 100 beneficiaries.

Nature of the small-scale commercial farming development

The Okongo Designated Area covers around 60,000 hectares and comprises Okongo East and Okongo West. Okongo East is characterised by individual farming, while Okongo West spans three villages: *Onghalulu, Okambali* and *Onane*. In developing small-scale commercial farms, through its development partners, the government provides the necessary "means to manage and utilise land as both a productive and market-oriented resource" (Meijs et al., 2014, p. 8). The support involves providing security of tenure through long-term rights of leasehold for agricultural purposes; investment in critical infrastructure, for instance, in water supply infrastructure; providing technical support on rangeland management, and providing marketing facilities.

In 2015, 17 long-term rights of leasehold for agricultural purposes (for 99 years) were granted to individual farmers in Okongo East. The sizes of the farms ranged between 373.7 hectares (the smallest), to 3,175.9 hectares (the largest). Six farms are larger than 2,000 hectares; five are in excess of 1,000 hectares; three are more than 500 hectares, and one is smaller than 500 hectares. In terms of age demographics of the beneficiaries, the majority had been born between the 1930s and 1960s; only one beneficiary had been born in the 1970s. The farms are held predominantly by men, with only one farm being held by a woman. This reflects the gender inequalities that exist in landholding, in particular, in the cattle economy, which is generally an arena for men.

In the notarial agreements of the leasehold, the state legally establishes and formalises, through registration, the relationship between the communal farmers, as the lessees, and itself as the lessor. Additionally, it sets conditions of use that guide the farmers towards commercially-oriented production. These conditions include the use of property for agricultural purposes only; practising sound methods of husbandry; following sustainable farming practices, and participating in capacity-building opportunities to enhance commercial success. The government has also set conditions for the use of all installations that supply water, including boreholes, windmills, pumps and water pipelines, which are all to be shared jointly by the farmers/lessees in the area, irrespective of whether the installations are situated within the boundary of a particular farm. This establishes an array of use rights between farmers/lessees, who have individual rights of leasehold to their respective units, but commonly share other resources.

Prior to the operationalisation of the small-scale commercial farming project, some farmers occupied their units with other farmers who had no land of their own. Additionally, some farmers keep cattle which do not belong to them in accordance with kin or even acquaintance-based arrangements through which access to land is gained and contextualised within the sharing economy. Such is the social context within which the use of natural resources operates in north-central Namibia. One of the most important conditions of the rights of leasehold is that which defines the conditions of occupation. The leasehold agreements stipulate that, in the event that leaseholders occupy their respective units with other farmers who had been living and farming on such units prior to the enactment of the Communal Land Reform Act, 2002 (Republic of Namibia, 2002), such arrangements shall continue. This stipulation is located within the context of recognising existing realities, in this case, the reality of land sharing. The lessees must notify the communal land board of any changes in the use patterns or changes in relationships with other farmers. Communal land boards are the management institutions for rights of leasehold for agricultural purposes, on behalf of the state. The lessees have to submit the names of farmers they share the landholding with, for land boards to recognise and ratify such arrangements.

The rights of leasehold for agricultural purposes that were granted in 2015 in Okongo East include two farms where the lessees share their land with more than 10 other farmers; on three, the lessees share their land with more than five other farmers, and on eight of the farms, the lessees share the land with between one and three other farmers. Only two farms accommodate a single leaseholder. In total, 75 farmers benefit from the small-scale commercial farming project in Okongo East, instead of only 17 farmers, if the process recognised landholders only. Recognising not only the rights of the leaseholders, but also that of other farmers on the land amounts to a group-based approach to tenure security. Across all the farms, about 15% of the beneficiaries are women, which although minor in percentage, reflects some degree of gender equity. Overall, seen from within the social equity framework, although the farms are individualised, the condition of occupation also legally secures other farmers' access to the land. This approach recognises not only landholders, but land users and as a consequence distributes the benefits derived from small-scale commercial farms more broadly. The designated areas are the only areas where commonage is legally protected and secured. This model could be expanded to areas outside the designated areas in order to broaden the equity benefits inherent in group rights, particularly to protect commonages, which are under threat of disappearing.

For Okongo West, the developments took on different arrangements. Okongo West spans three villages, *Onghalulu, Okambali* and *Onane.* Around 182 households hold registered customary land rights for the individual landholdings, and share a commonage area of approximately 11,000 hectares. The government's intervention in Okongo West involves securing the commonage area as a group right. The farmers in Okongo West have registered a cooperative (a legal entity) through which a group right leasehold for agricultural purposes is to be held. This group right has not yet been granted and registered, as the land on which the group right is to be registered is still to be surveyed. Challenges in this regard include how to register a group right on areas that are scattered, and areas which have units registered as customary land rights. This modality, however, will provide broad-based benefits to all farmers in the three villages through access to secured commonage and from infrastructural investments. Compared to Okongo East, the Okongo West model presents more equitable benefits. The approach in Okongo West has been adopted in other designated areas, such as Ongandjera and Amarika in Omusati Region. More recently, in Ohangwena Region, an area which had been involved in a protracted dispute to Supreme Court level, has been turned into a cooperative. This modality could be replicated across the board to realise the real and broad-based benefits of secured tenure.

In addition to securing the commonage, the government, with its development partners, provides support through critical infrastructure, for example, installations such as boreholes and water points for provision of water; fences to keep livestock within the perimeter boundary and to prevent livestock outside from grazing within the area, and animal handling facilities for good husbandry and improved animal health and productivity (Republic of Namibia, 2015). The conditions of use for this infrastructure are similar to those in Okongo East and other designated areas: Farmers must maintain good rangeland practices, practise sustainable farming methods, and participate in capacity-building activities to enhance their chances of commercial success. Supporting the small-scale commercial farming units with infrastructural development is in line with the long-held view that secure tenure alone cannot induce productivity on the land. It has to be accompanied by other support, in the Namibian case, infrastructural development, advisory support for farmers, and marketing facilities to enhance the chances of commercial success.

Reception and contestation

The development of small-scale commercial farming did not come without contestation. These disputes are described separately for Okongo East and West, and also, in general, at the scale of the intervention itself.

In Okongo East, the issues of contention revolved around the condition of occupation contained in the leasehold agreements or notarial leases. The notarial leases stipulate that, if the leaseholder occupies the unit with other farmers, such arrangements shall continue, and lessees must submit the names of all the other farmers to the land boards so that their access rights can be recognised. Some lessees did not submit the names of other farmers; others submitted only some of the names of the farmers occupying their units, and others included the names of their kin who did not occupy the land. This resulted in contestations between farmers themselves. Cases were brought to the communal land boards where unregistered farmers reported being excluded. Farmers used the date on which they settled in the area to assert their claims to land. Some asserted, "I occupied this land before the Communal Land Reform Act", others claimed that "He came to this area way after the Communal Land Reform Act was enacted", "He only came here because he heard people are getting small-scale farms", or "He wants to throw me off the farm, but we have been farming together for many years". The Communal Land Boards set up investigative committees for such cases. The committee members talked to farmers in the field and to the traditional authorities, as main witnesses. Some cases were resolved amicably, with all parties agreeing to inclusion in the notarial lease agreements. In other cases, the disagreements developed into fully fledged conflicts that were heard by land board meetings, where all parties presented their cases, and numerous witnesses were called to justify their claims. Some claimants lost their cases, some won and, for some, the land boards mediated for all parties to remain on the farms. Even after the rights of leasehold had been granted, disputes still emanate from Okongo East farms. Farmers use the conditions and/or the regulations which have been included in the leasehold agreements as weapons to evict other farmers. In response, land users whom we can refer to as "sub-leasing" farmers, respond to this in different ways: some report their cases to land boards, others approach and appoint lawyers and some use the condition in the leasehold agreements that leaseholders may not evict other land users. The leasehold agreements themselves become tools for claiming and defending access rights.

As in Okongo East, farmers in Okongo West also contested some of the set conditions. One of these conditions is the stipulation that no animals of any description which are not the property of the cooperative members may be allowed to graze in the commonage, whether for a fee, or gratuitously, without the written consent of the lessor. Additionally, village headmen are prohibited from allocating further customary land rights in the area designated as commonage to avoid reducing the commonage. This prohibition clearly reflects that the focus of the small-scale farming units and the infrastructural investment is on the livestock economy, particularly, because these areas are predominantly livestock areas. However, for many farmers in Okongo West, the regulation concerning livestock represented a restriction. Even representatives of the traditional authorities who served on land boards objected to this regulation. One, for example, asserted that

> Because of your rules, you want to say that I can no longer accept cattle from my kin? This rule contradicts our culture. In *eehambo* (cattle post) areas, we have always kept cattle for our kin. The cattle that you see in one kraal do not all belong to the owner of the kraal. Some are entrusted to him by his kin, some he has inherited from the clan, but they are not his property. Therefore, this rule is meant to limit us. It is not in line with our practices.

This quote reflects the embeddedness of land rights and land uses in north-central Namibia. Future research is needed to investigate whether the conditions of the lease agreements will, indeed, cause kinship and reciprocal relationships to disappear, or whether they will persist, regardless. Another concern raised by local people regarding the small-scale commercial farming units related to the true intention of the government and donors. Some farmers in Okongo West, in particular, believed that the government would develop farms such as those in central Namibia, and thereby, in the end, bring in farmers from outside, and relocate current land users. Some farmers were of the view that this was just the start of the process and, in the end, they would be moved, and others would occupy these small-scale farms. This belief reflects the fear people in the communal areas have of losing land to formalised individualised tenure in the name of development. Other perceptions are that the government is promoting commercialisation of cattle with the intention of exporting meat to Europe; as evidence, they refer to the fact that the project is supported by European development partners.

Equity in the development of small-scale commercial farming units

Fraser (2009) states that justice is not only to be understood or sought in "bounded" scales, but takes plural forms and may be achieved at different levels. On a broad scale, the development of small-scale commercial farming in communal areas aims to bring about parity of participation in the broader economy, so that communal farmers can also participate in the commercial agricultural economy. This parity is achieved by addressing unjust conditions that inhibit farmers from participating; it is done by creating a conducive environment for farmers to enhance production. Improving conditions is seen as a necessary precondition for enhancing market-oriented production, which represents recognition that production on communal land has the potential to be market-oriented and could go beyond subsistence.

Production has in fact achieved more than subsistence, however, a number of limitations, including lack of key infrastructure and, especially, markets, inhibits full maximisation.

My field research took place when the process was just being operationalised and, therefore, this study does not measure the extent to which farmers are participating in the market or include data on farmers' participation, leaving this avenue open for future research. However, I reflect on the conditions necessary for this aim to be achieved. As the process matures with implementation, further research is needed to determine the level and status of integration. The government provides the necessary infrastructure, the absence of which has long hampered production. This includes providing marketing facilities, the absence of which have limited farmers' markets within their own circles. I locate these interventions in the "affirmative conditions framework of equity" which Fraser (1995) conceptualises as one of the approaches to remedying injustice. Affirmative conditions refer to the "remedies aimed at correcting inequitable outcomes of social arrangements without disturbing the underlying framework generating them" (Fraser, 1995, p. 82). The support currently being provided works to improve and enhance production processes.

Equity in land distribution

While the development of small-scale commercial farms represents a process towards recognising the need for communal farmers to participate in the commercial agricultural economy, counterclaims emerge if we expand the geographical scale, and when we consider competing claims to the land. In other words, beyond the bounded entity of designated areas, or when using socio-economic space to understand equity, there are counterclaims to land rights. The gradual individualisation of land over the years has given rise to increasing concentration of land in the hands of a few. This trend has perpetuated exclusion of other communal farmers from using the same resources as commonages. Farmers who are outside the designated areas, but who have long taken their livestock for grazing there and who had used these areas as buffer zones in times of drought, now complain of scarcity of grazing land. They often stated that "There is no more land", "Everywhere you go, it is just fences after fences", "There is no more open land", "We are now grazing in the corridors of large farms". Appropriation of large tracts of land, fencing, and the development of small-scale commercial farms have affected the egalitarianism that used to be inherent in access to commonages. Providing legality, particularly with a focus on individual leaseholders of large landholdings, results in formalising of inequalities in land distribution. Appropriation of land produces maldistribution of land in communal areas, which exacerbates the problem of increasing scarcity of land. Providing legality on the basis of group rights is viewed as equitable, as it works to broaden the distributions of benefits from communal land reform. This is illustrated by the second model of leasehold rights for agricultural purposes granted to the Okongo West farmers and in other designated areas, or farmers in Okongo East who are not necessarily using the land alone. After all, this is communal land – *edu laaveshe* – hence, it should not be individualised on a large scale or at the expense of other land users. The benefits could be even more broadly distributed by extending this approach to other commonages outside the designated areas.

Conclusion

Securing Land Rights: Communal Land Reform in Namibia speaks to the reforms that are ongoing in north-central Namibia's communal areas as part of the broader communal land reform programme. These reforms are critical, not only as key remedies for undoing historical injustices relating to land relations and land rights on communal land, but more importantly because of the rapid transformations taking place in north-central Namibia's communal areas.

An economic restructuring is underway, whereby sources of livelihoods have diversified beyond subsistence farming. Sources of livelihoods now include wage incomes, pension grants, business earnings and remittances. Households in north-central Namibia's communal areas have been integrated into capitalist commodity relations. This means they are subject to the dynamics and compulsions of commodification which are internalised in their relations and practices (Bernstein, 2010, p. 103). This phenomenon is visible in both production and consumption. For example, production is no longer solely dependent on family labour. It is also "funded by wages, which are also used to buy food when own-farming is inadequate to supply household needs, whether on a regular basis or in bad years" (Bernstein, 2010, p. 104). The economic restructuring underway is not only about diversification of livelihood sources, but a transition from a socio-economic landscape of farming involving crop production and livestock rearing. The area now boasts a thriving economy based on many different kinds of activities, which reflect that agrarian reform from below is underway. In addition to economic restructuring, other processes in progress are territorial restructuring which includes proclamation of local authority areas, designation of areas for community-based conservation, and designation of areas for agricultural purposes. Furthermore, there is an emerging informal land market. Collectively, all these processes exert pressure on communal land, and redefine access to land. What is apparent are diversified land uses, and an increased need for land for various purposes, which sometimes entails competition for land. In view of these processes and their respective outcomes, and the fact that communal land remains a safety net, especially for the rural poor, communal land reform and, in particular, tenure reform for securing land rights, could not have come at a more opportune time.

To secure land rights, Namibia instituted a legislative framework, the Communal Land Reform Act, 2002 (Republic of Namibia, 2002), which is implemented through the communal land reform process. The goal of communal land reform is to bring about statutory security of tenure on communal land. Security of tenure is granted through registration of customary land rights and other land rights such as rights of leasehold for general business enterprises and for agricultural purposes. Namibia's communal land reform treats land rights on communal land as rights, not as defective rights. Customary land rights acquired through customary tenure systems are registered, recognised, ratified, and integrated into the national statutory system. With Namibia's communal land reform, gaining statutory recognition and security does not involve abolishing customarily derived rights and/or assimilating them into the dominant or preferred cultural norm, i.e., private titled rights to land, as has been the case in classical land reforms pursued since the 1960s. This approach, I conclude, is the basic element of social equity – recognising land rights acquired through customary tenure systems in their own right. Here, security of tenure is not defined by the type of right that one holds, but the longevity of rights and the lack of threats to these rights. Through this, the symbolic injustices manifested by cultural domination through favouring freehold tenure, are addressed. The customary and freehold tenure systems should not be seen in the light of dualism, but of duality. Duality, as derived from structuration theory, is a social theory of creation and reproduction of social systems without giving primacy to one over the other (Giddens, 1979). In this context, customary and freehold tenure are distinct kinds of tenure systems equivalent in the eyes of national law in their own respective rights.

Scholars such as Pauline Peters and, in neighbouring South Africa, Ben Cousins, are at the forefront of calls to cease denying full property rights to customary tenure, under which millions of resource users in Africa hold land. They demand adequate recognition of customary forms of tenure in land (Peters, 2013a, p. 556; Cousins, 2005). Cousins et al. (2005, p. 6), in particular, urge that

> we must build a better understanding of the complexity of multiple, informal tenures within the 'extra-legal' sector, in all their diversity, and acknowledge at the outset that they are fundamentally different to the individualised, exclusive, private property systems of Western capitalism.

The present recognition of customary land rights in Namibia has attained the first step towards that fundamental call. Another main strength of land rights registration – especially customary land rights in the communal areas – is gender equity in access to land and land rights, as well as the inclusion of women in communal land governance. Women's rights and in particular, the rights of widows, are legally protected through the Communal Land Reform Act, 2002 (Republic of Namibia, 2002). Given the choice to register land rights as a group, spouses can jointly register land rights, thereby enhancing equity benefits. The Act provides for a quota of women's representation on communal land boards, one of the key institutions in communal land governance. The aim is to close the gender gap that has long existed in communal land administration. While these achievements are progressive in relation to the general goal of gender equality in the country, there are still pockets of injustice against women regarding access to land and, in particular, widows who lose land when their spouses die. These pockets of injustice still need to be addressed.

In its initial design, the registration of land rights followed a model of identifying landholdings and linking them to individuals, the respective landholders. The process focused on rights-based mechanisms of access to land, and collapsed secured, statutory land rights to individuals, thereby cutting through the web of interests over land. In a context which involves various mechanisms for providing access to land, this approach excludes people who derive benefits from land through social and kin relations, or through relational mechanisms of access to land. The process does not consider the distinction between landholders and land users. Landholders' and land users' titles are not always held in one person, which means landholders are not necessarily land users and land users are not always landholders. Through registration, the process only recognises and registers the rights of landholders, even when these landholders are not the land users. In these cases, the process has fallen short in terms of land rights equity by failing to secure the rights of the people who are directly using the land. With this approach, the registration process produces a new layer of stratification where some people benefit and identify with state-recognised security of tenure, while others do not. It sharpens existing stratifications based on gender, as most land users who are not landholders are women. This is the risk inherent in the registration of land rights "as is", in whichever form and with whatever characteristics they currently possess (Wily, 2000).

The strength of Namibia's communal land reform is its flexible nature, its flexibility to accommodate amendments. New amendments have been made to Communal Land Reform Act to allow people to have the option to register land rights as individuals, groups, families, and juridical entities (Republic of Namibia, 2002). This provision holds the potential to distribute benefits from land rights registration broadly, and to bring about land rights equity. At the time of finalising this book, this provision is still new in implementation, and research is needed to analyse the extent to which this amendment has been put into practice.

By granting rights of leasehold for general business purposes and rights of leasehold for agricultural purposes, communal land reform recognises different transformations taking place in communal areas, through which land uses have extended beyond subsistence. Land uses are also now market-oriented and, therefore, these uses require appropriate land rights. Granting rights of leasehold for agricultural purposes, particularly, is key in the move to recognising farmers who are ready for market-oriented farming production. Registration of rights of leasehold in areas designated for agricultural purposes followed two models: registration of individual rights of leasehold and registration of rights of leasehold as group rights. More land users benefit from registration of rights of leasehold as group rights, than as individual rights. Registration of rights of leaseholds could offer greater benefits if it is extended to areas outside designated areas where commonages are being threatened by land alienation. The individual rights of leasehold for agricultural purposes are at odds with redistributive justice and contradict the approach to securing communal land for all. Thus, while registration of rights of leasehold for individual farmers may represent security, to other farmers, who have long used these lands as buffer zones, the process represents insecurity regarding access to land.

Communal land reform in Namibia forms part of the wider processes of tenure reform occurring in sub-Saharan Africa. Namibia's tenure reform takes a different route from classical tenure reform approaches which rest on the abolitionist approach to customary tenure. As a result of years of criticism of classical tenure reform, "states are being forced to recognise African tenure regimes in their own right" (Wily, 2000, p. 2). This process embodies "recognition", one of the central dimensions of social equity conceptualised by Fraser (1996). The process of recognition establishes a "difference-friendly world, where assimilation to majority or dominant norms is no longer the price of equal respect" (Fraser, 1996, p. 3). In classical tenure reform and in neoliberal views, assimilation to dominant norms means abolishing and/or assimilating customary land tenure systems into freehold tenure systems, as it regards freehold systems as the preferred model of tenure. Customary tenure in classical tenure reform is not "equivalent to full property" (Peters, 2013a, p. 537). The dominant narrative of tenure systems defines security of tenure by types of tenure, with private tenure being equated to security of tenure. This discursive landscape is underpinned by value judgement which leads to the perception that customary tenure is inferior. Communal land reform in Namibia today rejects this notion. While tenure reform in Namibia does not seek to replace customary land rights but to give them statutory recognition and protection, this protection does not prevent alienation of communal land, especially by government for purposes deemed important for the public, for example, the development or expansion of town lands.

While it is irrefutable that tenure reform in Namibia, as in other African countries "is offering Africa an unexpected opportunity to move into a more inclusive and equitable era of social transformation through decolonising property rights" (Wily, 2020, p. 57), security of tenure granted through these reforms can only be measured in relative and not absolute terms. The desired substantive protection of customary land rights is yet to be achieved.

References

Amanor, K. S. (2008). Introduction: Land and sustainable development issues in Africa. In K. S. Amanor & S. Moyo (Eds.), *Land and sustainable development in Africa* (pp. 1–32). London, UK: Zed Books.

Amoo, S. (2014). *Property law in Namibia*. Pretoria, South Africa: University of Pretoria Press.

Angombe, S. T., Naanda, M. T., Bloemertz, L., & Kuhn, N. (2016). Land use practices in north-central Namibia: A budding vehicle for improving ecosystem services in Namibia? In A. Kanyimba (Ed.), *Education for sustainable development in southern Africa* (pp. 24–51). Windhoek, Namibia: The Namibia Environmental Education Network.

Araghi, F. (2009). The invisible hand and the visible foot: Peasants, dispossession and globalization. In A. H. Akram-Lodhi & C. Kay (Eds.), *Peasants and globalization: Political economy, rural transformation and the agrarian question* (pp. 111–147). London and New York: Routledge.

Bassett, T. J. (1993). Introduction: The land question and agricultural transformation in Sub-Saharan Africa. In T. J. Bassett & D. E. Crummey (Eds.), *Land in African agrarian systems* (pp. 3–25). Madison, WI. and London: University of Wisconsin Press.

Becker, F. (2006). Development of space in independent Namibia: Deliberations on the projection of politico-economic and socio-cultural transformation. In H. Leser (Ed.), *The changing culture and nature of Namibia: Case studies* (pp. 17–35). Basel, Switzerland: Basler Afrika Bibliographien.

Becker, H. (2007). Making tradition: A historical perspective on gender in Namibia. In S. LaFont & D. Hubbard (Eds.), *Unravelling taboos: Gender and sexuality in Namibia* (pp. 22–38). Windhoek, Namibia: Legal Assistance Centre.

Becker, H. (1997). Women and land rights. In J. Malan & M. O. Hinz (Eds.), *Communal land administration: Consultative conference on communal land administration 26-28 September 1996* (pp. 56–60). Windhoek, Namibia: Ministry of Lands, Resettlement and Rehabilitation.

Bernstein, H. (2010). *Class dynamics of agrarian change*. Halifax, N.S.: Fernwood Publishing.

Borras, S. M. (2006). The underlying assumptions, theory, and practice of neoliberal land policies. In P. Rosset, R. Patel, & M. Courville (Eds.), *Promised land: Competing visions of agrarian reform* (pp. 99–128). Oakland, California: Food First Books.

Botelle, A. (2001). *A History of Marula use in north-central Namibia*. Submitted to CRIAA SA-DC (Namibia).

Boudreaux, K. C. (2010). *Community conservation in Namibia: Devolution as a tool for the legal empowerment of the poor*. Working Paper: No. 10-64. Mercatus Centre. Retrieved from https://www.mercatus.org/system/files/wp1064-community-conservation-in-namibia.pdf

Bourdieu, P. (1986). The forms of capital. In J. Richardson (Ed.), *Handbook of theory and research for the sociology of education* (pp. 241–258). Westport, Connecticut: Greenwood.

Brankamp, H. (2013). *This land is your land, this land is my land: Fairness perceptions in the arbitration of communal land disputes in Namibia* (Unpublished master's thesis). University of Tübingen.

Bruce, J. W., & Migot-Adholla, S. E. (1994). Introduction: Are indigenous African tenure systems insecure? In J. W. Bruce & S. E. Migot-Adholla (Eds.), *Searching for land tenure security in Africa* (pp. 1–13). Dubuque, Iowa: Kendall/Hunt.

Chimhowu, A., & Woodhouse, P. (2010). Forbidden but not suppressed: A 'vernacular' land market in Svosve communal lands, Zimbabwe. *Africa, 80*(1), 14–35.

Colin, J.-P., & Woodhouse, P. (2010). Introduction: Interpreting land markets in Africa. *Africa, 80*(1), 1–13.

Cousins, B. (1999). Invisible capital: The contribution of communal rangelands to rural livelihoods in South Africa. *Development Southern Africa, 16*(2), 299–318.

Cousins, B. (2005). Tenure reform in South Africa: Titling versus social embeddedness. *Forum for Development Studies, 32*(2), 415–442. https://doi.org/10.1080/08039410.2005.9666322

Cousins, B., Cousins, T., Hornby, D., Kingwill, R., Royston, L., & Smit, W. (2005). *Will formalising property rights reduce poverty in South Africa's second economy'? Questioning the mythologies of Hernando de Soto.* Policy Brief No. 15, October. Poverty, Land and Agrarian Studies (PLAAS).

Cousins, B., & Scoones, I. (2010). Contested paradigms of "viability" in redistributive land reform: Perspectives from southern Africa. *Journal of Peasant Studies, 37*(1), 31–66.

Cox, J., Kerven, C., Werner, W., & Behnke, R. (1998). *The privatization of rangeland resources in Namibia: Enclosure in eastern Oshikoto.* London, UK: Overseas Development Institute.

De la Hey, M., & Beinart, W. (2016). Why have South African smallholders largely abandoned arable production in fields? A case study. *Journal of Southern African Studies,* 753–770. https://doi.org/10.1080/03057070.2016.1265336

De Soto, H. (2000). *The mystery of capital: Why capitalism triumphs in the west and fails everywhere else.* New York: Basic Books.

Deininger, K., & Binswanger, H. (1999). The evolution of the World Bank's land policy: Principles, experience and future challenges. *World Bank Research Observer, 14*(2), 247–276.

Deininger, K., & Feder, G. (2014). *Land institutions and land markets.* World Bank.

Delgado, G., & Lühl, P. (2016). *The case for adequate housing for teachers in Windhoek.* Integrated Land Management Institute Working Paper No. 5. Windhoek, Namibia: Namibia University of Science and Technology.

Dobler, G. (2014). *Traders and trade in colonial Ovamboland.* Basel, Switzerland: Basler Afrika Bibliographien.

Fairhead, J., Leach, M., & Scoones, I. (2012). Green grabbing: A new appropriation of nature. *Journal of Peasant Studies, 39*(2), 237–261.

Ferguson, J. (2013). How to do things with land: A distributive perspective on rural livelihoods in southern Africa. *Journal of Agrarian Change, 13*(1), 166–174.

First National Bank Namibia. (2012). *Housing index: Namibia records 4th highest house price growth in 2012.* Windhoek: First National Bank Namibia.

First National Bank Namibia. (2018). *FNB residential property report.* Windhoek: First National Bank Namibia.

Fraser, N. (1995). From redistribution to recognition? Dilemmas of justice in a "post-socialist" age. *New Left Review,* (212), 68–93.

Fraser, N. (1996). *Social justice in the age of identity politics: Redistribution, recognition, and participation* (Lecture). Tanner Lectures on Human Values, Stanford University.

Fraser, N. (2009). *Scales of justice: Reimagining political space in a globalizing world*. New York: Columbia University Press.

Fraser, N., & Honneth, A. (2003). Introduction: Redistribution or recognition? In N. Fraser & A. Honneth (Eds.), *Redistribution or recognition? A Political-philosophical exchange*. London and New York: Verso.

Fujioka, Y. (2010). Changes in natural resources use among Owambo agro-pastoralists of north-central Namibia resulting from the enclosure of the local frontiers. *African Study Monographs, 40*, 129–154.

Giddens, A. (1979). *Central problems in social theory: Action, structure and contradictions in social analysis*. London, UK: Macmillan Press.

Graefe, O., Kuhn, N., & Dobler, G. (2012). *Communal land reform in Namibia: Implications of individualisation of land tenure*. Project No. 220519955. Freiburg: Deutsche Forschungsgemeinschaft.

Haidula, T. (2015, February 26). Address land issue – Analysts. *The Namibian*. Retrieved from http://www.namibian.com.na/index.php?id=134065&page=archive-read

Hall, D., Hirsch, P., & Li, T. M. (2011). *Powers of exclusion: Land dilemmas in southeast Asia*. Singapore: NUS Press.

Hamutenya, H. (1997). Development and communal land system. In J. Malan & M. O. Hinz (Eds.), *Proceedings: Consultative conference on communal land administration 26-28 September 1996* (pp. 31–34). Windhoek, Namibia: Ministry of Lands, Resettlement and Rehabilitation.

Hardin, G. (1968). The tragedy of the commons. *Science, 162*(3859), 1243–1248.

Hayes, P. (1993). Order out of chaos: Mandume ya Ndemufayo and oral history. *Journal of Southern African Studies, 19*(1), 89–113.

Hesselberg, J. (2005). The urban and the rural in the development debate: An overview. *Forum for Development Studies, 32*(2), 493–507. https://doi.org/10.1080/08039410.2005.9666325

Hinz, M. O., & Namwoonde, N. E. (2010). *Customary law ascertained: The customary law of the Owambo, Kavango and Caprivi communities of Namibia* (Vol. 1). Windhoek, Namibia: Namibian Scientific Society.

Iipumbu, S. (2012). Governors' welcoming remarks. In Research Department of the Bank of Namibia, *Unlocking the economic potential of communal land* (pp. 6–10). Windhoek, Namibia: Bank of Namibia.

Iivula-Ithana, P. (1997). Welcoming address. In J. Malan & M. O. Hinz (Eds.), *Proceedings: Consultative conference on communal land administration 26-28 September 1996* (pp. 11–12). Windhoek, Namibia: Ministry of Lands, Resettlement and Rehabilitation.

Informante. (2014, November 20). Land problem in Namibia – A time bomb. *Informante*. Retrieved from http://www.confidente.com.na/2014/11/land-problem-in-namibia-a-time-bomb/

Jauch, H., & Tjirera, E. (2017). The need for a developmental state intervention in Namibia. In G. Kanyenze, H. Jauch, A. D. Kanengoni, M. Madzwamuse, & D. Muchena (Eds.), *Towards democratic developmental states in southern Africa*. Harare, Zimbabwe: Weaver Press.

Kaapama, P. (2007). Commercial land reforms in postcolonial Namibia: What happened to liberation struggle rhetoric? In H. Melber (Ed.), *Transitions in Namibia: Which changes for whom?* (pp. 29–49). Uppsala, Sweden: Nordiska Afrikainstitutet.

Keesing, R. (1975). *Kin groups and social structure.* New York: Holt, Rinehart and Winston.

Kreike, E. (2004). *Re-creating Eden: Land use, environment and society in southern Angola and northern Namibia.* Portsmouth, NH: Heinemann.

Legal Assistance Centre. (1991). Communal lands in Namibia: The legal framework and its application on existing practices. In Namibia Economic Policy Research Unit: Office of the Prime Minister, *National Conference on Land Reform and the Land Question* (Vol. 1). Windhoek, Namibia: Republic of Namibia.

Levit, N., & Verchick, R. (2006). *Feminist legal theory: A primer.* New York: NYU Press.

Mafeje, A. (1976). *The study of land tenure conditions in South Africa.* Rome: FAO.

Maletsky, C. (2000a, February 16). Land Bill pushed through the NA. *The Namibian.*

Maletsky, C. (2000b, February 18). Anger at land Bill 'shame'. *The Namibian.*

Manji, A. (2006). *The politics of land reform in Africa: From communal tenure to free markets.* London and New York: Zed Books.

Meijs, M., Hager, C.-P., & Mulofwa, J. (2014). *Local level participatory planning: An approach towards tenure security and development planning.* Annual World Bank Conference on Land and Poverty 24-27 March 2014, Washington DC.

Meinzen-Dick, R., & Mwangi, E. (2008). Cutting the web of interests: Pitfalls of formalizing property rights. *Land Use Policy, 26,* 36–43.

Mendelsohn, J. (2006). *Farming systems in Namibia.* Windhoek, Namibia: Research & Information Services of Namibia.

Mendelsohn, J., Jarvis, A., & Robertson, T. (2013). *A profile and atlas of the Cuvelai-Etosha Basin.* Windhoek, Namibia: Research & Information Services of Namibia.

Mendelsohn, J., & Nghitevelekwa, R. (2016). *A study of land markets in Namibia's communal areas.* Consultancy Report. Windhoek, Namibia: Ministry of Land Reform.

Mendelsohn, J., Obeid, S., & Roberts, C. (2000). *A profile of north-central Namibia.* Windhoek, Namibia: Gamsberg Macmillan Publishers.

Migot-Adholla, S. E., Hazell, P., Blarel, B., & Place, F. (1991). Indigenous land rights systems in sub-Saharan Africa: A constraint on productivity? *World Bank Economic Review, 5*(1), 155–175.

Ministry of Environment, Forestry and Tourism & Namibia Association of CBNRM Support Organisation. (2019). *Facts and figures.* The State of Community Conservation in Namibia. Retrieved from https://communityconservationnamibia.com/node

Ministry of Land Reform. (2018). *The state of land reform since the 1991 national conference on land reform and the land question.* Report for the Second National Land Conference. Windhoek, Namibia: Ministry of Land Reform.

Moyo, S., Tsikata, D., & Diop, Y. (2015). *Land in the struggles for citizenship in Africa.* Senegal: Codesria.

Mufune, P. (2011). *The rural in Namibia: An introduction to concepts and issues.* Windhoek, Namibia: Solitaire Press.

Naidoo, R., Weaver, C. L., Diggle, R. W., Matongo, G., Stuart-Hill, G., & Thouless, C. (2016). Complementary benefits of tourism and hunting to communal conservancies in Namibia. *Conservation Biology, 30*(3), 628–638.

Namibia Statistics Agency. (2011). *Namibia 2011 population and housing census.* Windhoek, Namibia: Namibia Statistics Agency.

Namibia Statistics Agency. (2017a). *Namibia inter-censal demographic survey report.* Windhoek, Namibia: Namibia Statistics Agency.

Namibia Statistics Agency. (2017b). *The Namibia labour force survey 2016 report.* Windhoek, Namibia: Namibia Statistics Agency.

Namibia Statistics Agency. (2018). *Namibia household income and expenditure survey 2015/2016 report.* Windhoek, Namibia: Namibia Statistics Agency.

Namibia Statistics Agency. (2019a). *Namibia census of agriculture 2013/14 communal sector revised report.* Windhoek, Namibia: Namibia Statistics Agency.

Namibia Statistics Agency. (2019b). *The Namibia labour force survey 2018 report.* Windhoek, Namibia: Namibia Statistics Agency.

National Planning Commission. (1996). *The 1993/1994 Namibia household income and expenditure survey.* Windhoek, Namibia: National Planning Commission.

Nghitevelekwa, R. (2015). *Identifying, streamlining and harmonizing existing land rights and access arrangements to provide security of tenure in areas designated for commercialisation of land-based production: Case study: Okongo designated areas, Ohangwena Region.* Consultancy Report. Windhoek, Namibia: Ministry of Land Reform.

Nghitevelekwa, R. (2016). Land relations and property rights in central-north Namibia's communal areas. In M. Ramutsindela, G. Miescher, & M. Boehi (Eds.), *The politics of nature and science in southern Africa* (pp. 208–230). Basel, Switzerland: Basler Afrika Bibliographien.

Nujoma, S. (1997). Opening address. In J. Malan & M. O. Hinz (Eds.), *Proceedings: Consultative conference on communal land administration 26-28 September 1996* (pp. 13–15). Windhoek, Namibia: Ministry of Lands, Resettlement and Rehabilitation.

Nyambali, S. (2015, July 24). Land issue: Problem or crisis? *The Namibian.* Retrieved from http://www.namibian.com.na/index.php?id=139854&page=archive-read

Ochieng, C. M. O. (2020). Introduction. Rethinking land reform in Africa: New ideas opportunities and challenges. In African Development Bank (Ed.), *Rethinking land reform in Africa new ideas, opportunities and challenges* (pp. 13–18). Abidjan, Côte d'Ivoire: African Development Bank.

Odendaal, F. H. (1964). *Report of the commission of enquiry into South West Africa affairs: 1962-1963.* SARP Series No. RP 12/1964. Pretoria, South Africa: Government Printers.

Odendaal, W. (2011). *Land grabbing in Namibia: A case study from the Omusati Region, northern Namibia.* International conference on global land grabbing, 6-8 April 2011, Institute of Development Studies, University of Sussex.

Ondonga Traditional Authority. (2014). Oompango oompe dhomalelo gahetatu mOwambo. [New laws of the eight traditional authorities in Owambo; unpublished]. Oluno.

Peltola, M. (2002). *Nakambale: The life of Dr Martin Rautanen.* Finland: FELM.

Peters, P. E. (2004). Inequality and social conflict over land in Africa. *Journal of Agrarian Change, 4*(3), 269–314.

Peters, P. E. (2009). Challenges in land tenure and land reform in Africa: Anthropological contributions. *World Development, 37*(8), 1317–1325.

Peters, P. E. (2010a). Bewitching land: The role of land disputes in converting kin to strangers and in class formation in Malawi. *Journal of Southern African Studies, 28*(1), 155–178.

Peters, P. E. (2010b). "Our daughters inherit our land, but our sons use the wives' fields": Matrilineal-matrilocal land tenure and the new land policy in Malawi. *Journal Eastern African Studies, 4*(1), 179–199.

Peters, P. E. (2013a). Conflicts over land and threats to customary tenure in Africa. *African Affairs, 112*(449), 543–562.

Peters, P. E. (2013b). Land appropriation, surplus people and a battle over visions of agrarian futures in Africa. *The Journal of Peasant Studies, 40*(3), 537–562.

Peters, P. E. (2020). The significance of descent-based "customary" land management for land reform and agricultural futures in Africa. In African Development Bank (Ed.), *Rethinking land reform in Africa new ideas, opportunities and challenges* (pp. 70–82). Abidjan: African Development Bank.

Place, F., & Hazell, P. (1993). Productivity effects of indigenous land tenure systems in Sub-Saharan Africa. *American Journal of Agricultural Economics Association, 75*, 10–19.

Quan, J. (2000). Land boards as a mechanism for the management of land rights in southern Africa. In C. Toulmin & J. Quan (Eds.), *Evolving land rights, policy and tenure in Africa* (pp. 197–206). London, UK: International Institute for Environment and Development.

Republic of Namibia (1990). *Namibian Constitution, GG2.* Government Gazette, 21 March 1990, No. 2.

Republic of Namibia. (1991a). *Consensus document: National conference on land reform and the land question.* Windhoek, Namibia: Office of the Prime Minister.

Republic of Namibia. (1991b). *National Conference on land reform and the land question* (Vol. 1). Windhoek, Namibia: Republic of Namibia.

Republic of Namibia. (1992). *Local Authorities Act,* Pub. L. No. 23. Government Gazette, 470, 31 August 1992. http://extwprlegs1.fao.org/docs/pdf/nam82645.pdf

Republic of Namibia. (2000). *Traditional Authorities Act,* Pub. L. No. 25. Government Gazette 2456, 17 May 2001. https://www.lac.org.na/laws/annoSTAT/Traditional%20Authorities%20Act%2025%20of%202000.pdf

Republic of Namibia. (2002). *Communal Land Reform Act,* Pub. L. No. 5. Government Gazette 2787, 1 March 2003. https://laws.parliament.na/cms_documents/communal-land-reform-75a65055b0.pdf

Republic of Namibia. (2005a). *Key recommendations of the Cabinet retreat, Swakopmund.* Windhoek, Namibia: Republic of Namibia.

Republic of Namibia. (2005b). *Forest Amendment Act,* Pub. L. No. 13 (2005). Government Gazette 3564, 28 December 2005. https://namiblii.org/akn/na/act/2005/13

Republic of Namibia. (2009). *Compensation policy guideline for communal land.* Windhoek, Namibia: Ministry of Regional and Local Government, Housing and Rural Development.

Republic of Namibia. (2012). *Road map for the development of Small-Scale Farming Areas on communal land in Namibia.* Windhoek, Namibia: Ministry of Lands and Resettlement.

Republic of Namibia. (2013). *Communal Land Reform Amendment Act,* Pub. L. No. 13 (2013). Government Gazette 5264, 15 August 2013.

Republic of Namibia. (2015). *Programme for Communal Land Development (PCLD): Local level participatory planning (LLPP) in areas designated for commercialisation of land-based economic activities on communal land in Namibia: Site file: Okongo West.* Windhoek, Namibia: Ministry of Land Reform.

Republic of Namibia (2017) *Nature Conservation Amendment Act*, Pub. L. No. 3. Government Gazette 6344, 28 June 2017. http://www.lac.org.na/laws/2017/6344.pdf

Research Department of the Bank of Namibia. (2012). Preface. In Research Department of the Bank of Namibia (Ed.), *Unlocking the economic potential of communal land* (p. 5). Windhoek, Namibia: Bank of Namibia.

Ribot, J., & Peluso, N. (2003). A theory of access. *Rural Sociology, 68*(2), 153–181.

Schlager, E., & Ostrom, E. (1992). Property-rights regimes and natural resources: A conceptual analysis. *Land Economics, 68*(3), 249–262.

Shapi, M., Nghitevelekwa, R., Namupala, N., Likuwa, K., & Schier, C. (2017). *Baseline study: Women's land use, ownership and land rights in Ohangwena, Omusati, Oshana and Oshikoto regions of Namibia*. Windhoek, Namibia: Konrad-Adenauer-Stiftung.

Sherbourne, R. (2014). *Guide to the Namibia economy 2013/14*. Windhoek, Namibia: Institute for Public Policy Research.

Shigwedha, A. (2000a, May 18). NC rejects communal land Bill, says it will make the poor poorer. *The Namibian*.

Shigwedha, A. (2000b, May 19). NC explains its rejection of communal land Bill. *The Namibian*.

Shinovene, I. (2017, June 23). Traditional leaders' perks revealed. *The Namibian*.

Shiweda, N. (2011). *Omhedi: Displacement and legitimacy in Oukwanyama politics, Namibia, 1915-2010* (Unpublished doctoral dissertation). University of the Western Cape, Cape Town.

Siiskonen, H. (1990). *Trade and socioeconomic change in Ovamboland: 1850—1906*. Helsinki, Finland: Suomen Historiallanen Seura.

Tagliarino, N. K. (2017). Status of national legal frameworks for valuing compensation for expropriated land: An analysis of whether national laws in 50 countries/regions across Asia, Africa, and Latin America comply with international standards on compensation valuation. *Land, 6 (2)*(37), 1–28.

Tapscott, C., & Hangula, L. (1994). *Fencing of communal range land in northern Namibia: Social and ecological implications*. Windhoek, Namibia: University of Namibia.

The Namibian. (1999, October 14). Land Bill lands with a dull thud at Oshakati. *The Namibian*.

The Namibian. (2001, January 26). Land reform Bill amended. *The Namibian*.

The Namibian. (2014, October 29). Some Academia plots to be re-auctioned. *The Namibian*.

The Namibian Economic Policy Research Unit. (1991). Socio-economic conditions and attitudes to the land question. *National Conference on Land Reform and the Land Question, 1*.

Thiem, M. (Ed.). (2014). *A decade of communal land reform in Namibia: Review and lessons learnt, with a focus on communal land rights registration*. Windhoek, Namibia: Deutsche Gesellscaft für Internationale Zusammenarbeit (GIZ) GmBH.

Thiong'o, N. (1986). *Decolonising the mind: The politics of language in African literature*. London, UK: James Currey.

Toulmin, C. (2008). Securing land and property rights in sub-Saharan Africa: The role of local institutions. *Land Use Policy, 26*, 10–19.

Toulmin, C., & Quan, J. (2000). Evolving land rights, tenure and policy in sub-Saharan Africa. In C. Toulmin & J. Quan (Eds.), *Evolving land rights, policy and tenure in Africa* (pp. 1–30). London, UK: International Institute for Environment and Development.

Traditional Authorities from Owambo. (1997). Seven traditional authorities from Owambo. In J. Malan & M. O. Hinz (Eds.), *Proceedings: Consultative conference on communal land administration 26-28 September 1996* (pp. 68–69). Windhoek, Namibia: Ministry of Lands, Resettlement and Rehabilitation.

United Nations. (1951). *Resolutions adopted by the General Assembly during the period 19 September to 15 December 1950.* New York: United Nations.

United Nations Institute for Namibia. (1979). *Toward agrarian reform: Policy options for Namibia.* Lusaka, Zambia: UNIN.

United Nations Institute for Namibia. (1986). *Namibia: Perspectives for national reconstruction and development.* Lusaka, Zambia: UNIN.

United Nations Security Council. (1978). *Security Council resolution 435 of 1978 (Namibia).* New York: United Nations Security Council.

United Nations Security Council. (1982). *Security Council document S/15287 of 12 July 1982.* New York: United Nations Security Council.

Uukwaluudhi Traditional Authority. (2016). *Oofuto dhevi uuna omuntu a hala ehala [Communal land allocation fees].* Uukwaluudhi Traditional Authority.

Van Der Waal, B. C. (1991). Fish life of the Oshana Delta in Owambo, Namibia, and the translocation of Cunene species. *Madoqua, 17*(2), 201–209.

Verlinden, A., & Kruger, A. S. (2007). Changing grazing systems in central-north Namibia. *Land Degradation & Development, 18* (2), 197–197.

Vigne, R. (1998). The movable frontier: The Namibia-Angola boundary demarcation 1926-1928. In P. Hayes, J. Silvester, M. Wallace, & W. Hartmann (Eds.), *Namibia Under South African Rule: Mobility & Containment 1915-1946.* Oxford, UK: James Currey.

Wehrmann, B. (2008). *Land conflicts: A practical guide to dealing with land disputes.* Windhoek, Namibia: Deutsche Gesellschaft für Technische Zusammenarbeit (GTZ).

Werner, W. (1993). A brief history of land dispossession in Namibia. *Journal of Southern African Studies, 19*(1), 135–146.

Werner, W. (2001). The land question in Namibia. In I. Diener & O. Graefe (Eds.), *Contemporary Namibia: The first landmarks of a post-apartheid society.* Windhoek, Namibia: Gamsberg Macmillan Publishers.

Werner, W. (2008). *Protection for women in Namibia's Communal Land Reform Act: Is it working?* Windhoek, Namibia: Legal Assistance Centre.

Werner, W. (2011). *What has happened has happened: The complexity of fencing in Namibia's communal areas.* Windhoek, Namibia: Legal Assistance Centre.

Werner, W. (2015). Tenure reform in Namibia's communal areas. *Journal of Namibian Studies, 18*, 67–87.

Werner, W., & Bayer, C.-T. (2016). *Leasehold as a vehicle for economic development.* Windhoek, Namibia: Legal Assistance Centre.

Widlok, T. (2016). *Anthropology and the economy of sharing.* London, UK: Routledge Taylor & Francis Group.

Williams, F.-N. (1994). *Precolonial communities of southwestern Africa: A history of Owambo kingdoms 1600-1920* (2nd edition). Windhoek, Namibia: National Archives of Namibia.

Wily, L. A. (2000). Land tenure reform and the balance of power in eastern and southern Africa. *Overseas Development Institute – Natural Resources Perspectives, 58*(6).

Wily, L. A. (2011). *Customary land tenure in the modern world: Rights to resources in crisis: Reviewing the fate of customary tenure in Africa*. Brief #3 of 5. Rights and Resources Initiative.

Wily, L. A. (2020). Adjusting to new era agrarianism: Tackling the troubled interface of public and community property. In African Development Bank (Ed.), *Rethinking land reform in Africa: New ideas, opportunities and challenges* (pp. 57–69). Abidjan, Côte d'Ivoire: African Development Bank.

Winterfeldt, V. (2013). *Social implications of a total removal of the veterinary cordon fence*. Windhoek, Namibia: Ministry of Agriculture, Water and Forestry.

World Bank. (1975). *Land reform sector policy paper*. Washington D.C.: World Bank.

World Bank. (1989). *Sub-Saharan Africa: From crisis to sustainable growth — A long-term perspective study*. Washington D.C.: World Bank.

Zongwe, D. P. (2019). *International law in Namibia*. Bamenda, Cameroon: Langaa Research & Publishing Common Initiative Group.

Glossary

Local term or phrase	English translation/scientific names
okakefe	café
omaadi eengongo	marula oil
omahangu	pearl millet
omakaya (pl.) ekaya (sing.)	tobacco
omakove (pl.) ekove (sing.)	parts of landholding that are not cultivated
omalenga (pl.) elenga (sing.)	senior headmen
omaongo	marula brew
omalila	wide paths
omapata avali	two cooking places
omatala	open markets
omaumbo (pl.) eumbo (sing.)	households
omaumbo-hambo	cattle-post households
ombadu yekaya	a token of appreciation
ombelewa yelelo	traditional authority's office
ombelewa yomadu	land office
ombelewa yoshilongo	traditional authority office
ombidi	spinach *Cleome gynandra*
ombuga	open saline grasslands
Omeya oo haa shili ovanhu	water encourages people to settle
omifima	wells
omikunda (pl.) omukunda (sing.)	villages
Omikunda okwa li di na ondilo, ka kwali ha di dulika komapata keshe	villages were expensive, not all clans could afford them
omuhandjo	a part of a homestead (quarters used for different purposes)
omukunda (sing.) omikunda (pl.)	village
omukunda wa nge	my village
omukwiyu	*Ficus sycomorus* (sycamore fig)
Omulumenhu okwa li ha ke ongubu	The man who fortifies a fence
omulunga	*Hyphaene petersiana* (makalani palm)
omuve	*Berchemia discolor*

omwandi	*Diospyros mespiliformis*
omwoongo	*Sclerocarya birrea* (marula tree)
onde mu pa epitikilo a kale momukunda wange	I have given him/her permission to be in my village
Onde mu pa edu momukunda wange	I have given him/her land in my village
Ondi li moipundi ya tate/ ya tatekulu	I am on my father's/grandfather's/uncle's throne
ondobe	a pond of water
onhaulila	border
onhele yoilonga	place/land for work
oofuto	payments
ookapatashu (pl.) kapatashu (sing.)	representatives of village headmen
ootatekulu ovo va ka po omukunda ou	our great/grandfathers cleared/founded this village
oveta yomadu	land law
oovene vedu	owners of the land
oovene vomikunda (pl.) mwene womukunda (sing.)	village headmen
oshana (sing.) iishana (pl.)	drainage channels/shallow pan
oshilongo	human-created environment
oshini	milling station
oshinwa	marula juice
oshitauwa (also see omalila)	wide path
ositola	shop
otombo	local brew
ovapiya va vo	their servants
oveta yomadu	land law
tatekulu	uncle, grandfather
oshipe	thanksgiving
ouhamba	kingship

Index

A

abolitionist approach 146
access control 64
access mechanisms 63, 67, 86, 105, 126, 127
access rights 62, 135, 139
access to land xii, xiv, xvi, 1, 2, 6, 9, 22, 23, 24, 34, 35, 36, 43, 48, 53, 54, 60, 62, 63, 66, 67, 71, 72, 73, 75, 84, 86, 87, 90, 91, 93, 96, 104, 109, 111, 118, 120, 122, 123, 124, 126, 127, 129, 137, 143, 144, 145, 146
affinal 34, 69, 86, 87
affinal relations 68, 69, 87
agrarian change 4, 147
agrarian critical studies 46
agrarian economy 52, 54
agrarian reform 16, 143
agricultural extension 76, 77
agricultural households 37
agricultural intensification 9
agricultural investment 8
agricultural modernisation 11
agricultural producers 122
agricultural productivity 3, 4, 6, 8, 11, 94
agricultural season 85, 86
agro-pastoralists 30, 75
Alienation 20
areas designated for agricultural purposes 47, 129, 143, 146
arid landscapes 42

B

belonging 33, 41, 54, 71, 83, 127
buffer zones 7, 141, 146
bundles of rights 73, 121
business enterprises 36, 47, 131, 144

C

capitalist commodity relations 77, 143
cash cropping 9
cash income 48, 49, 76
cattle posts 30, 47, 76, 83
ceremonial economy 37
claims for redistribution 22
class formation 88, 104, 151
classical land reform 11
classical land reforms 144
classical tenure reform 146
collateral 3, 8, 11, 12, 13, 14, 132
commercial agricultural economy 27, 133, 140, 141
commercial agricultural sector 21
commercial agriculture 20
commercialisation 2, 7, 9, 48, 63, 110, 140
commodification of land 2, 63, 94
commodified space 42
commodified spaces 43
commonage 23, 38, 60, 63, 77, 78, 79, 112, 129, 130, 134, 138, 139
commonage rights 38
commonages 23, 31, 36, 37, 38, 58, 77, 83, 129, 130, 138, 141, 146
communal areas xii, xiv, xvi, 1, 2, 6, 8, 13, 20, 22, 23, 24, 27, 41, 43, 46, 47, 48, 50, 63, 80, 89, 90, 92, 94, 95, 96, 97, 99, 100, 103, 105, 119, 122, 129, 131, 132, 133, 140, 141, 143, 144, 145
communal conservancies 43, 44, 46
communal land xii, xiv, 1, 2, 6, 8, 9, 10, 13, 14, 15, 17, 19, 20, 21, 22, 23, 24, 25, 26, 27, 29, 33, 36, 40, 41, 42, 44, 46, 47, 48, 54, 61, 63, 88, 90, 94, 95, 97, 99, 100, 101, 102, 103, 105, 106, 108, 109, 110, 111, 112, 113, 114, 115, 118, 119, 120, 121, 123, 124, 125,

126, 128, 129, 131, 132, 133, 135, 136, 137, 139, 140, 142, 143, 144, 145, 146
communal land bill 24
communal land boards 14, 100, 101, 102, 103, 108, 109, 111, 112, 113, 114, 118, 119, 120, 131, 139, 144
communal land governance 144
communal land reform xiv, 1, 24, 27, 29, 88, 99, 110, 111, 114, 118, 119, 122, 123, 128, 129, 135, 142, 143, 145
Communal Land Reform Act xiii, 1, 2, 14, 23, 27, 36, 40, 61, 96, 99, 100, 102, 103, 107, 109, 110, 112, 113, 118, 120, 121, 122, 123, 126, 128, 129, 131, 137, 139, 143, 144, 145
communal pastures xiii, 2
communal tenure systems 10
community-based conservation 43, 46, 102, 143
community-based natural resource management 43
community conservation 36, 46
community forests 43, 44, 46
compensation 18, 38, 40, 41, 92, 94, 111
Compensation Policy Guidelines for Communal Land 40
compensation valuation indicators 41
competition for land 29, 143
compulsions of commodification 77, 143
consanguinity lines 34
consensus resolutions 21, 22
conservancies 44, 45, 46
conservation agriculture 75, 79
Consultative Conference on Communal Land Administration 13, 20, 24, 100
contract workers 34
credit markets 3, 11
crop production 30, 31, 37, 46, 49, 74, 83, 84, 118, 131, 143
cultivation season 75, 77, 115
customary land rights xiii, 99, 100, 106, 107, 108, 109, 110, 111, 117, 118, 119, 120, 121, 123, 128, 131, 138, 144
customary laws 23, 36, 123
customary practices 123
customary tenure xii, xiv, 1, 2, 3, 6, 8, 9, 14, 16, 17, 19, 22, 29, 48, 62, 67, 74, 97, 110, 122, 126, 128, 132, 144, 146
Cuvelai-Etosha Basin 29

D

dead capital 13, 48
de-agrarianisation 52, 53, 54
defective rights 144
Delimitation Commission 33
descent-based customary landholding 124
development planning 41, 150
disadvantaged communities 22
disturbance allowance 41
diversification 46, 53, 63, 143
domestic group relations 69, 71, 87
Dual grazing 22
dual land tenure system 3, 17, 20, 21

E

ecofeminist approach 102
economic growth 3, 12, 41
economic history 47
economic restructuring 47, 48, 143
economy of sharing 2, 66, 73, 81, 86, 87, 128
egalitarian distribution of land 109, 136
eminent domain. *See* juridical power
enclosures 4, 6
environmental history 57
environmental protection 44
evolutionary model 5, 14
evolutionary model of tenure change 4, 14
exchange economy 63, 76
exclusion 9, 40, 61, 63, 97, 104, 119, 120, 128, 130, 141
extra-legal property 16

F

family labour 143
food security 54, 118, 119
Forest Amendment Act 44, 152

formalisation of land rights 110, 127
formal property system 13
forum shopping 113, 114
freehold (agricultural) commercial land reform 1
freehold land tenure 3, 17, 19
freehold tenure 2, 3, 5, 8, 19, 132, 144, 146
fundamental human rights 18

G

gendered relations around land 125
gender equality 60, 102, 122, 145
gender equity 123, 124, 125, 130, 137, 144
gender gap 144
gender inequities 67, 126
generational history 124
generational inequities 124
globalised world 85
green grabbing 46
group rights 38, 128, 138, 142, 146
group tenure 37

H

heritagisation 43
homelands 17, 32
housing 14, 53, 94, 95
housing developments 95
human-created environments. *See oshilongo*

I

iifendela yedu. See land tax
illegal fencing 22, 25, 112
incentive for investment in land 132
indigenous population 6
indigenous trees 40
indirect rule 8, 32
individualisation xii, xiii, 2, 6, 9, 23, 24, 39, 62, 87, 127, 129, 141
informal economy 43
informal land market 143
informal settlements 42
informal tenures 15, 144
inheritance 59, 122, 123, 124
insecurity of tenure 4, 15, 23
institution shopping 113
investment in land 3, 48, 132
invisible capital 41

J

juridical power 41, 143

K

kinship xii, 32, 34, 58, 66, 67, 87, 125, 140

L

labour migration 32
labour reservoirs 8, 48
Land Act 25, 26
land administration 2, 13, 14, 23, 24, 25, 26, 36, 100, 102, 103, 107, 114, 145
land alienation 20, 121, 146
land allocation 22, 25, 36, 60, 89, 100, 101, 103, 105, 135
land appropriation 129
land banking 71, 75, 88
land-based resources 40, 64, 81
land concentration 129
land conflict 111
land delivery 53, 95
land dispossession 3, 21, 154
land disputes 59, 111
land fragmentation 31, 86
land inheritance 115, 124, 125
landlessness 12, 41, 97
land markets xvi, 2, 11, 43, 89, 90, 91, 93, 95, 96, 97
land ownership 4, 13, 25, 95
land policy reforms 5
land redistribution 21
land reform xii, xiv, 1, 5, 8, 11, 13, 16, 17, 18, 19, 20, 21, 22, 24, 27, 29, 99, 123, 124, 129, 131, 133, 135, 143, 146
land-related disputes 2, 41, 100, 114

land relations 2, 16, 19, 20, 23, 48, 54, 62, 63, 68, 69, 71, 73, 74, 87, 96, 126, 127, 129-130, 143
land rights xii, xiii, xiv, xvi, 1, 2, 4, 9, 10, 11, 13, 14, 19, 22, 27, 29, 35, 36, 38, 40, 42, 52, 61, 62, 63, 67, 68, 71, 72, 73, 74, 86, 88, 94, 96, 99, 100, 101, 102, 103, 104, 105, 106, 107, 108, 109, 110, 111, 114, 115, 117, 118, 119, 120, 121, 122, 123, 124, 125, 126, 127, 128, 129, 131, 134, 135, 138, 139, 140, 141, 143, 144, 145, 146
land rights registration xvi, 2, 35, 99, 101, 102, 107, 109, 110, 119, 122, 125, 128, 135, 144, 145
land tax 43, 62, 63, 93, 115
Land tenure 1, 3, 5, 99, 154
land use xiv, 2, 19, 23, 30, 41, 46, 48, 49, 54, 61, 63, 68, 73, 83, 94, 118, 119, 123
land-use planning 119
law reform 5
layered authority 36
legal empowerment 44
livelihoods 2, 15, 16, 23, 36, 37, 44, 48, 51, 52, 53, 54, 63, 67, 81, 82, 86, 87, 108, 110, 118, 127, 143
livestock economy 39, 47, 140
Local Authorities Act 39
local authority areas xiii, 31, 39, 40, 41, 42, 48, 63, 94, 121, 143
local-level decision-making 118
local-level participatory planning 135

M

maldistribution of land 3, 141
Mangetti Block. *See* Owambo Mangetti
marginalisation 41
marginalised communal farmers 26
market exchange values 90
marketing facilities 136, 138, 141
market-oriented economy 133
matrifocal relations 68
matrilineal descent relations 69
Matrilineal land tenure 69
matrilineal lines 32, 58
Matriliniarity 66
middle floodplain 56, 58, 82, 83
mixed economy 18, 21
mixed tenure arrangements 36
modern economy 6
modern governance system 33
modernisation of agriculture 129
modernising elites 68, 86
modernising land tenure 5
mystery of capital 13, 148

N

National Conference on Land Reform and the Land Question 21, 123
nationalisation of land 17, 20
national statutory system 144
native reserve 32
natural resources xii, 4, 30, 41, 44, 45, 46, 75, 137
nature conservation 46
Nature Conservation Amendment Act 44, 153
neo-evolutionary model of tenure change 15
neoliberal approach 20, 21
nested systems 69
northern floodplain 56, 58

O

occupational land rights 99, 100, 106
Odendaal Commission 6, 7, 8, 32
ofuka 2, 30, 31, 37, 47, 74, 75, 79, 83, 84, 134. *See also* wilderness areas
ombadu yekaya 34, 35, 37, 43, 49, 60, 62, 74, 89, 92, 115, 119, 120, 125
ombuga 38
oshilongo 30, 31, 37, 47, 82, 83, 84
overlapping land rights 105
Owambo Mangetti 6
ownership of land 3, 13, 14, 17

P

parity of participation 140. *See also* participatory parity
participatory approaches 12
participatory parity 15
patrilineal lines 59, 86
peasantry 5, 53
People's Land Conference 24
peri-urban centres 47, 85
political economy 3
population flight 56
Population growth 31
possession 1, 63
post-modern liberalism 12
poverty reduction 54, 97, 121
power of exclusion 119
primitive accumulation 42
private ownership 3, 14, 19, 42
privatisation 20, 21
privatization 5
Programme for Communal Land Development xi, xv, xvi, 89, 134
proletariat 42
property in land 3, 8
property rights 3, 4, 11, 12, 15, 18, 21, 48, 111, 144, 146
proprietary ownership 4
protectionist approach 97, 110

R

rangeland management 136
ratification of land rights 2, 105
ratification of rights 105
reciprocity 66, 87
redistribution 20, 24, 80, 95
redistributive justice 18, 146
Regional Land Boards 25
relational access mechanisms 64
representation of women 59, 60
resource users 16, 144
rights of exclusion 9, 61
rights of leasehold 2, 26, 83, 99, 100, 106, 108, 109, 110, 111, 117, 118, 120, 121, 128, 131, 136, 137, 144, 145
rural development 43, 133
rural economy 36, 46, 48, 133
rurality as a choice 43
rural poor 25, 67, 97, 110, 143
rural sociology 53

S

safety net 1, 21, 27, 97, 110, 143
scarcity of land 109
seasonal migration 30, 79
secondary rights holders 68
Second National Land Conference 111
security of tenure xiv, 2, 3, 19, 106, 127, 136, 143, 145, 146. *See also* tenure security
self-governing homeland 32
settlement history 57
sharing economy 137
small-scale commercial farming x, 6, 84, 128, 133, 134, 135, 136, 137, 138, 139, 140
social acceptance 126
social convention of vesting 124
social differentiation 74, 76, 79, 88, 104, 128, 130
social equity xii, xiv, 1, 2, 4, 11, 21, 22, 24, 25, 27, 126, 129, 137, 144, 146
social identity 15, 74
social inequities 9
socialist-oriented land reform 17
social justice 4, 11
Social movements 94
social progress 3, 4, 14
social relations 2, 38, 63, 66, 67, 72, 73, 74, 80, 87, 96, 97, 127
social support system 128
social vesting 69
socio-economic development 121
spatial restructuring 39
speculation in land 9
state laws 69, 71, 123

statutory land policy 71
statutory recognition of land rights 120
stock control barrier 22
stratification 145
structural adjustment 5
structural inequalities 15
structuration theory 144
subdivision of landholdings 71, 74
subsistence agriculture 21, 44, 47, 51, 54, 118
subsistence economy 6, 62
subsistence farming 50, 51, 52, 118, 143
surety for life 121
sustainable farming practices 136
symbolic beliefs 124
symbolic value 38

T

Targeted Intervention Programme for Employment and Economic Growth 134
tenure reform xiv, 1, 2, 3, 4, 5, 8, 9, 10, 14, 27, 99, 101, 143, 146
tenure security xii, 11, 15, 48, 121, 137. *See also* security of tenure
tenure systems xii, xiv, 1, 2, 3, 4, 5, 8, 9, 10, 11, 14, 16, 17, 19, 22, 67, 73, 74, 110, 122, 126, 144, 146
tenurial arrangement 119
territoriality 39
territorial restructuring 47, 54, 143
title deeds 3
titled tenure 1, 2, 132
titling of land 4
tradable property 14
trading stores 47, 48, 85, 118
traditional authorities xiv, 1, 19, 23, 24, 25, 33, 36, 38, 41, 47, 48, 59, 60, 62, 63, 73, 89, 90, 91, 99, 100, 101, 102, 103, 104, 105, 106, 107, 112, 113, 114, 115, 120, 121, 125, 127, 129, 131, 132, 139, 140
Traditional Authorities Act 33, 34
traditional laws 38
traditional leaders 25, 26, 33, 34
tragedy of the commons 4
trusteeship 63

U

unequal distribution 3
unitary land system 21
unutilised and/or underutilised land 132
urban housing 94, 95
urbanisation 42
urbanity 43
urban localities 31, 39, 48

V

vernacular land markets 91, 97
vesting practice 71

W

Western capitalism 15, 144
widows 69, 112, 122, 123, 124, 125, 144
wilderness areas 56. *See also ofuka*
wildlife conservation 44
women's access to land 123, 126
women's rights to land 122, 125
woodland areas. *See ombuga*

www.ingramcontent.com/pod-product-compliance
Ingram Content Group UK Ltd.
Pitfield, Milton Keynes, MK11 3LW, UK
UKHW051956041026
15590UKWH00009B/2334

9 789991 64262